Religious Education
as Social Transformation

Contributors

Allen J. Moore

Charles R. Foster

Mary Elizabeth Moore

Gerald F. Mische

James M. Wall

William Johnson Everett

C. Dean Freudenberger

Russell A. Butkus

Religious Education as Social Transformation

edited by
Allen J. Moore

Religious Education Press
Birmingham, Alabama

Library of Congress Cataloging-in-Publication Data

Religious education as social transformation.

   Includes bibliography and index.
   1. Christian education.   2. Sociology, Christian.
I. Moore, Allen J.
BV1473.R33   1989   207   88-36413
ISBN 0-89135-069-1

Religious Education Press, Inc.
5316 Meadow Brook Road
Birmingham, Alabama 35243
10 9 8 7 6 5 4 3 2

Religious Education Press publishes books exclusively in religious
education and in areas closely related to religious education. It is
committed to enahancing and professionalizing religious education
through the publication of serious, significant, and scholarly works.

PUBLISHER TO THE PROFESSION

Contents

Introduction

For the past several decades the major thrust of the literature in religious education has been primarily concerned with the personal, or with what professional educational literature calls the psychological foundations. Since the 1950s, we have benefited from a number of significant and formative books having to do with religious development and growth, interpersonal relations, and spiritual formation.[1] Although this literature has focused largely on the education of the individual, the social dimension has also been highlighted. Religious education, since the turn of the twentieth century, has shared with progressive education a social agenda that has included issues such as racial inclusiveness, peace and justice, and improved international relations.

In recent years, we have also benefited from an increasing number of social works in religious education although these have tended to focus on single issues and have not laid the foundation for a new social theory for religious education.[2] A major exception to this generalization would be the book of Thomas Groome in which he seeks to ground religious education, in part at least, in the critical theory and social analyses often associated with the German and Marxist sociologist, Jürgen Habermas.[3] Another exception is the emerging literature on education and the public church. Here the focus seems to

1

be on how religious education can enable persons within the religious community to participate effectively in the public dialogue that will lead to social policies that will serve the common good.[4]

Although all of these recent writings have made a significant contribution to the field of religious education and have led to a redefinition of the relationship between sociology and education, a book is yet to be written that lays out in a systematic way the sociological foundations for religious education. We still need someone who will reformulate for our time a social theory of religious education that will have continuity with the tradition of George Albert Coe and his successor, Harrison S. Elliott.[5] Although these two giants had a strong psychological awareness, they also sought to ground their religious education in sociological and social-ethical categories. They each sought to create a better world for better persons rather than believe that personal nurture alone would contribute to needed social reform. Coe was even more radical in this regard as he became increasingly occupied with the necessity for economic and political reform as a basis for a constructive theory of religious education. This desire for radical social reforms led him to be influenced more and more by the socialist movements in this country. He would not find the current interest in liberation education incompatible with his vision of religious education.

One might argue that Coe and his followers in the progressive religious education movement were key forces in keeping alive the liberal reform spirit in a social climate that became increasingly dominated by a variety of conservative forces and by the rise of religious fundamentalism. He set the stage for a long tradition in religious education to champion the causes of the social and economic oppressed. The history of religious education is rich in a tradition of giving leadership to social issues, such as racial integration, women's rights, economic justice, labor's right to organize, and world peace. Even as we celebrate this history of social justice in religious education we may also be in a time in which a new generation of religious educators may neither know this history nor have a theoretical base for understanding education as a transformative force in society.

Unfortunately, the reformulation of a social theory of religious education is too ambitious for an edited work, such as this book. Our purpose here is primarily to remind us that we as religious educators do have a social responsibility and to illustrate in a limited way the educational task that may be implicit in the basic orders of society. Each chapter addresses critical and ethical issues raised by our social world and suggests how some of these issues might be addressed by the religious education process. Naturally, in a book of this size, not all social structures are addressed and not all issues are identified. Likewise the educational opportunities are not exhausted by the chapters here. What we do hope to accomplish is to provide some models and to point to some directions for a social theory of religious education.

The book is intended to serve first of all the general reader who may wish to learn about some key social issues and to reflect from an educational point of view on ways to cope with these issues. Second, the book is prepared for use by directors of religious education in Protestant and Catholic churches. Finally, the book should be useful as a textbook for seminary and university courses in religious education. In addition to ample footnotes, each chapter has a selected list of other readings as well as resources that can enrich the learning experience. Hopefully, as a text the book will not be limited to an academic setting but will serve equally well learning groups in church or synagogue. They will find here issues that will stimulate not only discussion but will lead to action in the larger society. Although most of the writers are Christians, every effort has been made to make the chapters relevant to as broad a religious audience as possible. The chapters are also "educational" as they are written as a map to the issue rather than an exhaustive statement. Other points of view are possible. Most of all the chapters are designed to provoke discussion, to raise questions for further study and research, and to point beyond the classroom to praxis in and through the orders of society.

Although the several chapters are not necessarily uniform in their organization, each chapter, other than Chapter 1, does try to address similar elements or questions. A common approach to the book is shared by all the several writers in that each chapter addresses a social theme or concern that is fundamental to society and is of some sociological and ethical importance. Each chapter also attempts to discuss in some depth the ethical implications and the ways the issue or concern might be addressed from a religious education perspective. In this regard, the chapters are active in orientation and raise both social and pedagogical issues. No chapter is just a description of a problem but attempts to move the reader or a group of learners to a new social vision and to explore how religious education can participate in the work of social transformation.

The first chapter, written by the editor, serves not only to introduce the reader to a sociological foundation for religious education but seeks to provide a pedagogic frame for the chapters to follow. What is proposed here is that religious education can indeed be a means of social transformation. All education, including religious education, participates by interacting with all the basic institutions of society in shaping the social consciousness of the learner and in forming the social order that is most conducive to a productive life for all persons. The chapter looks at the historical work of Coe and Elliott in social religious education and seeks to explore new paradigms for a social theory of religious education.

Chapter 2 is written by Charles R. Foster who takes a historical approach to the changing patterns of family life. He shows that it is difficult to generalize on a family order that is normative to our society. In fact, his historical analysis leads us to conclude that there are many variations of the family and that no one form functions to serve all the needs and expectations of society. The forms and structures of family life always incorporate specific values and meanings, and, for Foster, religious education should serve to raise these assumptions to the surface for critical study. He is especially concerned that the excessive emphasis on the private nature of family life should be reexamined. He proposes a public role for the family that will serve to foster larger communities and the social good for all citizens of society.

Foster does not address in a specific manner the changing understanding of women in our society, but this does become the subject of the essay by Mary Elizabeth Moore. She describes the issue of sexism in the social order by showing how it has global significance. Sexism, in her opinion, results in the domestication of women and the assignment of women's roles primarily to the private sphere where power is limited. She proposes a religious education that helps to bring reality to how women are understood in society and how the structures that separate women from public roles and responsibilities might be challenged. This likewise requires new roles and different locations for men in the social order. Religious education in the order of men and women must help persons to choose a new language system, as well as a new symbol system. Religious symbols for God, for example, must be reformed to allow more inclusiveness in the life and practices of religious communities.

In spite of the rhetoric of a global society, Gerald Mische believes that a truly human world order has become increasingly elusive. His analysis leads one to look at the issue of national security and how this impacts the economic life of nations. Education here requires what he describes as "provolution," or a new human consciousness and a new vision of the forward movement of history. He expresses confidence in grassroot models and sees education serving to foster networking of persons working together for a truly global society. Mische is very pointed in how religion, especially fundamentalism in any one of the world's religions, can serve to promote nationalism and to block the structures of human solidarity.

The political order is examined by James M. Wall. He chooses to use literature, especially the novel, as a way of helping us analyze the value assumptions behind the American political system. His method is applicable to film and can readily be transferred to the classroom as an exercise to study what deTocqueville calls the "habits, attitudes, and values" of the people. Wall believes that religion should function to shape public opinion rather than to form laws that are parochial and that are enacted to force the values of the majority on a religious minority. He seeks in his chapter to show how religious education might function to redefine issues and to open up the social structure to be examined critically, especially with the use of the arts and the experience of the senses.

Work is related integrally to the economic order as well as

that of family. It may well be one of the most neglected issues in religious education. William Elliott demonstrates that work and education have a reciprocal relationship and that together they may form a partnership in the transformation of society. He proposes a theory that suggests that we are transformed "through the ways we are emotionally bonded to others" and that work is one of the places in which strong emotional bonds are formed. A role especially crucial for education is to create "bridge structures between religious communities and work-places." Elliott suggested that a critical issue is the need for religious organizations to critically examine their own life of work and the ethical and economic values that are informing the employment practices.

C. Dean Freudenberger shows us how all living life is interrelated and reminds us that we cannot address the issues of our humanity apart from having a concern for the whole of creation. For him, the natural order exists not only in humans but also for the earth itself. The ecological crisis is well-documented in this chapter, especially the global significance of the current abuse of the land. The problem of poverty and hunger in our society is not due to a lack of food but is related to an economic order in much of the world that is based upon cash crops rather than on farming that will sustain persons within their own environment. Here he shares a concern with Mische—the belief that world peace is largely an economic issue and that nations often turn to agriculture as a way to raise money for the purchase of military arms. Religious education for Freudenberger should serve the vision of a just, sustainable, and participatory social order in which the welfare of persons is served best by preservation of the natural order.

The closing chapter is by Russell A. Butkus and deals with what it means to do justice education within a public order. Drawing largely upon the history or memory of Roman Catholics he provides an educational model of social analysis that he believes has equal validity for Protestants and Jews. His chapter brings to the forefront critical reflection and praxis as a pedagogical strategy. Utilizing Metz's concept of "dangerous memory," he proposes a strategy by which persons can explore the middle-class values that are so pervasive in the public order and to call the new majority to remember what life is like at the bottom and what is required to become socially responsible. His chapter provides an entrance into a study of the need for a new moral order for modern society. For him education is a way to explore basic ethical and moral values of a society and to plan a course of action that will affirm a moral order that will serve more readily the common good of all humanity. Especially here is the opportunity to become more sensitive to the new people in our midst and how social structures are really designed to exclude such persons from the larger benefits of a just society.

John Dewey, who had so much influence upon the beginnings of modern religious education, believed that education had both the responsibility to eliminate from society those forces that have unworthy influence upon the learner and to engage in the reconstruction of society itself. Education is not just the accumulation of facts or even of experiences. Education is a way of life. For Dewey, education is a way in which the democratic way of life is realized and society is reformed.

Possibly our vision here is that religious education is an ethical way of life that serves to transform religious platitudes into concrete social structures that are just and serve the welfare of all people. Possibly Karl Marx is more to the point with his insistence that the dichotomies between the "ought" and the "is" should be overcome. Radical human learning is moving from the theories of a better society to human activity on behalf of that society.

NOTES

1. For example, Reuel L. Howe, *Man's Need and God's Action* (Greenwich, Conn.: Seabury, 1957); James Fowler, *Stages of Faith* (San Francisco: Harper & Row, 1981); Lewis J. Sherrill, *The Gift of Power* (New York: Macmillan, 1955); and James E. Loder, *The Transforming Moment* (San Francisco: Harper & Row, 1981).

2. For example, Brian Wren, *Education for Justice* (Maryknoll, NY: Orbis, 1977).

3. Thomas H. Groome, *Christian Religious Education* (San Francisco: Harper & Row, 1980); see Jürgen Habermas, *Theory and Practice* (Boston: Beacon Press, 1973) and Paulo Freire, *Pedagogy of the Oppressed* (New York: Seabury, 1970). Other attempts to ground religious education theory in social analysis and praxis are William Bean Kennedy's unpublished study on ideology and education, Allen J.

Moore, "Liberation and the Future of Religious Education," in *Contemporary Approaches to Christian Education*, ed. Donald E. Miller and Jack L. Seymour (Nashville: Abingdon 1982), and Malcolm L. Warford, *The Necessary Illusion* (Philadelphia: Pilgrim, 1974).

4. For example, Jack Seymour, Robert T. O'Gorman, and Charles R. Foster, *The Church in the Education of the Public* (Nashville: Abingdon, 1984).

5. See George A. Coe, *A Social Theory of Religious Education* (New York: Charles Scribner's Sons, 1919) and Harrison S. Elliott, *Can Religious Education Be Christian?* (New York: Macmillan, 1953).

1

A Social Theory of Religious Education

Allen J. Moore

The two kingdoms in the works of Martin Luther may give us insight into one of the major issues of religious education. Luther talks about the inner kingdom and the worldly kingdom.[1] Within modern religious education theory there is sometimes a tension between "matters of the heart" and "matters of the world." Is the central purpose of religious education to bring persons to conversion or to bring society to reform?

George Albert Coe, a pioneer theorist of modern religious education, was the first to focus attention on this issue by acknowledging that both individual faith and social reform are important, but one will always be more prominent than the other in the theory and practice of religious education.[2] Recent developments have tended to put the weight on personal religious development or faith formation rather than on the reformation of society or the social realization of humankind. How one views the central task of religious education will influence how religious tradition is appropriated and the way philosophical and learning assumptions are formulated.[3] This may be another of those debates about which comes first, the chicken or the egg, but the beginning point and the expected outcomes of education are both at issue. Do we seek to make better persons for a better world or to make a better world that will foster better persons?

Regardless of how Luther is interpreted, he did make it clear to many of his interpreters that religious experience is much more than the inward kingdom of faith and a righteous heart. For him, the kingdom also had to be social and political. The kingdom had to include what Pannenberg calls the "worldly powers."[4] Especially within Jewish thought, the kingdom of God is always understood as a social reality, and the full participation of persons is required for the fulfillment of the coming kingdom. Obedience, justice, and political awareness are all essential elements of the kingdom plan. God's kingdom is a coming reality that requires action on the part of the people. The kingdom of God is understood as the social manifestation of God's plan for a people, society, and even a nation state.

In a similar way, Luther understood personal religious piety to be inseparable from a social kingdom. The religious order, as represented by the kingdom language of the Bible, had both political (civic) and social (public) obligations. Pannenberg writes regarding Luther's ethical system that "the kingdom of God which the prophets promised and for which Jews hoped is political in nature."[5]

The human development approach to religious education tends to rely largely upon psychological categories and to focus upon moral and religious factors in personal growth. A social-functional approach would, on the other hand, be concerned with how religious doctrines and practices may be judged in accordance to their consequences for society. Religious education here shares much in common with social ethics and is concerned with how society may organize itself into institutions and communities in order that ethical actions may be carried out and the social good may be realized by the whole of society.

We are not proposing here that the early twentieth century debate between heredity and environment be reopened because our current understanding of reality is more interactive and dynamic. Our concern here is to give renewed attention to the sociological and ethical roots of religious education with the recognition that the social order continues to serve as an important focus for religious education. We can seek to learn from those early religious education theorists who found the new science of sociology to be a basis for theory formulation, and we can seek to benefit from our newer awareness of some fundamental social issues. For example, we have come to understand in our time that the context of the social experience includes the interaction between the local order and the global order. The structures of humanity cannot be limited to one region of the world because no society can be fully ethical and responsible apart from an awareness and a concern for the social well-being of the whole of God's creation. Social independence and cultural isolation seem impossible in a world order in which all persons are interconnected and are influenced and formed by the consequences of social decisions mf other people.

The Sociology of Religious Education

A revised social theory of religious education must be grounded in the works of George Albert Coe and the other progressive theorists who provided the first systematic theory of religious education written from a sociological point of view. Coe himself was not always consistent in his social formulations, largely because he was also an early leader in bringing psychology to religious education and because he held a deep commitment to the philosophy of personalism. In his teaching and writings, he increasingly formulated his theory of religious education around social purposes and inspired a whole generation of scholars who sought to integrate the social gospel movement into the movement in religious education.[6]

Coe was preoccupied in his professional career and in his retirement with social reform and a better society for all persons. He also emphasized the role that education had in the reconstruction of the social system, the making of a new world order, and the revision of traditional standards of religion and morality. He introduced a proposal for a religious curriculum based on the radical application of the ethical principles of Jesus.

Coe's concern for the social order led him to address some of the issues contained in this volume of essays, such as the issues of peace and justice, the rights of the poor and the racially oppressed, the rights of labor, and the causes of economic justice. Coe was less vocal on the issues of women's liberation and the protection of the natural order although one might guess that they would be central concerns of his today. In regard to women's rights he was somewhat ahead of his generation in his strong support of his wife's efforts to establish her own independence and to develop her own interests in what promised to be a brilliant career in music and teaching. Unfortunately, her life was cut short by an early death. Furthermore, Coe had the beginnings of a religious education for the natural order by his own practical concern for nature and the out-of-doors and in his efforts to formulate a modern doctrine of creation.

By Coe's own admission he leaned toward social radicalism, sometimes uncritically. Coe was active in some socialist movements and was deeply influenced in his social awareness by the left-wing socialist, Harry F. Ward.[7] Many of Coe's friends felt that he was somewhat naive in the way he readily embraced the communist or socialist ideology as it spread in the 1920s among the intellectuals in this country. At the same time, Coe was courageous in his willingness to submit capitalism and the American social order to the critique of non-Western philosophies and not be frightened by the threats of the "red scare" that became so prominent at the height of his academic career. He maintained an intellectual openness to the influence of a worldview that American isolationism had shut out. Coe would probably be very sympathetic today to social theories of religious education based upon neo-Marxist concepts of praxis, critical theory, and historical analysis. His concern for the poor and the underprivileged would lead him in this historical time to embrace the philosophies of liberation education that have become so popular in Latin America.

Coe's own social theory of religious education laid the foundation for a prophetic emphasis rather absent from modern religious education. He and others who followed him believed that religious education had a special responsibility to name social evil and to participate actively in the radical reconstruction of the social order. Coe remained a philosophical personalist throughout his career, but he also believed that persons are not realized apart from the realization of a new social order. His personalism was informed by his left-wing sociology, and he believed that persons were more fully realized by participation in community. Just as society teaches individuals, individuals learn to improve the society through education. Here again Coe's personalism influences his social theory. Society is composed of the interaction of persons.

The function of religious education is to create the kinds of social groupings that can expand into a new democratic order. The goal is to manifest the kind of cooperative living that would model what society could become. Even as society shapes the person, the educational experience moves always toward what Coe called "the democracy of God." Here Coe envisions a new inclusiveness of humanity in which the ethical principles of love and neighborliness taught by Jesus are realized socially. He preferred the metaphor "democracy" over that of "kingdom" because he saw the ethical teachings of Jesus not as abstractions but as something that could be realized in very practical and specific ways within the social experience of persons. The education experience seeks not only to address social reform but serves at the same time to create living examples that can be replicated by the larger society.

Ethical Basis for Religious Education

Coe's choice to succeed him at Union was Harrison Elliott, who was trained in the liberal religious education tradition and who shared Coe's passion for social reform. By the time Elliott was well-established as a professor at Union, he was the leading exponent of the ethical foundations for religious education. He moved beyond the character educators and the work of defining moral traits; he formulated a social ethic of religious education. He chose the model of the historical Jesus for the social reformers. His most important book, *Can Religious Education Be Christian?*, served as a defense against the onslaught of neo-orthodox theology against the religious education movement, but also as an occasion to introduce in a systematic way how social ethics could inform the theory and practice of the field.

Elliott was influenced by the "reconstructionists" at Teachers College who were seeking to revise progressive education and who shared his social-ethical consciousness. In religious education, the scholars had largely followed the lead of John Dewey's emphasis on child-centered education and the belief that education should basically lead to the growth of the self. The reconstructionists, on the other hand, believed that the progressive view of the individual was too limiting and that the self could never be fully realized independently of a reform of the society in which the self was located. Elliott wrote, "The social nature of the self makes evident the importance of a social theory of education."[8]

Elliott remained an experimentalist in educational philosophy and a liberal in theology. But he did approve of the reconstructionists' insistence on social reform as a function of the educational enterprise, and he sought to show how religious content could function in a program of change. Because of his posture he ran headlong into conflict with neo-orthodoxy, and the tension between him and his famous colleague Reinhold Niebuhr was well-known to the doctoral students in religious education at Union.

Like Coe, Elliott believed in the radical nature of love as the basis for social change and saw experimental strategies in education as a way of addressing social problems. Niebuhr, on the other hand, saw love as largely irrelevant to the larger social issues and emphasized that realism would deliver Christians from such a naive expectation. For Elliott, Christian love was to be the motivating factor in all acts of justice and social reform. The social acts of goodwill were grounded almost literally, for Elliott, in Jesus' commandment to love one's neighbor as one's self.[9] His high view of human nature and his belief that human action could incorporate values of love and good works dominated his theories of religious education.

At the time of Elliott's work, moralism was dominant in American Protestantism. He was influential in enlarging the Protestant attention to social issues to more than the usual platitudes about temperance and sexual abstinence. Elliott combined his experimental philosophy with a strong focus on Christian sociology that had been introduced a generation earlier by his friend Coe. Elliott was clear that the strong individualism that had been the hallmark of progressive education needed to be corrected with a social view of human life. He understood that a goal of religious education was the transformation of "individual strivings" into "cooperative efforts."[10] He wrote that persons can learn to create cooperative endeavors that will incorporate the ideals manifested in the New Testament view of the kingdom of God.

Elliott's view of the "kingdom" concept seemed to avoid the romanticism of the social gospel movement in the 1930s. In some ways, he foreshadowed the current view of the kingdom in religious education with its emphasis upon moving toward the vision of a coming kingdom rather than walking toward the literal realization of the kingdom of God in history.[11] Elliott wrote that he did not mean in his social theory of religious education "that the kingdom of God can be fully realized in the human scene. But it does involve the translation of the ideals of the kingdom into goals which are pertinent to human life."[12]

Like most liberal Christians of this era, Elliott saw religious education as a way by which persons learning and working in cooperation could achieve social progress in what he sometimes called "immediate goals" for social improvements. Lacking here is a utopian vision of society; he envisioned a society that is ever connecting its problems and leading toward a more hopeful life for its citizenry.[13] Elliott's social-ethical view of religious education led to expectations that people would experience and re-experience the ideals of a society as presented in the Jesus' stories of the kingdom. His experimental approach was strikingly similar to Dewey's problem-solving or project method of learning. He went beyond Dewey's method which was largely based on individual realization; he added an emphasis on cooperative work that could lead to social improvements.

Harper has outlined Elliott's social process approach to education:

1) The focus must be on social problems.
2) All possible solutions must be considered.
3) Solutions must be genuinely understood.

4) Accuracy in dealing with facts is basic.
5) Use church history, Bible, life and teaching of Jesus to develop a Christian perspective.
6) Examine Christian perspectives in light of the current situation.
7) Define proposed solutions in terms of action.
8) Test solutions and evaluate the results.[14]

Such social strategizing as an approach to religious education was considered by Elliott as appropriate to all age groups, and his immediate aim for social education was to develop a cooperative approach to society on the part of the learners. Discussion was to move from the abstract to the concrete and lead to cooperative action on the part of the group in an effort to make a difference in society.

Elliott believed that this cooperative endeavor was applicable to larger social systems, but we have no evidence that he undertook to experiment with groups where face-to-face dialogue was not possible. At his time in history, sociology was not fully informed on systemic issues and the role of power and conflict in social problems. Elliott, the idealist, was reluctant to move beyond his love ethic to the kind of power struggle articulated in the praxis movements of liberation. Futhermore, Elliott's method was largely to talk about the problem and its solution in society, rather than to do social analysis and to project how a group's action might collectively change the course of history.

Reconstructionism

Many of the religious educators educated under Elliott at Union and at Teachers College following World War II came under the influence of the reconstructionists, and especially the teaching and writings of the educational philosopher, Theodore Brammeld.[15] Basically, the reconstructionists sought to revise progressive theories of education and to shift the primary attention from the individual to society.[16] Elliott and others believed that persons were more than a product of their society but also participated in the creation of society. Influenced by the Chicago school of sociology and the work of Albion

Small, the reconstructionists believed that progressive education was out of touch with the massive needs of society and that education had a special role in social reform. They believed that the self could not be realized fully independent of the reform of society. The basic aim of education and of religious education was the reconstruction of society. Since education is a social institution that must function in interaction with the other basic institutions of society, the role of education is to begin to reconstruct itself at the same time that it participates in the fundamental reform of other social institutions. Educational reconstruction begins, for example, by addressing such issues as curriculum (the questions of what is learned and how knowledge is shared); governance (the question of who makes decisions about who is educated and how they are educated); schooling and (the question of how society is organized in order to educate).

For reconstructionists, the curriculum reflects the larger society with attention given to the relevance of knowledge to the practical affairs of the social order. Learning is often organized around the orders of society rather than subject matters. In this way classical knowledge has its relevance insofar as it is able to address the needs of society. The curriculum is sometimes organized around the orders or social structures, such as family, political, economic, world, and natural institutions basic to society. The basic organization of this book reflects the assumptions of reconstructionism.

The aim of reconstructionism is the reform and the remaking of the social order and the basic institutions of society. By social order is meant how society is organized in order to carry out the fundamental functions of human life in a reliable and somewhat predictable manner. Social institutions refer to those formal structures of society through which the basic needs and functions of humans might be organized. Institutions serve not only as a way to organize human behavior but to incorporate the values, attitudes, and belief systems that support social life and insure human fulfillment.

Social insititutions are the major structures of a social order, or the ways by which the needs of society are organized and served. An example is the family, which incorporates the social

relations between the generations and the cultural values and
beliefs. It also serves to regulate sexual activities of persons,
procreation, and nurturing of the young. The family provides
order for sexuality and procreation. Today, many would believe
that one of the reconstructive aims of education, including
religious education, is to reconstruct the myth of the man-
woman relationship in order to insure the equality of women
and to protect the human rights of the young. A new order is
required to structure the relationship between men and wom-
en, and this may not necessarily be institutionalized by the
family, at least as we have known it. Other institutional forms
may be proposed, such as communal structures in which relationships may be based upon religious values rather than sexual need.

The reconstructionists talked about "learning as social-self-
realization." By this they meant that, although personal experience is valuable and individual growth is important, education
needs to have as its central purpose the needs and requirements of society. This implies a social vision of the collective
life to balance the excessive individualism that is sometimes
expressed in the emphases on personal growth and development.

What is meant here is that education is not neutral. The ends
of learning are social and political in nature. Individual growth
is impossible apart from the reconstruction of the society in
which those individuals participate. Better persons require a
better social order. The purpose of education is to enable persons, or collective groups of persons, to take informed responsibility for the social order of which they are a part. This requires an awareness of the needs and problems, a growing
appreciation of the resources and value of corporate life, and
learning how to participate in the social order in order to bring
about needed change and to envision long-range goals that will
benefit the majority of the human race.

Education here is not just learning the beliefs of the past or
preserving the tradition of another generation, but it includes
reconstructing the heritage in light of present and future social
goals and formulating new beliefs and values to serve a society
that is in the process of becoming.

Contemporary Theories

Social transformation is a major concern in several recent approaches to religious education. The social-ethical dimension of religious education has been prominent in liberation education, in what might loosely be called lifestyle education, and in recent work in the practical theology of religious education. Each of these would have some continuity with the social theory approach of Coe, the social-ethical concerns of Elliott, and the social-psychological work of the reconstructionists. At the same time, there is no evidence that the persons working on these newer theories have tried to link their work directly to Coe or Elliott and, as we will note, there are some distinct differences in the current developments in religious education.

Liberation Education: A Social Change Approach

Although liberation education does not translate readily into the social experience of North America, several essays have attempted to use the dialectic philosophy and critical analysis as bases for a social theory of religious education.[17] The work of Paulo Freire has been especially influential in contemporary religious education.[18]

Liberation education has developed largely out of the Latin American historical experience where poverty and oppression are major social realities. Conflict between the social classes is a major source of content in liberation education, and the methods of social analysis, political change, and social *praxis* contribute to learning. Praxis in its historical meaning refers to the knowing that occurs in the midst of political action and radical social change. This also suggests that all liberation education is ethical in the sense that the meaning of justice is understood and implemented within the context of a concrete social or historical situation. Education is basically understood as *doing* justice rather than learning about the theories or principles of a just order. Liberation education is therefore primarily political action education.

Freire believes that individuals, regardless of their social plight, have the ability to probe critically their social reality, understand the conditions that control their lives, and deal with these conditions in a transforming way. For Freire, education is a *practice* of freedom and a means to restore dignity to people. His basic approach to education seeks to hold in unity theory and action, past and present realities, and thinking and doing in the social situation. Central to his view of education is the role of hard manual work as a method of social change. Because manual work is often not related to survival in the northern hemisphere, this is especially difficult to implement in the church or religious education experiences.

Freire's pedagogical methods were developed first in Brazil with persons who were extremely poor, illiterate, and disenfranchised politically. His imagination as an educator and his understanding of the psychology of the peasants are demonstrated in his educational praxis. Persons learned how to read, not with the usual primary readers designed to build vocabulary, but through political action in which they learned how to read the documents that are essential to their political welfare.

Similarly, Freire used photographs of the daily life of the peasants as a way to sharpen their perception as to what is going on around them and to stimulate what he called generative themes, or powerful symbols of the contradictions in their lives. He sought to create dialogue around what was most oppressing in their everyday life.

These inductive forms of education could readily be appropriated into patterns of religious education in our society. But as Freire suggests, taken from the cultural context in which these methods were formulated, they could serve only to reinforce a consciousness that is subjective and personal and would not lead to political revolution. Radical political action is possible only within a context in which radical change is urgently necessary to human freedom and personal dignity.

Freire also cautions against the idealization of liberation, either by abstracting the concept as a subject of discussion (e.g., a course *about* liberation rather than engaging in liberating acts) or in expecting all education to become liberation education. One only needs to observe the extent to which North Americans play the reformer role to know how great this temptation is. Poverty can become just another lifestyle in an affluent society where persons can afford to reject their material possessions and know that it is not a permanent condition.

For example, a textbook approach to a study of problems in the structures of society could make for interesting discussion but would serve to avoid the political action that is necessary for a liberation praxis view of education. As religious people, we are motivated by our view of charity to help the unfortunate people of the world to have a better way of life. We do this both by trying to identify with them and through programs of social service and other charitable acts. In this way we reach out to persons in need without making a far-reaching change in our own social position in society. We can also maintain an emotional and spatial distance which serves to limit real involvement in the human suffering of the world.

For most of us, our goal is the *reform* of the established social structures. Seldom do we within the North American scene envision the *total destruction* of the social system for the sake of political freedom and economic survival for others. The humanization of life for Freire requires radical, *new* political structures; for us it more often means new psychological structures and some basic, but not radical, changes in our society.

Liberation education has its grounding in a dialectic ideology that reflects the actual experience of people who have never known any way of life but oppression; for them social revolution becomes the *only way* out of the hopelessness of their situation. Few North American people can comprehend the true nature of total oppression much less identify with it. Oppression for us is often seen as the inability to do what pleases us or the failure to get our way. The common American ideology is that persons can help themselves and anyone can escape poverty and social repression with effort and hard work.

This is not to imply that there are not deep social injustices within the North American context and that there are not a host of persons who are being robbed of their humanity by an inequitable social system. What is being said here is that for affluent and politically franchised individuals, the idea of liberation may become more fashionable than a radical reexamination of political and economic structures. The very fact that we have a choice in how we live our life is, according to Freire, a sure sign that we are not really oppressed. Oppression is politi-

cal, and change calls for radical action that will not only challenge the establishment but will make change a requirement
for the political order. Our own liberating activities need critical
examination, and the function of religious education is to help
persons examine why they do what they do in order to find a
social witness consistent with their social context. Education
should serve also to examine the underlying ideologies in our
own political systems and to help persons make radical social
decisions that will have a positive impact on others.

Juan Luis Segundo has written that the adoption of the terminology of liberation by the churches has only served to water
down its content and to empty it of any significant meaning. It
is possible, as Segundo has suggested, to mouth the words
while at the same time going on as before.[19] The adoption of
the language and methods of liberation by religious education
runs the risk of fostering an inauthentic course of action and
leading the churches to believe falsely that they are on the side
of the oppressed.

The beginning point for a social education of liberation is a
critical awareness of the experiences of injustice within the
North American scene—including the injustices within religious institutions. To substitute the experiences of another time
and place only serves to be a stumbling block to the freedom
and self-determination of those who are really oppressed. As
Segundo argues, a theology of liberation begins, not with oppression of others, but with the questions which arise in the
present reality in which we find ourselves. It is only when
"profound and enriching questions are asked about a real situation"[20] that ethical decisions can be made for that situation and
education can begin to take place. We just cannot appropriate
the agenda of another people. This means, of course, that our
educational task is to perceive critically our own role in the
global oppression that leaves the majority of the world's people
in poverty and injustice.[21]

A major agenda for liberation education is to do a critical
analysis and radical reform of the educational order, including
schooling. Unless we become aware of the hidden values and
assumptions behind the educational structures, the attempt to
liberate learning will be self-defeating. Both public and reli-

gious education are dominated by materialistic and technological values. Look at those things that we feel are essential for a *good* education: paid professional staff; buildings with proper space allotments for each age group; equipment, including tables and chairs and technological hardware for teaching; printed resources, including books, story papers, and posters; and an organizational structure with teachers, superintendents, and committees. The crisis of the religious teacher today may be that there is too much material from which to choose rather than not enough. We are also inundated by bureaucratic leaders who offer abundant resources and guidelines, all for the cause of education.

William Pinar, Herbert Kliebard, and others have written about the materialistic base of current educational theory.[22] The "schooling" model of education that has generally been adopted by public and religious institutions is formulated largely around managerial and industrial concepts. Not only does such an education model assume large financial investments but it also requires heavy use of material resources, technological tools, and bureaucratic structures. Education is another form of production in which the end product is determined by behavioral objectives and in which control is central to the learning process.

Schooling is therefore designed to serve the socialization needs of a technological society and to insure that learners are adapted to conform to social expectations. In order to insure conformity, the church has adopted a grading or tracking system as the way to organize learners. Also, it has emphasized approved resources and curriculum materials, has sought to certify educational specialists, and has adopted a merchandising approach to educational programs.

Ivan Illich is very right when he suggests that our very language betrays the values inherent in religious education. We talk about learning systems, resource banks, superintendents and directors, learning objectives, educational standards, and so forth. Education is designed to serve the dominant minority and, through a process of certification, those who are dominated are not only eliminated but are proven to be unworthy because of the lack of a certificate. Illich goes on to say that the educational system is organized to insure the role of the "technocrat" in human affairs; those in charge are the ones who really benefit, not those who are supposed to be the benefited.

The materialistic base for education is not only found in its cost but also in the ways education serves to separate the haves and have-nots. Illich writes:

> Imperceptibly all countries, East and West, have adopted a system of knowledge-capitalism. Wealth is redefined in terms of hours of instruction purchased with public funds, and poverty is explained and measured by the individual's failure to consume. In such a society the poor are those who lag behind others in education. The rich man, the knowledge capitalist, cannot bridge the gap which separates him from Lazarus.[23]

Liberation education is based on a belief that persons are motivated by visions and by a consciousness that they have a role of self-determination. Education is not neutral as people face the changes that the future will require and as they develop awareness of their own role in making a radical, new social order. Educationally this requires a commitment to become active in the transformation of the old order. Such transformation begins with the social context in which the oppressed are located. They will learn by acting with criticalness toward the old order and by envisioning the new order toward which they will move.

Lifestyle Education: A Social-Psychological Approach

A second contemporary approach to religious education is consciousness-raising, or what I have called lifestyle education. This model of religious education shares some similar concepts and assumptions with liberation education, especially the influence of Paulo Freire. Lifestyle education focuses on the values and assumptions that influence how people live their public and private lives. In some ways, this approach to religious education domesticates the more radical features of liberation education and makes it more applicable to middle-class issues within North American society. The focus is on transforming the psychology or personal awareness of persons in the social context.

Conscientization, as used by Freire, means literally "making conscious." In religious education language, it is often translated as consciousness-raising to denote a process of apprehending one's reality and a vision of what one might become as a "liberated" person. Daniel Schipani has provided us with a very insightful study of Freire's understanding of conscientization. He writes, " 'Conscientization' can be defined as the process in which persons achieve a deepening awareness, both of the socio-culture reality that shapes their lives and their capacity to transform that reality."[24]

Lifestyle education serves to bring persons to an awareness of the value statement they make by their way of life. It includes a critical consciousness of how cultural forces dominate their thoughts and actions, and it encourages them to take control of their own existence as persons of worth. The goal is to transform the cultural contradiction in order that a synthesis between what people believe and do may take place.[25] Freire writes,

> In the antidialogical theory of action, cultural invasion serves the end of manipulation, which in turn serves the ends of conquest, and conquest the ends of domination. Cultural synthesis serves the end of organization, organization serves the end of liberation.[26]

The conclusion is obvious. Just as a dominating consciousness includes a planned program of socialization, freedom to choose and to live another lifestyle has to be a deliberate part of a larger plan and vision for social life. An example has been the struggle of women to be liberated from the space to which they have been assigned by society. Education has often defined what actions are appropriate for a woman and what roles are permissible. Women are socialized by family, school, and other social institutions to take their place in the home as wife, mother, and volunteer in the domestic functions of society (especially school, church, and child-serving programs, such as scouting and other nurturing agencies). Only with consciousness-raising enterprises have women come to protest the definition and place of women in society and to assume public and political roles in our society. The consequence has been the need to change attitudes and social orders of work, family, and politics.

Lifestyle also has both a social and moral dimension. The way one lives expresses what one really values. Social education therefore requires more than admonition, but also opportunities to reflect on how one is really living and what one's choices say about morality. This suggests that religious education in the future will certainly need to give greater attention to helping persons come to consciousness of the values they profess in relation to those they choose in everyday living. Most persons tend to be inconsistent in what they say they believe and in what they choose to do in public and private practice.

Lifestyle might be defined as a pattern of beliefs, values, and attitudes that are manifested in the way a person chooses to live; this pattern can be described and characterized. The private dimensions in that lifestyle are the unique and existential meanings that find expression in all the actions. Each person has value assumptions in the way she or he approaches the world.

Lifestyle is also a public life and a larger phenomenon than the idiosyncrasies of a single individual. The preoccupation of religious education with *the* individual has led to a neglect of those social or collective values and behaviors that become the shared way of life for a group of persons. Religious formation, for example, is usually more directed to the spiritual growth of the individual rather than to the development of a total group who have a common or shared approach to the world. The base communities in Latin America are examples of a collective formation of a shared public lifestyle; they are designed to bring about deep changes in the social order.

Max Weber introduced the concept of lifestyle into sociological literature by defining lifestyle as a subculture of people who are formed around a shared way of life based upon commonly held values and commitments. Lifestyle then can be understood as a way of describing the *ethos* or spirit of a people as they live in the larger society. It is that which marks a group and gives it recognition and acknowledgment.

Conscientization in Freire's works is apparently both an individual experience and a shared experience of a people who are acting together in history. A way of life is not determined from thinking *about* the world but is formed from the shared praxis. In this critical approach to the world, basic attitudes, values, and beliefs are formed and a people are humanized or liberated. *Conscientization,* therefore, leads to a life lived with consciousness of history, a life that denounces and transforms this history in order to form a new way of life for those who are oppressed.

What we are suggesting here is that lifestyle is both the way we live our lives and the subculture with which we identify; both are the product of choices. These choices can be made more conscious and deliberate through an educational dialectic in which the options are brought into direct conflict. Choices, then, are not made at random but are selected out of a matrix of possibilities. Something must be selected, and something rejected. Radical change requires something similar to a conversion experience in which psychologically a "super decision" is made that changes the course of one's life.

Let us conclude with some observations on the shape that lifestyle education might take in a program of religious education:

1. *Orientation to the World.* An emphasis on development sometimes separates the quest for fulfillment from the demands of the public sector. In the search for more meaningful experience persons not only turn in upon themselves but avoid any confrontation that calls into question the private values which are so difficult to give up in the face of community need. Lifestyle education must be an education that is oriented to the world—the space and history in which one lives—and the human need that calls out from the world. A person changes only in response to that which calls from beyond the self-seeking needs that get in the way of social responsibility. Social or public needs require attention in the choice of lifestyle.

2. *A Belief System or Ideology.* Considerable research has been done on the role of moral and religious belief in the behavior of persons.[27] Beliefs, first of all, satisfy the need that

most persons have for a coherent and rational view of life. In spite of the tendency to underrate belief in religious education, the need does exist to formulate belief statements that will give meaning to life and that will explain the social psychological realities in which people live.

In the second place, beliefs are more functional in a way of life when they are shared by members of a significant social group. Moral values and religious beliefs tend to change when persons who are important to us either advocate a new position or join us in searching for a more meaningful understanding of life and world.

John Wilson and others have pointed out that if we want persons to have a new moral view of the world, we need to instruct them in what they need to know.[28] Persons need information about lifestyle issues, organized and presented in such a way that it can be grasped intellectually and perceived as relevant to their own system of meaning. In addition, the cognitive alternatives for public life need to be explored in a group setting in which persons share a common quest for a better way of life. Lifestyle education requires accurate and challenging data that can inform decisions and be incorporated into one's pattern of thinking and acting.

3. *Construction of Visions.* Persons are also motivated by visions and by a consciousness that they have a role in the future of humankind. This is the essence of the biblical emphasis on the coming kingdom.[29] In the face of impending disaster, what is our hope and what is *my* role in that hope? Neutrality is not possible when one becomes aware of the changes that the future will require and the call to participate in the transformation of the social order.

Education, in the best sense of the word, really is concerned with envisioning. Although I would not want to take away from the dialectic emphasis on critical reflection as a form of knowing, I do want to suggest that imagination needs also to be emphasized. The arts and literature, especially biography, can serve to deliver a group from limited perspectives and to stimulate dreams of a new social reality. The power of vision in learning has again come to the attention of educators. Creativity—the transcendent reaching beyond the immediate concrete world—delivers the learner from the bland and mundane to a larger view of human life and the world.

4. *Education as Transformation.* As Richard Katz has suggested, transformation is a psychological process of change that we in the West have not always understood as an element of education. Within religious discourse, conversion has sometimes been emphasized as a goal of education, especially during the era of the evangelical movement. Coe sought to counter this limited goal in religious education. Throughout Christian history, persons who have come to a critical peak or psychological experience in their lives have often become social reformers. Conversion can be understood as a radical change in one's life orientation, or a turning point leading to a new state of being and a new posture in the world.

Transformation in much of psychological literature has a larger meaning than conversion, and the changes described by the conversion experience are usually as much social as personal. Katz describes transformation as not only a change of consciousness but also a personal reorientation that leads to new social connections and a new sense of responsibility within the community. Educationally, transformation involves the reorganization of information and experiences which leads to a change in perception and awareness. The result is a new sense of relationship to persons and social phenomena that may even have been rejected previously. For some, this new ecology of relationships may lead to a new sense of calling or purpose. Katz reminds us that outside the West transformation has also had a transpersonal or spiritual quality that can serve to restructure both the self and the self's relationship to the world.[30]

Lifestyle education has the possibility of bringing a unity to religious education that will unite personal or religious transformation with social transformation, and personal morality with social ethics.[31]

Practical Theology: An Integrative Approach

The last model that we will consider for a social theory of religious education is the practical theology of religious education. The revisionists of practical theology have generally sought to unify the many functional activities of the religious community and to center these activities within the cultural context in which the activities take place.[32] In a sense, practical theology in its contemporary meaning is no longer limited to the work of the clergy or to the inward life of the congregation; it is a socio-cultural approach to theology. A practical theology of religious education is focused on helping a people of faith to think critically about the social world and to form responsible actions for the concrete social situation. The most promising work on the future of religious education as social praxis is the work of Don Browning of the Divinity School, University of Chicago.[33]

Although Browning would not consider himself primarily a religious educator, he is among a small group of scholars who believe the reformulation of the discipline will best come from a revised theory of practical theology. Religious education, as a branch of practical theology, has many functions for the church-in-the-world, but a major one for Browning is to educate persons to think critically about ethical action in the world. He would locate religious education within what he calls the "fundamental discipline of practical theology."[34] Practical theology serves, therefore, to overcome the temptation for any one activity or function of the religious community to become imperialistic. It also affirms that all theology has a practical intention that requires the resources of all forms of praxis.

For religious education in particular, practical theology serves to create persons who are "capable of entering in a community of practical theological reflection and participating in the action that would follow from it."[35] In this regard, Browning draws upon the classical understanding of practical theology that is focused on moral theology and religious ethics. Ethics in this model becomes an important cognate discipline that helps to define a good social order and to form normative principles for moral action. In contrast to the ethical system of Elliott and Coe, Browning believes that social praxis should be grounded in ethical norms and that social action should not rely solely upon needs as defined by the situation. He is not opposed to gleaning insight from experience, but he does believe that these insights must be brought into dialogue with rules and theological and ethical principles.[36]

Browning, as well as a number of practical theologians, has been greatly influenced by the "revised correlation model" of David Tracy.[37] The revised correlation method seeks to bring into relationship data from multiple sources, including insights from theology or the Christian witness as well as insights from sociology and other human science sources. Browning, in his search for norms, does not begin with theology to be applied to a social situation but rather seeks to correlate descriptive material regarding the situation and interpretations from history and the social sciences with theological and ethical thought. The purpose is to formulate norms and to act upon them in the practical reality. Each side of the correlation asks questions, and each gives answers. The results seem to make practical theology an interpretative science in which truth claims may be made and a course of action formulated. Naturally, the new course of action and the assumptions behind it will also be subject to critical reflection and a new selection of responses. Religious education in this model becomes a form of hermeneutics in which truth claims are constantly being examined and articulated. Browning defines this process in religious education as the "critical correlation between the norms for human action and fulfillment revealed in interpretation of Christian witness *and* the norms for action and fulfillment implicit in various interpretations of ordinary human experience."[38]

Practical theology may be the way of the future for a theory and practice of religious education. It solves some basic problems and helps to clarify the discipline of religious education.

1. In the first place all the members of the religious community are involved and expected to be participants in the educational enterprise. The theological reflection or content of education is shared by all members and is not just the work of religious leaders. The revised model of practical theology seeks to move away from the clergy as the focus and makes the entire community of faith the subject of theological reflection. The separation between clergy and religious educators is overcome by this model when the focus is on the total experience of the faith community.

2. In the practical theology we have outlined, the separation of the church or religious community and the world is over-

come. One of the limitations of Coe's work is that his ecclesiology made it unclear as to who the Christian social reformers were. Apparently for him, the reformers were those who participated in the religious education program. Partly because of a dichotomizing of church and world, religious education theory has been divided between nurture of persons for the church and social action. In the religious education proposed here, the community of faith exists to serve the world. Some religious educators would describe this as the public nature of all theological discourse, and others would talk about it as the prophetic or political nature of theological praxis. In any case, the inner and worldly kingdoms are not mutually exclusive, as Luther discovered in his two-kingdom concept.

If religious education is to take a public role, then classes, forums, and other educational events should encompass public issues and should recognize them as having theological significance. Also, such studies need to prepare persons to participate in public debate, not for confessional reasons, but for the general welfare of society. A religious community is a group of persons who actively care for the social order and seek to make it just for all persons. The motivation of love, as understood by Elliott, becomes active in this model in the concern that persons extend to the social situation.

For persons in the faith community to take action around concrete social issues will also become the source for further theological understanding. To be involved as a faith community will lead to reforms in society influenced by some clear images of what it means to have a social order that is good for all people. As the church has discovered in Latin America, the liberation of the oppressed serves also to liberate the oppressor.

3. Practical theology as an approach to social religious education helps to deal with the problem that the progressive religious educators could never resolve. They either neglected theology because of a prior claim from educational functions or they chose a particular form of theology for religious education alone. The whole of theology is drawn into dialogue in the practical theology model. Even more important, practical theology insists that it is not just formal theology that is to be studied; the theological assumptions, beliefs, and values hidden in

action must also be examined and articulated. The act of doing theology and acting in the world as a people of faith leads to new theological conclusions and to new faith statements that must be in dialogue with historical statements.

4. This model of religious education provides the way to integrate all truth and to relate theological knowledge and secular knowledge around concrete issues and situations. The separation between theology and the social sciences can be overcome by more attention to the reverse correlation method. Questions can be asked by either side of the correlation, and answers may be derived from a multiple of sources. The method removes the dominance of one source of knowledge over all others.

CONCLUSION

In this chapter, we have sought to show the historical roots for a social theory of religious education. George Albert Coe is not only thought of as the father of modern religious education but he is the first to attempt a social theory from the discipline. Religious education for him was greatly informed by appropriating the insights from sociology. Harrison Elliott was not the first to introduce the ethical dimensions into religious education, but he was the one who tried systematically to demonstrate that social ethics and religious education belong together. He and many others of his day were influenced by the reforms in education introduced by the reconstructuralists. They sought to demonstrate that education was basically a social enterprise.

Some recent attempts to formulate the social aspects of religious education have been presented here also. Liberation religious education focuses on social action and even revolutionary forms of social change. Lifestyle education seeks to show the relationship between personal transformation and social change. Attention here is intended to help persons understand how society acts upon personal perceptions and how a new consciousness is required to change this action. The emphasis in lifestyle education is on making choices for life that have profound social implications. Such choices lead to a new sense of freedom and a vision of hope for all people.

A practical theology of religious education is still in a formative stage, but it provides a framework to integrate these modern emphases in religious education by a methodology that includes social analysis, action, ethical reflection, and theological thought. In this regard, practical theology is not only a method of correlation but seeks to integrate the social and the personal and to understand religious education as a way to help persons act in moral and ethical ways in the public and practical arenas of life.

NOTES

1. For a discussion of Luther's two-kingdom concept and its application to social ethics, see Wolfhart Pannenberg, *Ethics* (Philadelphia: Westminster, 1981).

2. *What Is Christian Education?* (New York: Charles Scribner's Sons, 1929), p. 29. Coe set forth a social theory of religious education early in his career and kept this viewpoint always in the forefront of his thinking. Cf. *A Social Theory of Religious Education* (New York: Scribner's, 1917).

3. The literary illustration of this point is in the classical debate between Harrison Elliott and H. Shelton Smith over the purpose of religious education. See Harrison S. Elliott, *Can Religious Education Be Christian?* (New York: cribner's, 1940), and H. Shelton Smith, *Faith and Nature* (New York: Scribner's, 1941).

4. Pannenberg, *Ethics*, pp. 7-8.

5. Ibid., p. 10.

6. The reader would enjoy reading a brief autobiographical statement written by Coe describing his development as a radical social thinker. See Coe's "My Own Little Theatre" in *Religion in Transition*, ed. Virgilius Ferm (New York, Macmillan, 1937); and "My Search For What Is Most Worthwhile," *Religious Education* 48 (1952), pp. 170-76.

7. See Harry F. Ward, "We Were Friends," *Religious Education* 47 (March-April 1952), pp. 88-91. Ward was a major leader in the Methodist Federation for Social Action and served as a colleague of Coe at Union Theological Seminary, and they continued to be dialogue partners around social issues until Coe's death in 1951.

8. Elliott, *Can Religious Education Be Christian?*, p. 219.

9. Ibid., p. 244.

10. Ibid, p. 212.

11. The idea of the vision of an anticipation of the kingdom as foundational to religious education theory is best developed in the work of James Fowler, *Becoming Adult, Becoming Christian* (San Francisco: Harper & Row, 1984).

12. Elliott, *Can Religious Education Be Christian?*, pp. 212.

13. I am deeply indebted to a very helpful study of Elliott by Frederick Nile Harper, *The Thought and Work of Harrison Elliott* (New York: Union Theological Seminary, 1964).

14. Ibid., pp. 209-210.

15. See especially Brammeld's definitive work on reconstruction-ism, *Toward a Reconstructed Philosophy of Education* (New York: Dry-den, 1956). Brammeld is usually considered the architect of social reconstruction in educational philosophy. For example, Walter Hol-comb of the Boston University School of Theology attempted to develop a religious education theory based on reconstructionism.

16. Clarence J. Karier chronicles the historical tension between the individual approach to education and the society-oriented view. See his *The Individual, Society, and Education* (Urbana University of Illinois Press, 1986), esp. pp. 184-257.

17. Allen J. Moore, "Liberation and the Future of Christian Educa-tion," in *Contemporary Approaches to Religious Education*, ed. Jack L. Seymour and Donald E. Miller (Nashville: Abingdon, 1982); Malcolm L. Warford, *The Necessary Illusion* (Philadelphia: Pilgrim, 1976); Alice F. Faiger, Robert A. Evans, and William B. Kennedy, eds., *Pedagogies for the Non-Poor* (Maryknoll, N.Y.: Orbis, 1987). This section is an adaptation from my chapter cited above.

18. Paulo Freire's writings are numerous, but three of his important books in English are *Pedagogy of the Oppressed* (New York: Herder and Herder, 1970); *Education for Critical Consciousness* (New York: Seabury, 1973); and *Pedagogy in Process* (New York: Seabury, 1978).

19. Juan Luis Segundo, *The Liberation of Theology* (Maryknoll, N.Y.: Orbis, 1976), pp. 3-4; see also Segundo's book, *The Hidden Motives of Pastoral Action* (Maryknoll, N.Y.: Orbis, 1978).

20. Ibid., pp. 8-9.

21. Religious education in North America takes place in a world context in which 20 percent of the people control 80 percent of the world's resources and in which two-thirds of the human family are in various states of starvation and hunger. We have conditioned our-selves to be immune to the fact that whites are haves and nonwhites are the poor. Much of mainline theology has served to justify this gross discrimination by overtones of "blessed" and the idea of stew-ardship, that is, we get because we are deserving.

22. See William Pinar, ed., *Curriculum Theorizing: The Reconcep-tualists* (Berkeley, Calif.: McCutchan, 1975).

23. Ivan Illich, "Education: A Consumer Commodity and a Psuedo-Religion," *The Christian Century* (December 15, 1971), pp. 1464ff.

24. Daniel Schipani, *Conscientization and Creativity: Paulo Freire and Christian Education* (Lanham, Md.: University Press, 1984), p. x. See also his discussion, pp. 25-52. See also Freire, *Pedagogy of the Oppressed*.

25. Freire, *Pedagogy of the Oppressed*, pp. 180ff.

26. Ibid., p. 185.

27. The behavioral or conduct component of a lifestyle is discussed more fully in James Michael Lee, *The Shape of Religious Instruction* (Birmingham, Ala.: Religious Education Press, 1971).

28. John Wilson, *Moral Thinking* (London: Heinemann, 1970).

29. A theme in the writing of James Fowler, "Practical Theology and the Shaping of Christian Lives," in *Practical Theology: The Emerging Field in Theology, Church, and World*, ed. Don Browning (New York: Harper & Row, 1983). See also Thomas H. Groome, "Christian Education for Freedom: A 'Shared-Praxis,' Approach," in *Foundations for Christian Education*, ed. P. O'Hare (New York: Paulist, 1978).

30. Richard Katz, "Education as Transformation: Becoming a Healer Among the !Kung and the Figians," *Harvard Educational Review* 51: 1 (1981), pp. 57ff. This entire issue is on the theme, "Education as Transformation, Identity, Change, and Development."

31. See Moore, "Liberation and the Future of Christian Education."

32. Scholars who have developed models of practical theology for religious education are Fowler, "Practical Theology and the Shaping of Christian Lives"; and Thomas H. Groome, "Theology On Our Feet: A Revisionist Pedagogy for Healing the Gap between Academia and Ecclesia," in *Formation and Reflection: The Promise of Practical Theology*, ed. Lewis S. Mudge and James N. Poling (Philadelphia: Fortress, 1987). John H. Westerhoff III has also sought to center religious education within a system of practical theology. Although he has a strong social consciousness, his work has been mostly classical in that he affirms the pastoral or clergy aspect of practical theology and the formational task of religious education for the life of the church. See especially John H. Westerhoff III and O.C. Edwards Jr., eds., *A Faithful Church* (Wilton, Conn.: Morehouse-Barlow, 1981), pp. 1-10 and 293ff; and *Building God's People in a Materialistic Society* (New York: Seabury, 1983).

33. See Don Browning, "Practical Theology and Religious Education," in *Formation and Reflection*. Browning's position has been developed more fully with pastoral care. See his *Religious Ethics and Pastoral Care* (Philadelphia: Fortress, 1983).

34. Ibid., p. 82.

35. Ibid.

36. For a discussion of the content and method of practical theology, see Seward Hiltner, *Preface to Pastoral Theology* (Nashville and New York: Abingdon, 1958); Browning, ed., *Practical Theology*; Schubert M. Ogden, *On Theology* (San Francisco: Harper & Row, 1986); Dennis P. McCann and Charles R. Strain, *Polity and Praxis: A Program for American Practical Theology* (Minneapolis: Winston, 1985).

37. The "revised correlational method" is a revision of Paul Tillich's method of correlation. In Tracy and Browning, the method is more ideological with questions and answers formed from both sides of the correlation. See Browning, *Practical Theology*, for a fuller discussion of method by Browning, Tracy, and others.

38. Browning, "Practical Theology and Religious Education," p. 80.

2

The Changing Family

Charles R. Foster

Few contemporary institutions receive more scrutiny than the family. The relationships of spouses, parents and children, and siblings have fascinated novelists, playwrights, and biographers. Marriage customs and child-rearing patterns dominate the attention of anthropologists. Sociologists intensively examine family structure and the relationship of the family to other societal institutions. Following the lead of Sigmund Freud, psychologists probe the pathology of family life. People in the so-called helping professions—clergy, educators, social workers, counselors—devote their lives to strengthening the quality of family life. Family advocacy groups engage in political action and public education with the intent to "save" and "protect" or to "challenge" and "reform" existing family patterns and resources.

All this attention has made us conscious of the complexity, vulnerability, variability, as well as the needs and pressures of families. At the same time, this attention creates a problem for people interested in developing a useful theoretical basis for social, educational, and religious policies related to family life and experience. One is confronted simultaneously by a cacophony of claims for the character and purpose of family life and an amazing lack of attention to the nature of the family itself. The experience may be similar to the attempts of the blind men to describe an elephant in the Indian parable. Each thought he had discovered the essence of the creature in the leg, side, tail, or tusk he was examining. Most of us have been raised in a family. We believe we know what the family is. Yet when we begin talking to each other across the varieties of our cultural experiences of family life, using language shaded by our own ideologies to evoke the meanings in those experiences and examining our personal experience against the conclusions of social-science research, we discover both the limitations in our experience and the difficulty we have in describing what we mean.

The language used to describe the variety of family forms compounds our problem. Some students of family life attempt to get at the meaning of the family through the *patterns of interaction* among family members. So Bernard Farber distinguishes among Puritan, Companionship, and Marxian models of family life, and Philip Grevin classifies families into evangelical, moderate, and genteel groups in a study of colonial child-rearing patterns. Other students of family life concentrate upon the *structure* of the family. Emmanuel Todd, for example, surveys the interplay of the concepts of liberty, equality, and marriage in families around the globe and discovers in the process seven distinctive variations of the nuclear family household and an eighth form that has a polygynous structure.[1]

The most familiar view of the family in the Western world emphasizes the *composition* of the family. This view tends to identify families as relational units including a father, mother, and children primarily in nuclear, but occasionally in extended, family patterns. The presence of all components becomes the norm against which all family experience is measured. Deviations from this standard have been variously called single parent, disjoined, step, blended, and serial marriage families. This nuclear image of the family has tended to dominate the imagination of social scientists, theologians, ethicists, lawyers, government officials, and religious educators in the Western world. As a norm this image of the family has been primarily used to preserve, protect, patch, strengthen, resource, support, and extend the values associated with the nuclear family. There are exceptions. Brigitte Berger and Peter Berger view the family as a social construct constantly in the process of being created. I share this point of view. In the pages that follow I intend to identify several sources for the confusion about the nature and function of the family, to begin to point our attention toward a theory of the family, and to conclude with several implications for developing a rationale and strategy for the religious education of families by churches.[2]

Why Is There So Much Confusion Over the Family

One source for the contemporary confusion over the meaning and value of the family may be traced to a set of conflicting messages found in the writing on the subject. The picture that emerges of the family emphasizes simultaneously its importance as an institution and its inability to fulfill the range of responsibilities historically identified with it. The family's strengths cannot surmount its weaknesses; its resources are inadequate to the challenges to be faced. This incipient cynicism toward the family is most evident in the discussions of divorce.

Divorce is not a new phenomenon. One can trace changing attitudes and regulations regarding divorce from tribal customs among the Hebrews to the attitudes of the early church in the Bible. The first divorce in colonial English America occurred shortly after the founding of the Plymouth colony. Contemporary divorce rates, however, undoubtedly contribute more than anything else to the perception of the family in crisis. Divorce is an increasingly familiar experience in American families. In 1880 only one of twenty-one marriages ended in divorce. By 1900 the ratio had changed to one in twelve. By 1916 it was one in nine. By 1976 one in three marriages ended in divorce. Although many now conclude that half of all marriages will end in divorce, a recent Harris poll calls the interpretation of this data "one of the most specious pieces of statistical nonsense ever perpetrated in modern times." Harris believes a more accurate reading of the data would indicate the ratio of marriages ending in divorce is closer to one of eight. Whether or not Harris is correct, the American public believes that the high divorce rate demonstrates the vulnerability of contemporary families.[3]

Over the years numerous suggestions have been made to reduce the divorce rate by strengthening the requirements of the marriage bond. In a survey of these suggestions, Elaine Fox traces an increasingly pessimistic view of the strength of marriage as the context for family life. As early as 1927, Judge Ben B. Lindsey proposed a couple enter a trial or "companionate" marriage. Bertrand Russell echoed the suggestion based on the conviction that a couple without sexual experience should not be planning for a family. Margaret Mead revived the notion in 1966 by proposing that marriage occur in two steps. A year later Virginia Satir suggested that couples enter into a five-year renewal contract for marriage. In 1972 Alvin Toffler anticipated a continuing disaffection with conventional marriage and the growing acceptance of temporary marriages. Psychologist James Henning brought this trend to its logical conclusion by calling marriage an out-dated institution.[4]

A more flagrant expression of this cynicism may be found in the rapidly growing industry that serves those caught in the upheaval of divorce. As Paul Bohannan observes, "Most of the people in that industry have nothing whatever to do with the quality of families. They hang on the fringe of collapsed families, providing commercial services, catering to divorce, and making a profit in its aftermath."[5] Bohannan correctly declares that we know a lot more about so-called "sick" families than we know about "well" families. Our preoccupation with the weaknesses and inadequacies of families focuses our attention on family problems rather than on family possibilities. This focusing on family problems draws our work with the family into remedial and therapeutic actions rather than creative and constructive ones and perpetuates our images of what we think the family should be rather than what the family is or could be.

The disparity in the rhetoric both celebrating family significance and decrying family limitations may also be seen in the discussions of the social utility or function of the family. Many follow the lead suggested by Talcott Parsons. Parsons observed that a major impact of modernization involved the removal of historic social functions such as economics and education from the family and the introduction of new functions having to do with the self-realization of individual family members and the development of individual rights. This shift of family function from public to domestic responsibilities required parents to learn a host of new roles and skills. The Carnegie Council on Children, under the leadership of Kenneth Kenniston, concluded that, in this shift, parenting became primarily a managerial task. The ability to choose programs and personnel to provide the services needed by their children, to negotiate their children's schedules, and to transport them from one activity to their next appointment dominated the parental agenda. The family, in this view, cannot fulfill the expectations of contemporary society regarding their children's educational, social, medical, and religious needs. The intervention by schools, churches, and professionals in a variety of fields is required.

Christopher Lasch also depicts the reduction of the role of the family in public life. The primary function for the family is to provide a haven or refuge for men, women, and children from the hostility they face daily in the megastructures of school, work, and government. Because the family serves to nurture personal well-being, it continues to be a crucial agency in the community. The reduction of family purpose, however, to functions promoting personal identity, managing personal schedules, and creating havens of calm and tranquility leaves the family without a moral contribution to the well-being of humankind.[6]

A second source for the confusion over the family may be traced to our lack of understanding the influence of radical technological and social changes on family structure and function. In a review of the adaptations of the family to the industrial revolution, Bohannan reveals the family's flexibility and innovativeness.[7] In the rising middle class, for example, men took jobs outside the home to become providers. Women became nurturers concentrating their efforts in the home and, through a host of community voluntary societies, promoted the efficacy of the new domesticity. Children, with more discretionary time on their hands, spent more of it in school and in activities supervised by adults who were not related to them. Improved medical care and changes in the economic value of children contributed to a decreasing family size. These shifts in function dramatically altered the ways in which women, men, and chil-

dren viewed and related to each other. The image of the nuclear family emerging from this social situation dominates most
expectations of the family in contemporary literature and media. This image does not reflect the corresponding urban working class adaptation to the industrial revolution in which men,
women, and children, as soon as they were able, all worked
outside the home. Only later did child labor and compulsory
schooling laws prevent the majority of lower-class children
from entering the world of work. Working-class family patterns
and relationships contrasted with those of the middle class—a
point made with increasing vigor by the advocates of middle-
class domesticity. At the same time the emergence of these two
patterns of family life indicates something of the capacity of the
family for innovation and adaptation.[8]

Perhaps less visible to us are the changes in family life due to
what Bohannan has called the biological revolution. This current transformation of the family has to do primarily with an
increased potential for controlling the processes of reproduc-
tion. This change does not simply alter the role of women in
the family; it alters their status and power in the community.
This shift has made possible the alternation of economic and
nurturing roles associated with industrial society family patterns; it also has made possible the consideration of marriage
without children. Furthermore, this change has stimulated and
intensified the momentum of the feminist and the rights of
children movements. This shift has also precipitated considerable creativity among those in the vanguard of the revolution. A
new vocabulary consisting of phrases like househusband, cler-
gy-couples, test tube babies, and day care as well as the extension of much civil rights legislation to women indicate something of the character of this revolution.

This revolution is far from over. Geneticists continue to explore the processes for starting life. Medical researchers persist
in their search for new techniques to facilitate and to hinder
fertility. Projections of the future point to alternatives for parenting, challenging in the process popularly held conventions
regarding family life. In the meantime families continue to
make specific decisions in response to these biological and
social changes, thereby shaping family forms and functions we

have discerned only in the most preliminary ways.

The ideological conflict over the meaning of the family also contributes to our confusion. Actually, as Stanley Hauerwas points out, little attention is given to the ideological content in the views people have of the family. Therein lies our problem. Bohannan observes that " 'family' is a code word for our deeper views of the place of women and of men and of children in the social world." Emmanuel Todd, in a provocative analysis of the relation of family structure to political structure, suggests that these codes are reflected in beliefs about the meaning of social relations integral to the cultural and political constructs of a society. Consequently, when people of western European ancestry in the United States speak of the family they usually have in mind a particular view of the nuclear unit of parents and children.

The ideological content in this view of the family begins to become self-evident when Brigitte Berger and Peter Berger call this family pattern *bourgeois*. In their claim that the bourgeois family is the necessary social context for the emergence of the autonomous individuals, the empirical foundation of political democracy becomes obvious.[9] The Bergers, along with Todd, Hauerwas, and a few others recognize, of course, that no view of the family is neutral. Whatever its form, the family shapes and reinforces what people value about the meaning and structure of society, about the basis of a society.

Recent anthropological and historical research challenges the view, however, that the bourgeois nuclear family is either predominate or normative in human experience. Todd's research for example, identifies at least eight family patterns, each with its own distinctive ideological basis. Philippe d'Aries, in his landmark study of the family in fourteenth-century France, concluded that childhood is not an innate human experience but is instead a social construct reflecting the values and commitments of people in a specific historical situation. This conclusion challenges many cherished convictions about the relationships of adults and children.

The family, in other words, is more than the extension of our experience. The family takes on a variety of forms and functions; it embodies a wide range of values regarding authority, freedom, and responsibility which in a pluralistic society often exist side by side. This means the student of family life, the architect of family social policy, and the religious educator can no longer assume a consensus regarding the meaning of the family.

A fourth source for our confusion about the family is rooted in our lack of attention to the influence of economics upon our understanding of family life and structure. In some Caribbean cultures, for example, elaborate and expensive ceremonial rites underscore the social significance of marriage. In this regard cultural practice supports the church's commitment to the importance of marriage. Most couples, however, cannot afford the cost involved. So they set up housekeeping and have children until the time, if ever, when they can afford to marry. Governmental and ecclesiastical laws and regulations are adapted to social conventions. Fox has also observed that low income intensifies the vulnerability of marriage commitments. "In terms of simple exchange theory, when a marriage is surrounded by poverty," she concludes, "the rewards outside the marriage may frequently surpass a lifetime of bills."[10] In an era of great economic fluctuation, such as the one in which we live, the patterns of feast and famine in many industries tests the resilience and adaptability of the nuclear family. The greater financial freedom of working women has provided new options to conventional family roles and expectations. One can only conjecture what the influence on family life will be from the shift in our nation from an industrial to a service economy, the probability of required retraining for ever new and changing jobs, the increased amount of leisure time, and the continuing devaluation of the meaning of work.

The church also has added to the confusion over the family. One source for Christian views on the family may be traced back to the pervasive sense of the interdependence of family, religious, and national identity in Jewish thought and practice and expressed most explicitly in the covenantal theology of the Puritans. Another source may be found in the elevation of celibacy as a higher form of devotion, first, in the early church's expectation of the return of the Messiah and the establishment of a new kingdom in which old patterns of marriage and family would be irrelevant and, second, in the influence of monasticism upon the medieval church. The interplay of these two themes in the history of the church has left its mark on church polity (as in the debates over the ordination of women), liturgy (as in the debates over the meaning of baptism and the role of children in the community of faith), and theology (as reflected in the variety of views regarding the role of the family in the kingdom of God).

In Karl Barth's lecture fragments on the Christian life we may discern a clue to the dilemma for the religious educator who turns to theology for guidance. Barth's intention in these lectures was not to examine family life and experience. Instead he draws upon familial relationships to illuminate the character of the Christian life. The opening petition of the Lord's Prayer—"Our Father"—establishes the pattern. In "fatherhood," Barth contended, we may most fully discern the meaning of the word "God." In this petition we also may recognize our own relationship to God as children. God consequently is "the founder and head of a family, a society of beings who are related by nature, physically to him and to one another, and who thus belong to him and to one another."[11] Although Barth's concern is not programatic, his theological analysis draws upon common human experience. Barth's analysis strangely makes no mention of the function of mothers in the social economy of the Christian life other than in the obvious implication of their role as childbearers. This is not the family experience of people. Unconsciously perhaps, Barth consequently perpetuated patterns of unreflective patriarchy, denigrated the role of women, and suggested an autocratic, albeit sometimes benevolent, view of social relationships.

The lack of awareness among most theologians of the cultural bias in their writings compounds the dilemma for the religious educator seeking a theological framework for understanding the family that responds, at the same time, to the cultural diversity of the church. Joseph Allen's discussion of the covenant as a model for social relationships illustrates the problem. Allen observes that from a Christian perspective all of humanity participates in one covenant community. This covenant community exists prior to any human agreement, yet the covenant community awaits human trust and loyalty before it is fully present. People cannot will the covenant out of existence. They can only decide whether or not to participate in the covenant. This basic covenantal relationship establishes the context for "special covenants" that arise out of specific historical transactions. Hence the covenant functions as a social structure binding people into families, churches, and political communities. Allen's exposition of the concept of the covenant in the Bible emphasizes the corporate and inclusive character of covenant. When Allen moves to a discussion of the special covenant of marriage, however, his conclusions are limited to images and experiences associated with the industrial middle-class version of the nuclear family. Allen does not consider the possibility that his discussion of special covenants might be culture specific. In spite of an inclusive paradigm for understanding family life, Allen's interpretation of the meaning of this special covenant circumscribes that inclusivity with Western values and commitments. The approach easily perpetuates the possibility of imposing these cultural views on the people of other cultures without recognizing the personal or social cost involved.[12]

No more help may be found in the theoretical literature in religious education. Most religious education writing on the family is programatic. This writing tends to project an uncritical commitment to the values of the middle-class nuclear family that emerged with the industrial revolution. The most explicit theological discussion of the family in religious education has its roots in the nineteenth-century controversies over the relationship of nurture and conversion in the faith of children. This debate centered upon the character and quality of the influence of parents upon the faith, values, and behavior of their children and also had to do with the extent to which the home environment might nurture human faith and character. The debate has continued into the present, although the metaphors have changed from nurture and conversion to development and transformation. The names involved are familiar: Horace Bushnell and Bennett Tyler in the nineteenth century and James Fowler and James Loder in the present.

The debate runs deeper than the description of alternate

routes to faithfulness; it has to do with the social constructs or contexts in which development and/or transformation occurs. Hence the debate has to do with the character of both church and family life. Bushnell recognized this fact, drawing heavily upon Puritan commitments to the family, church, and school as the primary organisms for the *nurture* of the faith and character of family members. For Bushnell this process was not confined to individual piety and character. The process was integral to the building up of both church and public life. The role of the family in the religious development or transformation of persons and of churches has not been a major focus in either Fowler's or Loder's research and writing. However, his lack of attention to the influence of agencies like the family in these processes makes it difficult to translate either Fowler's or Loder's theoretical work into policies to guide the social dimensions of religious education in either the family or the church.

Perhaps the ambivalence of the church toward the family is nowhere more evident than in the repeated attempts of religious educators to enlist the help of parents in the church's efforts to educate their own children. The pattern was set by nineteenth-century Sunday school leaders—Frederick Packard, Henry Clay Trumbull, John Vincent, among others. These individuals proclaimed the primary authority of parents in the religious education of their children. They also taught Sunday school teachers how to enlist parents in the support of the Sunday school's efforts and, later, promoted the development of standardized denominational curriculum that removed the authority for teaching from both congregation and home. This gap between religious education rhetoric and denominational practice has persisted into the modern era.

During the 1950s many Protestant denominations sought to enlist parents in a so-called educational partnership of church school and family. The intent of this educational strategy was to awaken parents to their religious education responsibilities, primarily by providing them with magazines discussing Christian parenthood and with a family curriculum resource augmenting the lessons of the church school. James Smart identified the intent of these religious educators in *The Teaching Ministry of the Church* to encourage "parents to do a little religious teaching in the home," but even more, to work toward "the recovery of the divine order for the home."[13] In actuality the strategy did not address the depths of the despair felt by religious educators over the ineffectiveness of the family in the religious education of children. This strategy perpetuated the notion that the family as a viable force for religious education had irreversibly declined and could function only with the intervention of the congregation. The promotion of a partnership of church and home in religious education only revealed the extent of the collapse of the mutuality of these two community agencies.

Toward a Theoretical Framework for Religious Education of the Family

Two views dominate most church discussions on the family and education. Both begin with the assumption that the contemporary family is under stress and in need of outside help. Each view responds to that assumption differently however. The first is primarily a reductionist perspective which seeks to reclaim patterns of family life and experience received often uncritically from the past. For the most part this response celebrates the industrial middle-class nuclear family both as the most viable family form and the model against which all other family experience should be measured.

Perhaps the popular lecturer and writer James C. Dobson most clearly represents this perspective. Dobson contends the home should be organized around the spiritual and moral authority of the father—a view based on a combination of biblical prescription and corporation images of executive leadership.[14] The ideal role for mothers is in the home. The primary authority for family decisions belongs to the father. Parents relate to children as role models and guides with the expectation that children will emulate and incorporate family values, ideals, and skills. Dobson acknowledges the reality of working mothers and single parents but views them as symptoms of the contemporary problems in the family. The family is nuclear in composition, hierarchical in structure, and primarily transmissive in function. Those who hold this view believe deeply in the constructive role of the family in society. They limit the family's contribution, however, to social images based on biblical in-junctions and the values of an industrial middle class.

The other dominant perspective is primarily reactive or de-fensive. This approach to the family also values the traditional nuclear family structure but views the family as existing under the siege of modernity. The family consequently is hurt, frag-mented, and unable to cope alone with the variety and the extent of the demands placed upon it. Among the most familiar of the works on the family from this perspective is drawn from the research on adolescents and their parents by Merton and A. Irene Strommen. The title of their work reflects the point of view: *Five Cries of Parents.* As the cover of the hardback edition claims, the book seeks to guide families "weathering the inevi-table problems of adolescence" and to help "parents build a more satisfying life." The most pervasive concept informing the book has to do with parental *need*. In this case parental need includes their fears about the dangers their children face from drugs and alcohol, child abuse, and social violence. The as-sumption of the Strommens and others who view families un-der siege is that intervention by schools, churches, and social service agencies can strengthen the family to withstand the negative influence of the infections.[15]

A third approach to the family is taken by Brigitte and Peter Berger. Their study of the family entails a thorough survey of the social science and historical literature related to the family. The Bergers are cognizant of the great variations in family form and function around the world and work from the premise that society and its various components are social constructions. The form and function of the family consequently is not to be assumed. For the Bergers the question runs deeper than whether or not one can strengthen or perpetuate existing fam-ily forms. The question has to do with what kind of family will be constructed for the future. The Bergers answer their ques-tion unapologetically. Their study of family research leads them to the conclusion that the nuclear family is a family structure deeply rooted in human history. In its recent and Western form, the nuclear family has functioned as the "agent and conduit of modernization"—promoting especially the modern emphases on individuality and rationality. The nuclear family has also shaped, through an intense socialization process, the consciousness of each succeeding generation. The resulting "domestication education," as the Bergers call it, "made it possible to socialize precisely the sort of responsible, competent, and morally sensitive individuals that bourgeois values demanded."

Historically, the primary purpose of the bourgeois family centered on this educational mission. The recent loss of clarity about the meaning and purpose of family life, the Bergers contend, is due in part to the diminishing commitment of people to this understanding of the family. The result tends toward social decadence and anarchy—all in the name of freedom and change. For the Bergers the bourgeois family has been one of the "foremost human achievements" because it provides an appropriate balance between "freedom and restraint, between individual self-realization and social responsibility."[16] Consequently the Bergers advocate an explicit social commitment to the primacy of nuclear families in the task of providing stable environments in which people might fashion a world to enhance their own sense of well-being and to nurture their contribution to society. The Bergers move beyond strategies to save, protect, or guide family members. They advocate, in the midst of the pluralism of family forms, approval of social policies to enhance the national commitment to the strengths of the bourgeois nuclear family.

I would like to suggest a fourth approach to the family to guide religious education theory and policy. This approach is similar to that of the Bergers in seeking to take seriously the insights of history and social science into the durability and variability of family form and function. This approach also takes seriously the connection between the structure and the ideology of family life. In contrast with the Bergers' point of view, however, this fourth approach begins with the quality and character of the human community rather than with the forces undergirding individual identity and vocation. Our approaches are essentially reversed. We both recognize the necessary interdependence of personal and social phenomena, but my premises begin with the nature of community and move to personal values.

To begin we must first distinguish between our use of the

terms family and household. The two have been equated for much of Western, and Christian, history. Biblical writers, for example, used family and household interchangeably. So does the United States Census Bureau. Contemporary experience of the meanings associated with the two terms, however, is often divergent. Emmanuel Todd's use of the phrase "family household" points to the possibility that the two are no longer necessarily interchangeable. While it may be true that most families may be identified with a household, the reverse is not necessarily true. An increasing number of households do not contain families.

Family encompasses specific ways of viewing the relationship of men and women and children. As stated earlier, family is a code word gathering up, for specific social and cultural entities, sets of expectations regarding the nature of that relationship and its function within the larger social milieu. Family is a temporal word because through the family societies envision their continuity. Stanley Hauerwas makes this same point. We do not choose to be a part of a family. There is, instead, for every person an inescapable sense of being "stuck with" the history of a particular people. People tell stories to help them make sense out of the good and the bad in that history. The act of storytelling consequently involves the "moral affirmation of what it means to be a part of a family." Hauerwas concludes by observing that "the family is morally crucial for our existence" because the family is "the only means we have to bind time." Through the intergenerational ties of the family we discover "what it means to be historic beings." A strong sense of family identity acts as an antidote to the appeal of whatever ideologies dominate the popular imagination. The family establishes the link between our sense of responsibility for the relationship of the past we have inherited and the future we have the power to help create.[17]

Family has to do with kinship. This means that the family is concerned with "the ways in which mating is socially organized and regulated, the ways in which parentage is assigned, attributed, and recognized, descent is traced, relatives are classified, rights are transferred across generations, and groups are formed."[18] Although most views of kinship have a strong biological basis, this definition emphasizes kinship's sociological character. This definition also reflects the experience of those cultures in which biological ties make up only one facet of kinship. In some African cultures, for example, all women and men of a village function as aunts and uncles for all the children of the village. Responsibility for the supervision and care of children is thereby expanded beyond the typical patterns to be found among the descendents of northern Europeans.

Kinship structures are one of the primary components in society. As a primary structure for relating men, women, and children, kinship structures engage people in the exercise of power; they embody patterns of authority, control, and freedom. Kinship structures build and extend corporate indentity—often through stories and rituals; they pattern ways of educating. These family actions encompass a range of intentional and unintentional activities; their function, however, is to historicize family experience by linking family heritage and family possibilities and to socialize family life by linking the experience of family members with the institutions and social structures of the larger community. In this regard the family acts in developed societies as a mediating structure.

Peter Berger and John Neuhaus have described the function of a mediating structure as making possible the ongoing migration of people back and forth between the private and public spheres of their lives. The family role in society is crucial to the welfare of both individuals and society. The family reduces the isolation of individuals caught up in the impersonal and unresponsive megastructures of school, industry, and government. Together with other mediating structures, such as the church, the neighborhood, and other voluntary societies, the family facilitates the involvement of people in this public world by generating and maintaining values integral to the welfare of both.[19] This view of the family reclaims for parents a designated community role beyond the popular notions of nurturing identity or managing schedules.

As a mediating agency in the community, the family may or may not be an economic or political institution. In its patterns of governance, however, the family introduces children to moral values and social practices associated with the political life and cultural institutions of the larger community. The family also provides a wide range of relational, educational, and liturgical services for family members. The family initiates successive generations into the public ideals of the community. The family participates in the larger social milieu both as an agent of the community's identity and heritage, and as an agent of the community's future. The family, in other words, is basic to the continuing vitality of the community.

In contrast to the temporal character of the family, household is a spatial term having to do with the dwelling places of people. A household locates people in a place, as specific as the corner of First and Main streets or as general as the region around Hebron or East Tennessee. Setting, climate, and memories of events and relationships associated with the particularity of a place give household its meaning. The household may gather several generations to a common place for meeting and remembering, thereby reinforcing the connections often made between household and family. For others, household is associated with the belongings that make any place home.

Household patterns vary even more than families. In biblical times a household such as that of Jacob included his wives and their children and their sons' wives and children, his concubines and their children and their children's children, as well as his servants and their "families." Jacob's household included married and unmarried adults, children, residents, and sojourners. In contrast a household in the United States today may include a "family." Just as likely, a household may include a single adult living alone, or two or more adults who have consented to share for a time the responsibilities of a household. The members of a household may be ever-changing. Children may or may not be included. Perhaps most significant is the fact that there is no necessary connection between the generations.

A household is a social structure. Members consent to patterns of power and authority, freedom and responsibility. These, however, tend to be situational and discrete, voluntary and changing. In spite of this variability, the household fulfills certain social functions. The household provides shelter, protects dwellers from natural elements and societal dangers, establishes boundaries between the public and private worlds of persons, and often serves as a retreat or refuge from the public world. Christopher Lasch describes this latter function of the household. In the process he illustrates as well the contemporary tendency to reduce the concept of the family to the experience of the household.

The household is also a center of hospitality; it is the place where the rituals of eating, intimacy, and mutuality exist at their most elemental levels. As such the household stands over against the human predilection for isolation in the public world. The household gathers people into ritual activities that enhance mutuality. The traditions of hospitality are deeply rooted in the Jewish and Christian experience. Henri Nouwen and John Koenig convincingly argue that, for the church, household hospitality has been a primary strategy for the establishment and maintenance of communities of reconciliation in a hostile world.[20] The household, in other words, is more than a place for sleeping and eating; it is the location of the most basic of human activities involved in the care and protection of others. Consequently the quality of the household is critical to the well-being of family life. The quality of the household is also critical to the significant proportion of the nation's population who are not gathered into family communities. The household provides a nonfamily social structure that legitimates the decisions of adults who choose not to marry or to have children. The concern of the church for the household, in other words, is not confined to the issues of family life.

Both family and household experience stress whenever the interdependence of the various mediating agencies of the community become dysfunctional. In our own time this stress is evident in urban and rural, advanced and developing, Christian and Buddhist societies. Stress is evident in the family in the fluidity of family relations. Divorce becomes a symptom of the collapse of the marriage vow as the special covenant of the family. The mobility of family members inhibits the ways families perpetuate and reinforce family traditions and stories. The consistent interventions into family life by the megastructures of government, school, industry, and media intensify the stress upon the continuity of family identity and function.

The stress on the household is often economic and political. Common burdens have to do with finding and paying for adequate places of shelter. Zoning ordinances increasingly restrict the locations where people may live. Even as racial barriers limiting the access for housing to certain peoples are disappearing, new boundaries emerge clustering people into age-segmented and income-segregated communities. Public policies continue to contribute to the dehumanization of the poor and to the isolation of the elderly and the young. High-rise housing projects and nursing homes, for example, may provide shelter but, equally, hamper the exercise of hospitality. Shelters for the homeless are only respites in the desperate quest for places of safety and havens of compassion.

The family is not only a social institution. The family functions conceptually, informing and, at the same time, standing over against that reality. Todd reminds us that "the family by definition reproduces people and values. Unconsciously but inevitably, each generation absorbs those parental values which define elementary human relationships: between parents and children, between siblings, between husband and wife."[21] These operating assumptions take on ideological content as people participate in a complex but "highly organized intellectual apprenticeship" in cultural agencies assigned the responsibility of transmitting formally the values and beliefs of a society. The school, religious traditions, and religious institutions, as well as voluntary societies, contribute to the formation and extension of a society's ideals of the family. That the most familiar ideological perspectives on the family are identified with economic systems—capitalism and Marxism—is intriguing. These two, however, are not the only such perspectives among the people of the world.

The power of ideology is located, in part, in its ability to be translated into an image which serves people as a model for their actions and aspirations. In the United States and much of the Western world, the culturally established image of the family promoted by church, state, media, and family professionals includes "a married couple, and their minor children, living together in their own home, forming an intimate and protective environment, providing nurture and care to the individuals concerned."[22] Any deviation from this image tends to be perceived as abnormal. The negative view taken of these deviations is reflected in such phrases as "broken-home," "illegitimate" children, and "unwed" mother. The cultural content of this nuclear image was dramatized for me by a friend from India who sympathized with my wife and myself for having to find someone to love rather than to enjoy the benefits of an "arranged" marriage.

As an image the nuclear family has functioned constructively as a model for family life. This image has contributed significantly to the advances of Western society—a point the Bergers make convincingly. At the same time, any family image viewed normatively for all of human experience can be destructive as well. Students have often explored the contribution of this Western middle-class image of the family to the social, political, moral, and religious life of other peoples around the world. A corresponding critique of the social disruption and corruption created by the imposition of that image on family practice in societies having other views has yet to be done.

Family also functions symbolically. Particularly is this true within religious traditions. Christianity, for example, hallows the Holy Family even though the traditions around the birth of Jesus create problems for understanding the relationship of men and women and of men and children. Dietrich Bonhoeffer points to a more helpful way the family functions symbolically. For Bonhoeffer the family relates the world to God. The family participates in the creative activity of God in the creation of children who live to give glory to God and who serve Jesus Christ by helping to extend the kingdom of God. The family thereby symbolizes the creative and educative will of God. That relationship is made concrete and active in the expectation that parents are "for the child the representatives of God."[23] One might say that from this perspective the family functions paradigmatically as the community of faith and parenthood as the primal expression of the priesthood.

Hauerwas makes another claim for the power of the symbol of the family. The family distinctively embodies hope for people who have "a growing distrust of our ability to deal with the future." For Jews and Christians, having children makes a moral claim on the future. The action is not unlike that of Jeremiah buying a piece of property just as the enemy is ready to destroy the city. "It represents our willingness to go on in the face of difficulties, suffering, and the ambiguity of modern life." Such an action declares we have something of value to hand on to the future.[24] And such action dramatizes our sense of responsibility for the decisions we make affecting the quality of that future.

Implications for the Religious Education of Families

The family is a historical, social, and pluralistic phenomenon. Hence we are confronted with varieties of family forms and ideologies from our collective past, our global present, and our emerging future. We make choices among these options. As Hauerwas aptly observes, there is no "great moral issue" involved in a choice among particular family forms, because "families find ways to exist" despite external conditions.[25] We do have, however, a responsibility regarding our view of the meaning of the family; it is that decision which will influence the way we approach family religious education. As participants in the Christian tradition those choices are governed in part by the Christian tradition's values and vision. As one participant in that tradition I would like to suggest several claims for the family that we who call ourselves Christians should be making. In this regard I share the Bergers' conviction that, because the family is a social construct embodying both tradition and ideology, we need to attend consciously to the point of view we will use to guide the approaches we take to family religious education.

1) *The family is the basic institution of society.* The family is basic in the sense that it exists as the first and most enduring institution in which the perceptions, values, ideals, and behaviors of people take shape and are given expression.[26] The family opens up the world to its members. As such the family contributes to the public life of a society. This means that the roles of family members are not confined to the private realm of relational intimacy. Instead these roles are crucial to the quality and character of public life. In this regard the church needs to reclaim an ideology for the family that affirms the

social contribution of the family. Bushnell's conviction that the three "great forms of organic existence" appointed by God—the national life, the church life, and the family life—functioned interdependently illustrates this perspective. For Bushnell the resourcefulness of a society depended upon the mutual strength of all three. If any one of the three proved to be weak or dysfunctional, the whole suffered. Bushnell believed the weak link in the social order during the mid-nineteenth century was located in the family, in part, because people had forgotten its distinctive contribution to the whole. Today the problem is more serious; the church, and to an even greater extent the government as well as a new social configuration—the family professional—has assumed increasing responsibility for traditional family roles. Hauerwas claims this appropriation of family roles and functions may be traced in part to the "individualistic ethos of democracy" and the fascination of Christianity with the "idea of singleness." If correct, the task of reclaiming the communal nature and public function ·of the family will be a major undertaking. The impetus to this task, however, is equally rooted in the historic Jewish and Christian commitment to the interdependence of family and public life.

2) *The formation of families embodies the mutuality of partners imaged in the covenant.* Contrary to Western middle-class family ideology, the purpose of the family is not to create individuals; it is to create communities. The nature of the family is relational—between man and woman, between parents and children across successive generations, and among siblings. The nature of the family involves a binding action that builds community, emphasizing a relational rather than a psychological source for identity. We discover our distinctiveness in the context of family, church, and community identity.

In Jewish and Christian theology this process has been identified most clearly with the covenant. At this point Joseph Allen's description of the inclusive character of the covenant is appropriate. Initiated by God the covenant includes all people. Allen's description of marriage as a "special covenant" is also helpful. Through the marriage vow a man and woman publicly affirm the covenant of God in the structure of the family. The mutuality of the covenant is internal. The unequals of the covenantal relationship are man, woman, and children, not in the structure of their relationships to each other, but as they stand together in the family community before God.

Each participant in the covenant has both rights and responsibilities to help the family community participate in the gracefulness of the covenantal relationship with God.[27] The particular structure of those relationships is historical, cultural, and changing. The structure of family life in the Bible did not remain the same through the ages. Obvious differences may be observed in a comparison of nomadic and urban, patriarchal and early church experience of family life. Family structure, in other words, adapts to contemporary conditions. At the same time, the persistence of patriarchal notions in the relationship of family members into our time reveals more about the persistence of cultural values than such persistence does about God's graciousness. The persistence of patriarchal notions is a historical, and therefore time constrained, structure of the family community. The issue for the family community today—as in any age—has less to do with holding on to any given family form, which may be identified with Abraham and Sarah or some other historical prototype, than with discerning what to be faithful together in our own time and situation means. As we face the challenge of that task, the power of tradition cautions us from cutting ties with past forms and functions too quickly. Similarly the call to participate in the creation of the future challenges our corresponding tendency to idolatrize that which is familiar.

3) This brings me to my third claim. *The family is the primary agency for the re-creation of the community.* The continuity of church, cultural, or global human community is dependent upon families. The task is seen in the description of childbearing as "pro"creation. Unfortunately, in the tendency to reduce the social role and function of the family, this term has also lost much of the breadth of meaning it has had in the past. Allen reminds us that procreation has meant through the history of the church, not only the task of "bringing children into the world, but also bringing them up to responsible maturity."[28] This latter task involves grandparents, parents, older siblings, and other family members in *handing on* the stories, traditions,

values, beliefs, and behaviors central to the identity of the family and of the associations and institutions that sustain, extend, and renew family, religious, cultural, and national identity. This task involves *introducing and initiating* family members into the moral beliefs, overarching ideals, and social roles central to the identity of the institutions of the larger community and includes actions that *shape* the beliefs, values, attitudes, and behaviors of family members through instruction and advice, the establishment of limits, and the reinforcements of selected responses.

These educational tasks emphasize the socialization of the young and the uninitiated into the life of the family and of the larger community. Such socialization does not mean the blind perpetuation of the past. Instead this socialization reminds us that our images of the future are drawn from the intensification of our collective memory, that the depth of our convictions and the power of our knowledge and skill are connected inextricably to the meanings we associate with experiences shared with those who have significance for us, and that our ultimate sense of purpose in life is enlivened by our ability to participate in it. Our images of the future are resources for engaging the content of contemporary experience and are central to the processes of making meaning and valuing. Hence these images enhance the potential for personal and social transformation which depends, in turn, upon the vitality of the interplay between our concern for continuity and our openness to change.

A second implication for the religious education of families has to do with educational strategy. The depth and quality of the educational efforts of mediating structures depends upon the extent of the mutuality among them. Mediating structures should overlap. Each has its own distinctive function in the community but is dependent upon the support of the other mediating structures to make that contribution. Current formal, religious educational practice in congregations, however, contributes more to the fragmentation and isolation than to the reinforcement and support of families. Congregations either approach the family as a composite of individuals rather than as a community bound together by a common purpose, history, and identity or as autonomous social units who come together in response to an appeal to a personal interest or need. These approaches negate the essential mutuality among families and between congregations and families. Any educational strategy must therefore be directed to the interdependence of congregation and family. With these comments in mind I would like to ask three questions that might be used to guide congregational planning for family religious education.

1) *Where are family members instructed in the content of the Christian faith? Where do they have the opportunity to explore the meaning of the Christian faith in relation to their contemporary experience? Where are family members trained to be agents of the gospel in the larger community beyond family and church?* I raise this set of questions because the most effective way congregations engage in family religious education is to attend first to the distinctive congregational responsibilities as mediating structures. The quality and depth of congregational religious education sets the context and expectations for any specific programatic strategy directed toward families. The religious education of families requires solid biblical, theological, and ethical teaching. By solid teaching I mean adequate *instruction* in the content of faith, sensitive *interpretation* of that content for the explicit issues and questions women, men, and children face in their daily lives, and plenty of opportunities to *practice* the insights, knowledge, and skills received in the educational process in the congregation's mission. If a congregation insists upon effective teaching, teachers must both know the content of their teaching and possess enough skill to communicate that content's vitality, for the Christian church and for them personally, to those they teach. A congregation's religious education of families could be said to begin with the congregation's commitment to the continuing education of its teachers. Hence congregations seeking to strengthen the religious education of families should begin with an assessment of their own teaching programs.

2) *Where and how is the congregation building family networks?* Contemporary congregational life perpetuates a program organization that emerged when people assumed, at least, that extended family ties and neighborhood associations were much closer than they are now. Few families have the full

range of resources to respond to the issues faced by the family
unit as a whole or by the family members individually. These
resources are most adequately supplied in the give and take of
families who share the bond of kinship, neighborhood, or fellowship. Family strength and resourcefulness depends significantly upon the extent and intensity of these overlapping relationships. The mobility and fragmentation of contemporary life
works against the establishment and support of these networks.
Consequently congregations no longer assume the presence of
such networks and seek instead to supplant them with programs external to family life. Bureaucratic and age-segregated
congregations, however, lack the flexibility and adaptability to
respond to the daily dynamics of family life. This suggests that
family religious education depends upon the creation of networks among families to provide mutual support and encour-
agement, to uphold standards and values against external pressures, and to share responsibilities for the nurture and care of
family members. The intimacy of family networks, moreover,
helps to reduce the sense of family isolation and to give to
children a variety of adult friends and role models. Such intimacy intensifies as well the mutuality critical to the vitality of the
sense of community in the congregation.

3) *Where does the educational, liturgical, and missional life of
the congregation spill over into family life thereby modeling and
resourcing the ministry of the family community?* Most programs
and activities in the congregation are designed to be self-suffi-
cient and self-contained. Worship occurs between 10:30 and
11:30 a.m. The educational program is limited to designated
classes and scheduled times. Most outreach programs tend to
be isolated from other congregational activities. This programatic structure subverts the interdependence of ministry and the
mutuality of church and home. Congregational approaches to
education, worship, and mission can spill over into the life and
work of families in such a way that they participate as "house
churches" enlivening in turn, the larger faith community.

An example may illustrate my point. Many congregations
encourage families during Advent to make use of an Advent
wreath to encourage family worship. The congregation may
send out a leaflet describing how one may be made and pro-

vide a devotional guide. The readings and prayers accompanying this ritual activity may be common for both home and church. Any connections made between the liturgical life of home and congregation, however, depends upon the interest and the will of individual people.

A different sense of the relationship of congregation and family occurs, however, when members of the congregation are invited to participate in a special worship event on the first Sunday of Advent. Members of the congregation are involved in the preparation of a worship and study guide to be used in the weekly ritual. Scripture readings in the guide either are drawn from the lectionary or have been chosen because they will also serve as the texts for congregational worship. Members of the congregation gather prior to the special worship event to create their Advent wreaths. During worship each family unit lights a candle from the flame on the candle used in the congregation's worship. The corporate character of this family event is reinforced by singing familiar hymns. The scripture lessons are read and interpreted. A class for youth and adults is organized to run through the church season to facilitate a study of the weekly scripture lessons. A way for families to participate in this ritual is modeled. The mutuality of families in the congregation and between families and congregation is made visible. Parents and other family members are drawn into a ritual of priestly and teaching activities that reinforces the educational and liturgical responsibilities of families and dramatizes at the same time, the mutuality of congregational families in the cycles of church life. Family religious education can take place in special programs. My own belief, however, is that family religious education is most effective in those times and places where congregational leaders plan for the worship, education, and missional life of the congregation to spill over into the experience of families.[29]

NOTES

1. Bernard Farber, *Family and Kinship in Modern Society* (Glenview, Ill.: Scott, Foresman, 1973), pp. 128-32; Philip Grevin, *The Protestant Temperament: Patterns of Child-Rearing, Religious Experience, and the Self in Early America* (New York: New American Library, 1977); Em-

manuel Todd, *The Explanation of Ideology: Family Structures and Social Systems* (Oxford, England: Basil Blackwell, 1985).

2. This chapter is necessarily limited by the constraints of space. Consequently the complexity of issues related to the religious education of the contemporary family cannot be fully developed. Some of these would include the influence of extended life span, the growing public acknowledgment of relationships based on homosexual patterns of intimacy, the impact of recent immigration from Asia and Latin America on views of family life, the influence of adults who choose not to marry, or the fear precipitated by the AIDS crisis on our cultural expectations and attitudes toward marriage, children, and the function and character of family life.

3. Elaine Fox, *The Marriage-Go-Round: An Exploratory Study of Multiple Marriage* (Lanham, Md.: University Press of America, 1983), pp. 164, 141, 6.

4. Ibid., p. 165.

5. Paul Bohannan, *All the Happy Families: Exploring the Varieties of Family Life* (New York: McGraw-Hill, 1985), p. 11.

6. Cf. Kenneth Kenniston and The Carnegie Council on Children, *All Our Children: The American Family Under Pressure* (New York: Carnegie Council on Children, 1977); Christopher Lasch, *Haven in a Heartless World: The Family Beseiged* (New York: Basic Books, 1977).

7. Bohannan, *All the Happy Families*, p. 1.

8. In Diane Gittens, *The Family in Question: Changing Households and Familiar Ideologies* (Atlantic Highlands, N.J.: Humanities Press, 1986), pp. 35-72 and Jane Douglas, *The Feminization of American Culture* (New York: Avon, 1978), these changes are developed in detail. Considerable attention is also given to the development of the ideology of the middle-class nuclear family that led to repeated efforts to reform the family patterns of the working-class poor.

9. Bohannan, *All the Happy Families*, p. 3; Todd, *The Explanation of Ideology: Family Structures and Social Systems*, p. 13; Brigitte Berger and Peter L. Berger, *The War Over the Family: Capturing the Middle Ground* (Garden City, N.Y.: Anchor/Doubleday, 1983), p. 172.

10. Fox, *The Marriage-Go-Round*, p. 168.

11. Karl Barth, *The Christian Life: Church Dogmatics IV, Four Lecture Fragments* (Grand Rapids, Mich.: Eerdman, 1981), pp. 53, 56, 149.

12. Joseph L. Allen, *Love and Conflict: A Covenantal Model of Christian Ethics* (Nashville: Abingdon, 1984), cf. pp. 16-17, 32-42.

13. James D. Smart, *The Teaching Ministry of the Church: An Examination of the Basic Principles of Christian Education* (Philadelphia: Westminster, 1954), p. 185.

14. James C. Dobson, *Straight Talk to Men and Their Wives* (Waco: Word, 1980), pp. 64-65.

15. Merton P. Strommen and A. Irene Strommen, *Five Cries of Par-*

ents: *New Help for Families on the Issues that Trouble Them Most* (San Francisco: Harper & Row, 1985), pp. 3-4.

16. Berger and Berger, *The War Over the Family,* pp. 146, 115-16, 133, 164.

17. Stanley Hauerwas, *A Community of Character: Toward A Constructive Christian Social Ethic* (Notre Dame: University of Notre Dame Press, 1981), p. 165.

18. Gittens, *The Family in Question,* p. 64.

19. Peter L. Berger and Richard John Neuhaus, *To Empower People: The Role of Mediating Structures in Public Policy* (Washington, D.C.: American Enterprise Institute for Public Policy Research, 1977), pp. 2-7.

20. Henri J.M. Nouwen, *Reaching Out: The Three Movements of the Spiritual Life* (Garden City, N.Y.: Doubleday, 1975); John Koenig, *Hospitality in the New Testament: Partnership With Strangers as Promise and Mission* (Philadelphia: Fortress, 1985).

21. Todd, *The Explanation of Ideology,* p. 12.

22. Berger and Berger, *The War Over the Family*, p. 60.

23. Dietrich Bonhoeffer, *Ethics* (New York: Macmillan, 1961), p. 75.

24. Hauerwas, *A Community of Character,* pp. 165-66.

25. Ibid., p. 173.

26. See Berger and Berger, *The War Over the Family,* p. 204.

27. See Allen, *Love and Conflict,* p. 221ff.

28. Ibid., p. 224.

29. Similar examples may be found in other faith traditions, such as the celebration of Hanukkah within the Jewish family.

3

Women and Men
in the Social Order:
Challenge to Religious Education

Mary Elizabeth Moore

Women's liberation has galvanized much attention in the past twenty years, especially under the leadership of the feminist or womanist movements. In fact, the attention has increased to the point that most people feel compelled to have some opinion on the subject. Rarely is the subject mentioned without persons in the conversation offering their various opinions. In a recent international meeting of theologians and church leaders, I introduced myself by naming some of the courses I teach, including feminist theology. This was by far the most interesting and disturbing fact about me for the group gathered. I have grown accustomed to such nervous reactions, as well as to the jokes that are common responses when someone expresses feminist concerns. In this chapter we are not dealing with a nonissue or with the issue of a vocal minority, but with an issue that touches deep passions in most people's lives.

The first purpose of this chapter is to probe sexism in the present social order, and in the religious communities in particular. Since the author stands within the North American Christian context, the analysis undoubtedly will be affected by that context, but some attention will be given to how the issues rise in different forms all over the world and in various religious communities. The second purpose is to propose a social vision for the future, and the third, to propose how religious education can foster movement toward such a vision.

PICTURING THE PROBLEM

The problem is not an easy one to define because definitions cannot capture the richness of human life that is involved and the depth of human pathos. For this reason, the problem of sexism will be approached through story, reminding the reader that the stories are only partial and could be multiplied a thousand-fold.

Problem of Disparate Agendas

In a world meeting of church leaders in 1986, someone had the idea of gathering the women participants together for conversation. The meeting itself involved a few thousand people, but the number of women delegates was small enough that the women could sit in a circle in one large room. When the appointed time came, we introduced ourselves one by one, telling what we did in our home countries and what we hoped from this international organization. The informal convenors of the meeting then suggested that we might want to address some issues of common concern since this would be the only opportunity for women to gather together.

The meeting erupted into heated debate, reflecting the different agenda of the participants gathered. Some were angry that the convenors would want to focus on issues at all because they were more interested in sharing stories about their work. Others were angry about the way in which women had been underrepresented and closed out of the larger meeting, and they wanted to deal with those issues while we had opportunity to exert some political influence on the future. Still others felt that North American and Anglo women were dominating the agenda and that they were raising questions that were irrelevant in other parts of the world. (In fact, the convenors of this particular meeting were all from North American or Anglo-heritage countries, and the total delegation of men and women from North America was far larger than delegations from other parts of the world.)

Given the disparate agendas, the meeting time was occupied in identifying what those agendas were, and none of the agendas was actually addressed. The meeting, instead, was involved with a more basic problem of knowing what the issues *are* in a complex of many diverse agendas.

Identifying and understanding the issues is a very complex problem, and the problem is intensified by the passion and concern attached to the differing agendas in various parts of the world. The issues include the plight of poor women, the unique problems of women in nations at war, the tensions that exist between women from oppressed and oppressor racial groups, the power of sexist language to name reality in sexist terms, the stereotypes that exclude or minimize women's leadership in the social order, and patriarchal worldviews that perpetuate partriarchal social structures. This list of agendas is only partial, as any list would be, and that is part of the problem being raised here. One can never summarize the concerns inclusively or conclusively.

To complicate the picture still further, the separate agendas are sometimes used by others to minimize or negate the voice of women; people point to the differences as evidence that certain agendas are irrelevant because they do not concern all women. This adds a particularly grave problem to the list above because it becomes a way to devalue women's voices, or to "divide and conquer."

Some *educational challenges* arise out of the issue of separate agendas. The most obvious is the need *to listen to one another in dialogue and hear how others define the agenda.* For example, some Hispanic feminists believe that the most important agenda is to work together as families for social and economic change, rather than to focus solely on dynamics within family structures as if they were independent of oppressive social systems.[1] Some black and Hispanic feminists emphasize the interconnectedness of the issues of sexism, racism, and classism.[2] The test of liberation efforts for many of these women is the effects of the efforts on poor, racially oppressed women.

The second educational challenge grows naturally from the first. *Women and men with feminist concerns need to seek realistic ways to be in community with one another*, recognizing that alliances will vary from issue to issue and struggles will occur among those who struggle together for justice for women. The diversity and struggles should not be taken as a sign of inauthenticity or hopelessness in the movement, but of honesty and vitality. The time when feminist thought is controlled by white, North American, middle-class women is past, and the remnants of it must be left behind as soon as possible. Likewise, the time when differences within the feminist movement are taken as a sign of weakness and ineffectiveness is also past, and those with feminist concerns must avoid collusion with such destructive habits of thought and action. Women in society and in religious and academic institutions are too often divided by such dynamics to the point that mutual hearing and cooperation are thwarted.

Problem of Prejudice

A woman applied for a job as a postal carrier. She took the necessary civil service tests and scored higher than anyone else who had applied. The postmaster of her small town was alarmed about how to handle the situation because all of the other applicants were men and his rural community had never had a woman delivering the mail. He called in the woman's husband and, explaining his dilemma, asked for advice. The husband said that he was not going to give him a good reason for not hiring his wife; the postmaster would have to make this decision on his own.

In another situation, a woman had been serving a local church as an ordained Protestant minister for several years. She had carried all of the responsibilities of the ministry and had met very little resistance from her parishioners. When she became pregnant, the picture changed. One day after the worship service, a man in the congregation came up to her and asked her to let the other minister conduct the communion service while she was pregnant. He explained that her impure state was a reminder of sexuality that did not belong in the service of Holy Communion. This story, taken alone, seems to be an anomaly, but stories abound of women who have been asked by parishioners to cease certain ministerial activities, including preaching, during their pregnancies.

These are stories of prejudice that are used to discriminate against women by limiting what they are allowed to do. The limitations are sometimes rationalized by the desire to protect women from certain responsibilities or to protect the home for which women are responsible. The limitations are present, however, whatever reasons are given. Someone has made a stereotypical generalization that the women are not capable or interested in certain activities, or someone has decided *for* a woman that her spouse or family would be negatively affected if she did certain things.

The dynamics of prejudice do not operate simply in relation to getting and keeping a job but also to opportunities and privileges within a job. The statistics in the late 1980s are still alarming in terms of job opportunities, salaries, and advancement for women. Some of the economic disadvantages are very subtle, related to maternity and divorce practices in the United States.[3] These, of course, are the visible signs of discrimination, but many more signs are invisible.

To complicate the picture still further, women in both domestic and career roles have often been limited to the private sphere, the sphere of tending to the internal dynamics of the family or business or institution. The small proportion of women in academic administration is one small measure of this problem. In most professional groups, even in the late 1980s, women are more likely to be asked to serve as secretary and less likely to be invited to chair the group. The prejudices that support this discrimination become intensified when women are encouraged to stay in the private sphere and when the private sphere is isolated and devalued. The public and tangible rewards for the privatized duties are usually much smaller than the rewards for the duties of the public sphere, and the potential influence of persons working in the private sphere is smaller.

The situation is further intensified by the very large responsibilities and expectations placed on that same private sphere. Rosemary Radford Ruether has pointed out how frequently the private sphere is required to correct the problems of the public sphere, such as engage in ecological measures in the home to correct the ecological abuses of industry.[4] Another example is the expectation placed on mothers to guarantee the happy, well-adjusted personalities of their children. This expectation is so well endorsed by Western culture and by modern psychology (especially under the Freudian influence) that people living in the Western world tend to assume that crediting mothers with their children's strengths and blaming them for their flaws is simply common sense. Only very recently has this bit of common sense been revealed as culture-bound ideology.[5]

The double-edged consequences of prejudice begin to reveal themselves. Women are often limited to the private sphere, where their freedom and power are limited, but they are often burdened with responsibilities beyond the coping capacity of the private sphere. They are often expected to cure the ecological crisis or the complex problems of human development with little or no help from the social structures, institutions, and culture.

The primary educational challenge in this issue of prejudice is to recognize the prejudices which are fostered in the social order, even by ourselves. The challenge is to begin with the points of pain, however small they may seem by themselves, and then, to probe the larger picture: What other pains are connected, and what attitudes contribute to the pain? Dialogue is very helpful in this process because one becomes more conscious of others and of oneself in mutual hearing. Identifying prejudices becomes a step to other challenges, including especially the resolve to cease participating in the stereotyping that puts people into categories and limits their existence.

Problems of Poverty and Violence

Poverty and violence represent two of the most devastating oppressions of women. The United States is now being confronted with the feminization of poverty, with women being the fastest growing population of the poor. Furthermore, the objectification of women as sex objects and the exploitation of women through media and pornography contribute to a culture of violence toward women. The violence is expressed in rising statistics of wife-battering and rape in the United States.

In warring countries the poverty problem for women is close-ly linked to problems of violence and loneliness. One of the most devastating consequences of war is the way in which families are often pulled apart, and women suffer the oppres-sions of losing husbands and sons to the war effort, carrying responsibility for support and care of their families (while en-joying fewer rights and privileges than men in the same soci-ety), and being vulnerable to rape and assault by soldiers and others in a war-torn society. One of the most devastating re-minders of this complex of problems is Caroline Allison's col-lection of stories from women in Namibia.[6] The women of Namibia are poor and black, and they live in a country ravaged by the South African racial, political, and military conflict. Alli-son documents the situation in the words of women who live in isolated rural areas, responsible for the family farm and the care and feeding of several children. They carry that responsibility at the same time that they are subject to a curfew which prevents their seeking help from neighbors. They are limited in the per-mission to hold public meetings, cut off from human services and protection, and regularly at the mercy of South African soldiers who attack and rape them, pillage their homes, and even kill their children.

These stories in the United States and Africa are grim remind-ers that the issues of poverty and violence are global and that they often affect women with unusual intensity. Women often suffer the consequences and responsibilities of social malignan-cies in magnified ways; thus, the oppressions are multiplied.

The educational challenge of this social fact is to recognize the life and death nature of some aspects of sexism. The severity of the oppressions puts into larger perspective the problems that were first vocalized in public by white, middle-class, North American and European feminists. In fact, the multiple oppres-sions remind those same white, middle-class feminists that they are themselves a part of an oppressor class and that women are among the victims of their own participation in racism, class-ism, and militarism. The issues of poverty and violence are cries waiting to be heard so that the invisible protest of the power-less will be given voice.

Problem of Limited Participation

Another problem is women's less than full participation in social decisions and actions; this might also be called the problem of a tight center of leadership. Since leadership is often passed down in informal ways, many subtle influences keep women out of the center of influence, even in the presence of affirmative action programs and good intentions. For example, studies of women in academic institutions reveal that women are less rewarded and less advanced than men on all measures of formal status—employment, rank, salary, and tenure.[7] This has been evidenced in many studies, revealing only modest changes in the past twenty-five years (even when researchers controlled for variables, such as rank, in studying salary or tenure).

When asked why the pace of hiring women for theological faculties has not increased with all of the attention to the issue, one woman professor explained that she believed the senior male professors in her own institution tend to be drawn to the young candidates who are more like they were in their younger days. Unconsciously these men are often biased toward male candidates, even though they give reasons in terms of the candidate's style of scholarship or some other seemingly objective measure. This pattern is often repeated in the religious communities where church leaders and theological representatives of the church in global and ecumenical dialogues are almost always men, even in churches where women have been ordained or have served in public leadership for several decades.

The small percentage of women holding public office in the world is another reminder of the lack of full public participation among women. This is an ancient problem and is complicated by the fact that women have often held a great deal of power in the private sphere while holding minimal power in the public sphere. Karen Torjesen, for example, has discovered that women were often quite powerful in their homes during the early centuries of the Christian era. They were reprimanded, however, if they entered into the public arena, crossing boundaries inappropriately.[8]

This distinction between private and public power is important to help us understand the competitive dynamics that often plague the relationships between men and women. The private power held by women is sometimes used as justification for keeping women out of the public, in order to preserve some kind of balance between women and men. On the other side, one common argument of women who oppose the feminist movement is that they do not want to give up their own power in the family and in the private realm. They see the liberation of women into the public realm as a partner movement to the liberation of men into the private realm. They fear that men will begin to exert more power in private arenas. Their suspicion is justified because the liberation of women does begin to break down the sharp dichotomy between private and public and the sharp role differentiation. This is welcomed by many women and men as truly liberating, but breaking down the dichotomy is also threatening, especially to women and men who want to preserve their unique place on one side of the dichotomy or the other.

Another aspect of the problem of limited participation is the narrow range of leadership styles that are accepted as viable within the tight center. This problem is much more complex than it may seem on the surface, and a story may serve to raise some of those complexities. A few years ago, a Protestant woman pastor was called to a new church. She made an intentional decision not to initiate discussion about her femaleness. She did this in part because the congregation had already called her, and she assumed that they had worked through the major issues of having a woman for a pastor. More than a year passed, however, and she began to experience resistances within the congregation. In discussing these resistances with them, she discovered that they were related to her leadership style. Further, she realized that her leadership style was very much related to her being a woman. Among other things, she spent more time in consulting with various groups in the congregation and in consensus building than this congregation expected from their leader. This was particularly problematic for those who had long been in the tight center of the congregation's leadership and who began to see their own decision-making power spread more broadly through the congregation.

What was happening in this story (and in many stories like it) was not only the problem of bringing a woman into the tight center, but also, the problem of introducing a leadership style that was personally disarming to those in the tight center and threatening to the very existence of centralized, nonconsultative authority.

The obvious educational challenge in this problem of limited participation is to build inclusive participation throughout the community. The challenge is not only threatening but also difficult to implement without alternate visions. Looking at some concrete possibilities may at least open some new avenues for participation.

One concrete possibility is to try different ways to expand participation and resist the temptation to assume that only one way is possible. Within the Christian tradition some churches have focused on the ordination of women (bringing them into the tight center) and have been surprised to discover that the problems of sexism did not disappear from their theology or their social order. In fact, the ordination of women sometimes obscures the problem by making people think that the problem is solved and by allowing only those ordained women into the tight center without considering who is still being excluded.

Other churches have focused on building nonhierarchical leadership structures, decentralizing and spreading leadership as widely as possible. People engaged in these efforts are often surprised also, especially when they discover how much power still resides in the hands of a few people who have broad personal influence or access to leadership in several parts of the decentralized structures.

Yet another approach is to put emphasis on informal networking and communication between people in the core leadership group and people engaged in all aspects of the community's ministry. This approach, also, works only if people in the core leadership group are willing to listen to others and to give up the tightness of the center. Consultation processes are often only cosmetic if the results of consultation are ignored, or if people in the central leadership function primarily by veto. What is needed is not one of these approaches taken as a panacea, but multiple approaches complementing one another.

Another concrete possibility is to break down the barriers between public and private arenas. This would include giving more public responsibility and recognition to those engaged in works that have been largely privatized, like education. Religious educators, for example, need to reflect with the people on the whole church or synagogue and its ministry; they need to take leadership both in nurturing the congregation and in inspiring the active reflection and service of the congregation beyond the walls of its buildings. Breaking the public-private dichotomy ould also include more interaction between those engaged in leading public ministries and those engaged in leading more internal ministries.

And because men have often been given the public leadership, and women, the private leadership, breaking the public-private dichotomy would involve bringing women more actively into the public realm of finance committees and administrative councils, and bringing men more actively into the private realm of preparing church suppers and teaching children.

One last concrete possibility should be mentioned here: that is, the decision *to seek and receive leadership from persons with very different styles.* The person whose style of participation is to quote poetry can work side by side with another person whose participation is to make financial projections, and another who draws analogies between ministry and rearing children. The person whose style of participation is to lead meaningful liturgy can work side by side with another person whose participation style is to minister with individuals struggling with personal problems, and another who is able to arouse and empower people to serve in the community.

Problem of Exclusive Language

Exclusive language takes many forms, such as ethnocentricism, classism, or racism. The particular type of exclusiveness that is highlighted here is sexist language that excludes women, particularly the use of masculine language for humanity and for God. The language question raises very strong feelings, which should come as no surprise. Language is the way we name our world, and it holds together our social systems. A community cannot change its language without becoming aware of a whole set of cultural practices, such as the exclusion of women from certain roles in the religious community or selective interpretation of the role of women in the Bible. Just as one cannot pull on a loose thread without disrupting a garment, one cannot pull on the thread of language without disrupting some basic beliefs and values and practices.

I became acutely aware of the emotive power of the language issue when attending a workshop on inclusive language led by a woman in ministry. The woman articulated the issue calmly and clearly, giving some examples of how sexism creeps into language. She also described ways that sexist language could be changed, even drawing from some resources within Christian tradition. She distributed some sheets with biblical quotes in which feminine images of God were employed, and she led us in singing a couple of inclusive language hymns. The responses began to flow very quickly in this large group, made up largely of women who did not know one another before the day of the workshop. One woman stood and spoke of how good her father had been; she said that he was the best person she had ever known and that calling God Father communicated something that no other language could communicate. Almost immediately, another woman stood in the back of the room and said that her father had been the most abusive person she had ever known, and she could not relate to God at all if she had to use masculine or father language. A man sitting near me stood next, and trembling with emotion, he said that we could not possibly change language if the change meant upsetting the Trinity.

Not only was each of these people speaking with great feeling, each of them was raising a significant theological issue. The first woman raised the issue of analogies or metaphors for God that help us relate to a mystery that we cannot fully understand. The second woman raised the issue of the limits of those same analogies and metaphors, and more specifically, the limits of anthropocentric metaphors for God. The man raised a theological question that is particularly important within the Eastern

Orthodox traditions of Christianity; that is, the meaning and value of trinitarian language for God. On this last matter, Deborah Belonick has emphasized the centrality of the Trinity for the Orthodox tradition. The Trinity calls attention to the community of God, so that the relations among the persons of God become a model for human community.[9]

What are our challenges, then? *One challenge is to be more conscious and critical of our language and more willing to probe the theological issues that are raised by language change. Another is to be willing to face the terror of language change.* Benjamin Whorf put forth the thesis that language grows out of a culture and reinforces the culture by shaping the way persons see the world.[10] Because of these strong bindings between language and culture, language is highly resistant to change, and any change in language is threatening to the whole cultural system. For these reasons, people need not only to question their language in the religious education process but also to find support in facing the terror of discussing and implementing change.

TRENDS THAT REINFORCE SEXISM IN THE CHURCH

Here the focus will be on trends within the Christian church that reinforce sexism. These are not unlike trends in other religious traditions or within cultures at large. Speaking for other traditions would be presumptuous, however, and it would also be an undertaking beyond the scope of this chapter. In order to explore some new possibilities for Christian religious education, some analysis of the Christian tradition is needed, though even that can be done only summarily. What follows, then, is a brief description of three trends that reinforce the problems of sexism outlined above. Each trend carries an implicit challenge for education, just as the problems described above challenge educational ministry in some new directions.

Literalizing

Literalizing is a mode of theological reflection in which words and images are taken to mean exactly what they say. To speak of God as Father, then, is not to say that God is like a father, but that God *is* a father. This trend is discussed cogently by Sallie

McFague as she seeks to make a case for using and analyzing metaphorical language in theology, alongside the more commonly used conceptual language.[11]

Some of the common literalizations in Christian tradition reinforce the sexist patterns described above. One is the idea that since woman was created after man in the Genesis 2 creation account, then she is obviously inferior to man; another is the identification of women with evil based on the Genesis 3 account.[12] Another common literalization is the argument that women were not among the twelve apostles, and therefore women should not be ordained and cannot be part of apostolic succession. These examples, of course, could be multiplied, and the problems are not simply in limited thinking but also in the ways such literalizations are used to reinforce sexist patterns of life.

The trend of literalizing calls forth some *religious education challenges*, most important of which is *to name the literalizations that are prominent in your own community and to analyze the social consequences of those literalizations*. Flowing from such consciousness would be theological discourse on such significant questions as the nature of God, the nature of creation, and the meaning of ministry and apostolic succession.

One further challenge is to draw more richly from images and metaphors in theological reflection. To recognize that the historical tradition offers various metaphors for God is to realize that God is larger than any name or image. God is most commonly addressed in the Bible as Yahweh (Lord) and Father, but God is also addressed as Elohim or Ruach (both feminine gender words translated as Spirit) and is likened to a woman searching for a lost coin (Luke 15:8-10). In addition, the historical addresses for God include Mother, friend, companion, rock, and so forth. Sallie McFague's work is helpful here, and in fact, her most recent work is an attempt to analyze and evaluate certain metaphors for their adequacy in relation to social and ecological issues of the modern age.[13]

Dichotomizing

Another trend within the Christian church that reinforces sexism is the tendency to dichotomize. Some of the common dichotomies are mind and body, thinking and feeling, practical politics and mysticism, and nature and divine reality. These dichotomies are almost always associated with a tendency to value one side of the dichotomy more than the other, and very often the more valued side is associated with men and the less valued side, with women. For example, mind has been associated with men and has been valued over the body, which has been associated with women. Similarly, thinking has been valued over feeling. Just one obvious example is the argument that women should not be given certain leadership positions because their thinking is too often clouded by their feelings. Such an argument belittles women and feelings in one grand swoop.

Similar associations are made between men and practical politics, and between women and mysticism. These associations are connected to the problem discussed earlier as the separation of public and private arenas. The work of practical politics is seen as men's work, and it belongs in the public arena. Mystical activity is usually understood as a private and sacred activity; it has usually been associated with women and a few unique men who are called to enter the private mystical realm themselves.[14]

A look at the dichotomy between nature and divine, transcendent reality also makes connections with the problems described above, such as the problem of prejudice. When the pregnant woman was told that she should not serve the elements of the Eucharist, a dichotomy was being assumed and perpetuated. Her pregnancy was somehow a reminder of the natural world, and that reminder seemed inappropriate to her parishioner in a divine act such as Holy Communion.

These dichotomies are not simply distorted ways of thinking, but they serve a social function to label men and women and to value one over the other. *The challenge* that bursts forth from the trend of dichotomizing *is to think more holistically*. Dichotomies perpetuate themselves when one side is overemphasized at the expense of the other. The challenge, however, is not simply to balance and give equal attention to both sides of the dichotomy; the challenge, rather, is to see them as a whole. We need to recognize how mind and body are interconnected, as are thinking and feeling, and practical politics and mysticism, and nature and divine reality.

Further, we need to seek ways to integrate these different dimensions of reality in our own lives so that our feelings can inform our thinking and vice versa. In other words, moving beyond dichotomous thinking involves a recognition that thinking and feeling are inextricable; what we normally call thinking is always felt and what we call feeling is thought. Furthermore, a move beyond dichotomous thinking encourages us to nurture the mutual influence between thinking and feeling and to avoid tendencies to value one over the other or to value one group of human beings over another. As we learn to transcend the dichotomies named here and to nurture the relationships among different dimensions of human existence, we will not feel such need to label women and men into categories that we value differently.

Patriarchalizing

Patriarchalizing is another trend that reinforces sexism within the church and society. The biblical witness already reflects the patriarchal culture from which it springs, such as the genealogies that trace family history and Israel's history through the men. The same biblical texts reinforce the patriarchal structures, as these texts offer a view of God and the world and a pattern for living.

The early church added further layers of patriarchy. One clear evidence of this is the way that women's leadership and offices were gradually eliminated. For example, Prisca's leadership of the house church and the office of widows in early Christianity were not carried into later eras.

Another example of patriarchalization is the way in which many strong women of the Bible are not remembered by name and are not even remembered for their strength through the trajectories of interpretation. Martha, for example, who urged Jesus so strongly to come and care for her dying brother Lazarus, has been remembered much more often by biblical interpreters as the woman who made the less wise choice in the story of Mary and Martha. Elisabeth Moltmann-Wendel has demonstrated how the trajectories of interpretation have underplayed Martha's strength and have emphasized the story in which Jesus tells Martha that her sister Mary has made a wiser choice to sit and talk with him rather than to scurry about the kitchen.[15] Such interpretations disparage Martha (a strong woman) and housework (woman's work) at the same time.

The trend to patriarchalize does not end in the early centuries, however. One clear example of the continuing trend is the way in which biblical translators of recent centuries have translated the Greek word *anthropos*, which means person. Four times out of five, *anthropos* is translated into English as man rather than person.

The challenges begin with recognizing the trend in Christianity to patriarchalize, as well as biblical movements against that trend. If we try to ignore or obscure the patriarchal character of the biblical and later Christian traditions, we will be blind to the way those traditions shape our own patriarchal structures. Likewise, if we cannot uncover the radical countercultural movements within Christian tradition, we cannot appreciate and claim the power within the tradition itself to move away from patriarchal organization.

The work of Elisabeth Schüssler Fiorenza has been devoted in large part to uncovering those countercultural movements, such as the discipleship of equals and the house church in early Christianity that functioned as a community of equals.[16] Another countercultural movement that has received considerable attention is the way that Jesus interacted with women, even appearing to them and entrusting them as witnesses of the resurrection. Paul also entrusted leadership to women, even though some of his writing is often quoted as testimony to the limits of women. (1 Corinthians 7; Ephesians 5).

What is our challenge, then? It is to study our traditions with questions of suspicion and hope, asking what in the tradition actually contributes to the patriarchal character of the Christian community and what in the tradition promises liberation.

Another challenge is to seek ways to change the blatant and subtle patriarchal structures and relationships within the Christian church. This effort includes questioning the church's regular and systemic exclusion of women from decision making, as well as what it does to idealize women and put them on a pedestal. A pedestal, after all, is a very small place with very little room for movement.

Finally, we need to find ways to move toward a ministry of partnership, rather than a ministry of patriarchy and hierarchy. Letty Russell has put forth a vision of a church guided by its eschatological mission and empowered by people working together with one another and with God.[17] Such a vision suggests that the church needs to educate the whole people, not just the leaders, and that the education needs to be empowerment for a collegial ministry where the gifts of each person and community can be brought together with the gifts of others for the sake of mutual ministry. Such emphases as the ministry of the laity, or peer ministry among youth, need to be encouraged at every opportunity.

VISION FOR THE FUTURE

A vision for the future is already implicit in the challenges named throughout this chapter. The large vision is for a social order based not simply on equality in opportunities and rights but based on an *ethic of life*—an ethic of caring for all of life. An ethic of life is grounded in caring for life in creation; hence, ethical decisions are based on what would give and nurture life in the whole of creation—female and male, human and nonhuman. Emerging from an ethic of life is a strong sense of gender justice in which discrimination based on gender and all forms of sexist ideologies would be rejected for its destructive power in the lives of women and men.

Some more specific hopes for the social order are the reverse side of the problems named above. Both in the church and in the full social order, consciousness of the problems can become a first step in recognizing new possibilities. The problem of disparate agenda points to a hope that persons and communities would hear one another with respect and would work collaboratively on their multiple agendas. The problem of prejudice points to the hope that persons would be respected as subjects, rather than be categorized and treated as objects or be defined in terms of gender or any other distinguishing feature, such as race or cultural heritage. The problem of poverty and violence signals a hope that problems of sexism would be addressed in relation to other social problems, such as racism and classism and war. The problem of limited participation creates a hope that the fullest possible participation would be possible for women and men in the social order, including full public participation for women and full private participation for men. And finally, the problem of exclusive language points to the possibility of inclusive language, more particularly, a continual critique and reform of language to include the forgotten, the under-represented and the oppressed.

These hopes are all seen as important to a social order based on an ethic of life. The future vision is that these and other hopes might be realized possibilities in the social structures and patterns of relationship.

RELIGIOUS EDUCATION AS A BEARER OF VISION

If religious educators are to be true to their inheritance, they will assume responsibility to lead people out (e-*ducere*) from the limitations and life-destruction of a sexist social order to the freedom and life-nurture of an inclusive social order. This includes drawing out the deepest hopes that people hold for the social order and leading people to share their hopes for the sake of a communal vision and communal work. Within the context of a religious community, this educational enterprise is carried forward in relation to the community's tradition and vision.

A warning should be sounded in any discussion of religious education in relation to the social order. The revolutionary potential of religious education can easily be ignored, and in fact the religious communities have often expected religious education to play a domesticating role, making good little boys and girls who fit into the social order. The danger is that we may not be sufficiently suspicious of ourselves as educators to release the revolutionary potential of the educational enterprise. When, for example, we teach with a vision of women and men in community, we must examine our own educational practices. Are women doing most of the teaching, or have men assumed teaching roles as well? Is the educational ministry seen as a subordinate, privatized aspect of the ministry, or is it valued and made public? Is education being used for social control or for envisioning and building more liberating social structures?

If religious education is to bear new vision regarding women and men in the social order, it will be revolutionary. This will involve acts of teaching that create a spirit of search, critique, vision, and action. Some possibilities for religious education practice follow.

Rehearse The Memory

The Jewish and Christian memories are themselves revolutionary. The story of the Syro-Phoenician woman who came to Jesus to heal her daughter is one such revolutionary memory (Mark 7:24-30). When Jesus quipped to the woman that he should not take food from the children and give it to the dogs, she retorted that even the dogs could get the children's scraps under the table. Jesus' answer to the woman was, "For this saying you may go your way; the demon has left your daughter" (Mark 7:30, RSV). In this story, even Jesus was open to being revolutionized, and the story is one of the early reminders that this gospel message is revolutionary. The social conventions of keeping the blessings of God within a particular community were being upturned, and the upturning was being led by a foreign woman who dared to correct Jesus. The revolutionizing capacity of such a text is part of the memory Christians bear.

Examples of revolutionary memory abound—in the witnesses of Esther and Ruth, in the liberating features of the Deuteronomic law, in the leadership of women like Prisca in early Christianity, and so forth. These biblical examples are multiplied manyfold when one considers the full range of Jewish and Christian history and memory. One has only to develop eyes for seeing and ears for hearing. The challenge for religious educators is to seek out these passages for study, recognizing that some of them have been underplayed in the tradition of interpretation. The additional challenge is to learn to ask questions of any text, such as: What is the revolutionary element here? How does this text question my world and my world-view?

Wrestle with Texts until They Bless You

Sometimes texts seem to speak much more loudly to rein-force patriarchy than to point to a revolution in the social order. These texts are also part of the Jewish and Christian heritage, and due to their formative power, interpretation and critique are vital to the revision of a sexist social order. These are the texts with which we must wrestle if we are to bring critique to them and to the world that they have helped to form. Phyllis Trible calls these "texts of terror," and she suggests that we wrestle with them until they bless us, as Jacob wrestled with the angel.[18] In fact, she herself has wrestled with such stories as Hagar, Tamar, and the daughter of Jepthah who was raped and dismembered.

The challenge for religious education practice is to seek out difficult texts and difficult events in the tradition for wrestling. If nothing else, these texts and events will raise significant faith issues and will encourage persons to question and face their doubts.

Listen To the Silences

One way to bear a new vision is to allow time for silence—to counter our educators' instincts to fill every moment with words. Religious education also includes listening to silence. It includes meditation in silence before God.[19] It includes listen-ing to the silence that so often characterizes women in our society.[20] It includes what Nelle Morton has called "hearing others into speech."[21] To hear others to speech is to listen to them and to give priority to listening rather than speaking. Silence is a pathway by which mystery is revealed, and it is a pathway for discovering the voices of the voiceless. Through mystery and through new voices, we may experience revela-tion, and our perceptions and visions may be transformed.

Silence can be planned, as the silent day for women planned during Advent by one Anglican church. The women were asked to make no preparations, not even to bring a sack lunch.

They were to come only with themselves and their openness.

Silence can also be unplanned, as the moment in discussion when no one has anything to say. That time may be more alive than we think, and educators need to learn to be comfortable with silence, even when it comes unexpectedly and uninvited.

Allow Yourself To Be Vulnerable

Many sexist dynamics have been described in this chapter, such as categorizing people by prejudice or literalizing or dichotomizing. These are really means of social protection and control. People use these mechanisms to keep other people at a distance, or to distance themselves from what they do not know or understand. To be vulnerable is to allow those distances to shrink—to dare to know and be known by others, and to dare to face what one does not know or understand. When persons are vulnerable as individuals and as congregations, they are open to receive from others and, also, to change. They are open to receiving one another as persons. A vulnerable community is not a healthy environment for sexism because, in such an environment, people relate humanely rather than categorically.

Vulnerability can be planned in religious education. Educators can allow themselves to be vulnerable and encourage others to be so. One can plan for vulnerability by creating opportunities for persons with different gifts to express themselves, by nurturing an accepting climate, and by creating opportunities for small groups to face issues that are tender or unknown for them.

One can also be open to the unplanned, unexpected moments of vulnerability. This is especially important in a community that intends to be inclusive of women. Women are often socialized to be more vulnerable in their relationships than men and are often more comfortable in relating to a community where their vulnerability is accepted and respected as a strength.

Empower Others for Ministry

Religious education that bears a new vision for an inclusive social order is education that empowers people for ministry. It is education that helps persons to recognize and nurture their gifts, to understand themselves as called to ministry, and to find avenues for using their gifts in service to the church and world. This is different from an education that seeks to pour out the gifts of a few leaders onto everyone else. This is an education in which the work of the leaders is to share their own wisdom, yes, but also to respect the wisdom of everyone in the community and to help other persons discover and utilize their wisdom in God's service.

This kind of religious education is especially important for women, whose wisdom has often been ignored and belittled, and whose avenues of service have often been limited to designated arenas. To plan for empowerment education requires that a community be prepared to take seriously the wisdom of the household where much of woman's work has been done. Such education would be *vocational education*, which would include self-assessment, study and prayerful reflection on vocation, critical analysis of needs in the church and world, and networking of persons with one another and with opportunities for service. Such education would be *community education* in the sense that the congregation would also study its vocation as a congregation and would seek new avenues for congregational service.

Furthermore, the congregation would need to do critical reflection on the opportunities for service that it offers to women and men. If women are only serving in traditional women's roles and men in traditional roles for men, something is wrong. Liberation and inclusiveness are possible only when communities live and model role flexibility, as discussed earlier, engaging men to prepare and serve church suppers and women to serve on the finance committees. Liberation is possible only when all persons are able to discover and use the variety of gifts in ministry.

Engage in Social Analysis and Critique

To engage in the religious education practice that is described above requires social analysis and critique. A congregation needs to spend time reflecting on the social dynamics within its own community life and in the surrounding community. Who is hurting? Who is oppressed? Who is powerless? What is the gospel speaking to this situation?

To plan for social analysis and critique in educational ministry is to provide opportunities to study systematically the structures of the church and the ways in which women and men fit and interact in those structures. Also important would be opportunities for persons to analyze the structures and relational patterns in their own lives and to learn as much as possible about the larger community. This kind of analysis can be a source for review and revision of one's own actions within those social arenas.

Seek God's Wisdom and Vision for a New Future

In conclusion, religious education can only bear a new vision of women and men in the social order if people are willing to dream and hope. To dream of a new creation is to take seriously the tradition of a kingdom or monarchy of God which gives hope for a more just and righteous social order and which stands in judgment of the present unjust, unrighteous order. To dream of a new creation is also to take seriously the Jubilee tradition which urged a periodic release of captives and return of property so that every fifty years society would be reordered more equitably. To dream of a new creation is to be willing to admit that our world is not in ideal form and need not be protected from change.

Persons can seek God's wisdom in silence as we discussed above. Persons can also seek God's wisdom in the traditions of new creation found in biblical and historical sources. And persons can seek God's wisdom in their own experiences and intuitions of the world and its possibilities. What is important is that we educate in ways that will give persons courage to seek wisdom. What is important is that we offer resources to persons for their searching and visioning and that we support their actions in the direction of new futures.

NOTES

1. Maxine Baca Zinn believes that the political action of families in the social arena (political familism) can contribute to sex role equality within the families themselves. See Maxine Baca Zinn, "Political Fami-

lism: Toward Sex Role Equality in Chicano Families," *Aztlan* 6:1 (Spring 1975); Zinn, "Chicanas: Power and Control in the Domestic Sphere," *De Colores* 2:3 (1975). Other Hispanic feminists share Zinn's analysis, and still others propose different agendas.

2. See for example Delores S. Williams, "The Color of Feminism: Or Speaking the Black Woman's Tongue," *Journal of Religious Thought* 43:1 (Spring-Summer 1986), pp. 42-58; Delores S. Williams, "Women's Oppression and Lifeline Politics in Black Women's Religious Narratives," *Journal of Feminist Studies* 1:2 (Fall 1985), pp. 59-71; Magdalena Mora and Adelaida R. Del Castillo, eds., *Mexican Women in the United States: Struggles Past and Present* (Los Angeles: UCLA, Chicano Studies Research Center, 1980); Margarita B. Melville, ed., *Twice a Minority: Mexican American Women* (St. Louis, Mo.: Mosby, 1980).

3. Sylvia Ann Hewlett, *A Lesser Life: The Myth of Women's Liberation in America* (New York: Warner, 1987).

4. Rosemary Radford Ruether, *New Woman-New Earth* (New York: Seabury, 1975), pp. 22-23, 196-204.

5. See, for example Julius Segal, "Mothers: Saints or Sinners," *A Child's Journey* (New York: McGraw-Hill, 1978), pp. 73-74; Judith Arcana, *Our Mother's Daughters* (Berkeley: Shameless Hussy Press, 1979).

6. Caroline Allison, *It's Like Holding the Key to Your Own Jail: Women of Namibia* (Geneva: World Council of Churches, 1986).

7. Angela Simeone, *Academic Women Working Towards Equality* (South Hadley, Mass.: Bergin & Garvey, 1987), pp. 27-49.

8. Karen Torjesen, *Women's Leadership in Early Christianity*, manuscript in progress.

9. Deborah Belonick, *Feminism in Christianity: An Orthodox Christian Response* (Syosset, N.Y.: Dept. of Religious Education, Orthodox Church in America, 1983), pp. 26-29. Belonick raises some of the problems in changing conceptions of the Trinity or shifting away from the word "Father" for God, and she analyzes these from an Orthodox Christian perspective.

10. Benjamin Lee Whorf, *Language, Thought and Reality: Selected Writings of Benjamin Lee Whorf*, ed. John B. Carroll (Cambridge, Mass.: M.I.T. Press, 1956), pp. 134, 252. See also: Mary Elizabeth Moore, "Inclusive Language and Power: A Response," *Religious Education* 80:4 (Fall 1985), pp. 603-614.

11. Sallie McFague, *Metaphorical Theology* (Philadelphia: Fortress, 1982), pp. 1-29.

12. Ida Raming, "From the Freedom of the Gospel to the Petrified 'Men's Church': The Rise and Development of Male Domination in the Church," in *Women in a Man's Church*, ed. Virgil Elizondo and Norbert Greinacher (New York: Seabury, 1980), pp. 4-5, 7.

13. Sallie McFague, *Models of God: Theology for an Ecological, Nuclear Age* (Philadelphia: Fortress, 1987).

14. The association of sacred with private and secular with public is a major problem for religious communities, and not just for the women who are often thwarted by being restricted to the private, sacred realm. A fuller development of this idea is offered in Mary Elizabeth Moore, "The Unity of the Sacred and the Public: Possibilities from Feminist Theology," *Religious Education*, date to be determined.

15. Elisabeth Moltmann-Wendell, *The Women Around Jesus* (New York: Crossroad, 1982), pp. 15-48, esp. 15-28.

16. Elisabeth Schüssler Fiorenza, *In Memory of Her* (New York: Crossroad, 1983), pp. 140-154, 251-279; and Fiorenza, *Bread Not Stone* (Boston: Beacon, 1984), pp. 65-92.

17. Letty M. Russell, *The Future of Partnership* (Philadelphia: Westminster, 1979).

18. Phyllis Trible, *Texts of Terror* (Philadelphia: Fortress, 1984), pp. 1-5.

19. Mary Elizabeth Moore, "Meditation at the Center of Congregational Life," in *Congregations: Their Power to Form and Transform*, ed. C. Ellis Nelson (Atlanta: John Knox, 1988).

20. Mary F. Belenky, Blythe M. Clinchy, Nancy R. Goldberger, and Jill M. Tarule, *Women's Ways of Knowing* (New York: Basic Books, 1986), pp. 23-51. These authors document the experience of silence that is common among many women.

21. Nelle Morton, *The Journey Is Home* (Boston: Beacon, 1985), pp. 54-56, 127-129. Nelle Morton suggests that hearing to speech is a very deep hearing that empowers people. It is accompanied by an image of God as "the hearing one" (p. 129) or as a "great Listening Ear" (p. 55).

4

A Human World Order

Gerald F. Mische

A central question confronting us today is how we should read the signs of the times. Much is at stake—not only for the individual person, but also for the future of the human community. The vision which is held of the future will influence how we conceive the structures of human life in the world. In seeking to interpret the crisis around us, we must deal with the power of a self-fulfilling prophecy. If we judge that history is closed, that we are living in end-times, we will act in certain ways. If we judge that we are living in-between-times, that history is open to our initiatives, we will respond in other ways. One reason so many advocates of justice, peace, and social change in the late sixties and early seventies have "dropped out" from efforts to be forces for positive social change is that—having once judged that history was open to their initiatives to shape the future—they now judge that same history to be closed.

Whereas a just, peaceful, and more human society once seemed to be a realistic goal, the status quo seems to have solidified its roots. Crises have multiplied. Problems seem too complex, institutions too heavy. Furthermore, the national security complex has strengthened its grip on national economics around the world.

Efforts for peace and justice continue, of course, but the

impact of such efforts on public policy seem to remain relatively peripheral. Even the encouraging progress presently being made by the superpowers in deescalating their arms race is tentative and marginal.

The recent arguments by the superpowers to eliminate intermediate and short-range nuclear weapons will not end the threat of nuclear war. Intercontinental nuclear missiles would still remain, even if the superpowers later cut long-range, intercontinental missiles by half. Also, an increasing number of smaller nations have gained nuclear capability.

Further, decreases in nuclear weapons may well result in *increased*, rather than decreased, military expenditures. The reliance on nuclear weapons is cheaper than maintaining conventional weapons, and war is actually paid for at the expense of Third World nations who are forced for a variety of reasons to expend an unusually high amount of national budgets on arms sold to them by either the East or the West or both.

Arguments for greater expenditures on conventional weapons and on larger armies and navies will grow as national, economic, and monetary insecurity increases. Such insecurities will surely increase, and will continue to increase as long as nations compete in an increasingly integrated, but lawless, global marketplace. In a world in which nations are ever more dependent upon foreign sources for natural resources and on foreign markets for both jobs and international currency, no nation can be expected to substantially disarm.

Recognizing this sobering reality is frightening enough. But there is a litany of other global-scale crises—environmental breakdown, a trillion dollar global debt crisis, world hunger and poverty, the drying up of international credit, worldwide overcapacity of production, growing unemployment, terrorism, international drug trafficking. It is a litany before which national leaders and traditional assumptions, expertise, and policies—of the right, center, or left—stand increasingly powerless. Small wonder that the burnout rate of persons working for a just, peaceful, and environmentally viable future is increasing. For many people of the world, the central issue is not nuclear disarmament, which is sometimes viewed as a First World agenda, but creating structures of human order which will allow all of humanity to live in dignity. We live in a world in which no human life can survive unless all of human life will survive.

This new megacrisis is causing many people to lose nerve. Millions are interpreting the megacrises as a sign of an imminent societal breakdown, too massive for human institutions to handle. Taking initiative to effect positive social change is judged to be fruitless. This reading of the signs breeds confusion, fear, cynicism, paralysis, hedonism, addiction, and growing numbers of suicide, in addition to starvation, loss of natural resources, and the spread of new incurable diseases.

End-Time Theologies

Such confusion and loss of a positive vision of the future has given rise in some religious traditions to what might be called "end-time theologies." Such theology is represented by the rise of fundamentalism and even fanaticism in both Christian and non-Christian traditions. Apocalyptic teachings have emerged with an emphasis on the end of this world and dispensationalism. For some Christians the new deliverance is in a belief in the imminent Second Coming of Christ. For them, the future of the world does not rest in practical human endeavors to resolve problems, but in prayer and the works of God or the Holy Other.

Central to this reasoning is a belief that "countdown" for human history is clearly stated in the sacred literature or "scripture" as interpreted by the leaders of these end-time interpretations of religious traditions. A case in point can be found in some Christian "nuclear dispensationalists."

This way of reading the signs proclaims that Satan has been, and continues to be, in control of the present era. His reign began with the Fall of Adam and Eve, at which time he became the "Prince of the World." With the power of Satan and his legions ruling life on this planet and with human beings having been corrupted by a "fallen" nature, a just and peaceful society is an impossible dream. This era of Satanic rule, however, is seen as now approaching its preordained end through a nuclear confrontation that, "providentially," will result in the destruction of communist power.

All these events are said to have been foretold in the Bible. As God's plan for human history, a cataclysmic nuclear confrontation is perceived as being inevitable; it *cannot be prevented*. To work for peace and a new world order, therefore, is seen as a type of "heresy," or as disbelief and a lack of faith in God's order beyond this world.

The "final tribulation" is seen as a necessary prelude to the Second Coming. Christ's glorious coming cannot take place until these horrendous "Last Days" run their course . . . and the forces of the Antichrist are destroyed in history's final battle on the plains of Armageddon in Israel. The Tribulation will end with the dawning of the millennium, a thousand-year era of peace under a "spiritual aristocracy" of the New Christian millennists. After the tribulation period is over, born-again believers who will have been "raptured" (lifted up in the heavens to avoid the nuclear cataclysm) will return with Christ to destroy God's enemies and administer the government of the Millennial Kingdom.

Fortunately, nuclear dispensationalism is not universally embraced by evangelical Christians, just as Khomeini's Jihadic Holy War is not shared by all Muslims. Many reject the view that a loving God would deliberately sacrifice billions of lives and destroy the wonders of the earth that are so praised in all religions. Nonetheless, the number of people ready to accept some form of an end-time interpretation—be it religious or secular—of today's crisis-filled world is large, and as the numbers grow the self-fullfilling dynamic gathers steam.

Presenting an Alternative Reading

The Chinese concept of crisis provides an alternative framework for reading today's megacrisis. They use two characters to express the concept: WEI, meaning "danger," to express the possibility of *breakdown*; and CHI, meaning "opportunity," to express the possibility of *breakthrough*. This twofold dimension is a reminder that, rather than reading today's crises as signs that human history is winding down, i.e., as end-times, we can read them as signs of "crisis of growth," a crisis out of which, through imagination and bold initiatives, solutions can emerge.

What is the nature of this crisis-spawning growth? It is an

explosive growth of global interdependence, building upon the quantum jump in global-scaled technologies which occurred during World War II. Transportation, communications, and computer technologies have shrunk the world into an interdependent village in which all nations are intertwined and impacted by a global economy. Human institutions, however, have not kept pace with this explosion of global interdependence. They have remained circumscribed by national boundaries as the peoples of the world have continued to worship the illusion of unlimited sovereignty.

The result is a *structural lag*. The crisis of growth is rooted in this lag, a lag that, with imagination and commitment, can be overcome. In our interdependent, global marketplace, individual nation-states, acting alone, are increasingly unable to provide peace, justice, and security for their citizens. Although the nation will continue to be a major vehicle for problem solving and goal setting, it is too small to solve some problems and too large to solve others.

Today's global-scale crises defy traditional expertise and assumptions. The explosive growth of economic and monetary interdependence has created a whole spectrum of rampant global forces that are devastating local and national development efforts, threatening international economic collapse, destroying the earth's environment, and perpetuating the rise of the National Security State around the world. These crises bear witness to the *birth of a new era*, requiring new modes of thinking, acting, and institution building.

A birth image is apt. The healthy delivery of our shared future is not automatic. Nor will the delivery be without pain. New birth seldom comes without pain. The greater the life reality seeking to be born, the greater the pain that may accompany the birth process. In the birth process, if the birth passage remains rigid and does not widen, the pain intensifies. The unborn life is imperiled, and the mother's life is endangered.

The birth image provides insights into the pain being experienced in the human community today. Existing socio-political structures are too rigid and narrow to allow healthy delivery of the new stages of human growth and development struggling to be born. *But more than human development is at stake. The constriction threatens human survival.*

Our religious education task then is not to fight against our pains and crises, reacting against the symptoms and in so doing making present structures more rigid than before. Rather, our task is to recognize the positive pregnancy of a new world order, to work with the birth spasms, giving our energies to a widening of the birth passage, *making ready the way for a viable human future.* Our labor now is to create the consciousness and structures through which a more just and human order can be born—a labor not of tearing down but of a new creation. The great task before us is not of revolution. Rather, the task is what Jürgen Moltmann calls *provolution.*

The *re* in revolution focuses on return:

> Revolutionary terrorism directed against the old order always turns into the absolutism of the new order which is revengefully directed against its critics and thus against its own future.

The *pro* in provolution focuses on the new, forward movement, on the creation of that which has not yet been present in history:

> In provolution the human "dream turned forward" is combined with the new possibility of the future and begins consciously to direct the course of human history.

Within this transition context, a context of giving birth to a new era which is transnational in scope, the importance of how we read the signs of history becomes starkly clear. To denounce negative readings of history, it does not go far enough. The real challenge is to take Mahatma Gandhi seriously in his call to become *"satyagrahi"*—that is, seekers-of-truth regardless where that search might take us. This is the same admonition that Jesus gave to his followers when he said that "truth will make you free." How can we overcome "end-time thinking" in both religious and secular thinking?

There is no simple answer. Some cite an inability or unwillingness to think seriously about new and complex problems. Others believe the problem is a *dualistic worldview*—a worldview rooted in the West in Hellenic philosophy and dualistic theology that see history as an ongoing battle between "good" and "evil," between forces of light and forces of darkness, between spirit and matter, between body and soul.

There are those who say that born-again Christians have a psychological need for certainty in today's confusing, crises-filled, and rapidly changing interdependent world—certainty that they are saved, certainty about how things will turn out in the future, and certainty that they will personally escape the horrors of nuclear war or global institutional collapse. There is, however, another factor that merits serious consideration. That factor is a *vacuum of realistic analysis*. Most people lack an analytic framework capable of offering a practical basis for hope amid today's global chaos, survival crises, and institutional breakdown. The end-time theologies fill the emptiness of this vacuum.

Millions of people are accepting the end-time explanation that "evil empires" and "Satanic forces" are the primary roots of the chaos and breakdown they see all around them. One reason for this acceptance is that many, perhaps most, people are fed up with negative approaches that merely denounce. They are looking for analyses that can both help them make sense out of the turmoil and confusion they see all around them and *announce* concrete positive alternatives. With few exceptions, these analyses and solutions assume that territorial sovereignty is still an adequate framework for solving today's global-scaled crises. Popular common sense is increasingly rejecting such an assumption.

Although few clearly understand the parallel between today and the breakdown of the feudal system in Europe, many *do* correctly perceive that today's global crises are too large for national states and institutions to handle. Having been taught that the emergence of the territorial nation-state represented the *culmination* of human history, this perception is devastating. If the today's global megacrisis—which impacts so profoundly on our personal lives and on the life of our nations—cannot be resolved or controlled by *national* institutions, where can we turn?

A Faulty Analysis Is Mutual

I suggest that some of us who actively commit ourselves to justice, peace, and human liberation are partly responsible for the vacuum of analysis that underlies much of this vulnerability. Could it be that we also are working out of a too limited—and, therefore, out of a faulty—framework for analyzing the events of today's interdependent world?

Permit me to share several reflections on why some efforts toward a new world order seem inadequate:

1. Many of us mainly *denounce*. We are not taking time to do the hard work needed to *announce* alternatives, alternatives that are commensurate to the global dimensions of the crises and opportunities of our interdependent planet.
2. When we do announce alternatives, they are usually designed to operate *within the framework of unlimited territorial sovereignty*—at a time when such sovereignty is rapidly breaking down under the assault of the explosive growth of global interdependence. Too often, we also erroneously assume the nation-state is the culmination of political process; or at least the only framework available at this period of history.

As we noted already, what is required is another view of a world that is not out of control of human reasoning and human effort. An alternative to the rejection of the world, as articulated by a host of fundamentalists within Christian, Jewish, and Moslem traditions, is a holistic vision of human life in which the creation of history becomes new possibilities for a world in which all people may find a common life together. A repeated issue in all religions is whether to stand against the world or to embrace the world. To say it another way, is the task of religion to serve a divine world outside the practical realities of political and international order or to work for human structures that will insure life for all people regardless of religious belief?

The task, then, is not primarily to *denounce* the militant evangelization of the Armageddon reading of the signs of the time. Rather, the task is to provide an alternative framework for interpreting the events of this pivotal, transitional period in history—a framework based on social analysis of history and world events and in accord with a holistic and comprehensive understanding of all religious traditions.

For example, if we believe that nuclear weapons will be the instruments by which the "final tribulation" prophecies in the books of Daniel and Revelations will be fulfilled, then efforts to resolve the escalating arms race between the two superpowers will be judged to be doomed from the start. However, if we believe that many of today's global crises are growing pains of a historic transition from national self-sufficiency to an economically and environmentally interdependent world community, we have a basis for moving beyond the demonology of the Cold War confrontation toward a framework of cooperation based on mutual self-interest.

In fact, one of the new educational directions for global understanding is a new appreciation of the inclusive nature of all the world's religions. God may indeed have many names. John Hick has suggested that all major religious traditions have inherent values that move human life toward a world based on peace and justice.

One result of this lag is a *structural powerlessness* of national societies and their leaders to deal adequately with mounting domestic and global problems. This powerlessness cannot be simply explained by ideology or demonology.

At first glance, to talk about a "structural powerless" may seem to contradict our assumption that there is an alternative reading to the end-times reading of the signs of the times. Quite the contrary! The key word here is *structural*.

Structures are not immutable; they are not constants in history. Rather, structures are variable, susceptible to change, even breakdown. Such is the case of the present nation-state system which is breaking down under the pressures from today's rampant economic/monetary forces and technological weapons. These forces are making a mockery of national boundaries and declarations of sovereignty. The challenge is to mobilize human imagination, human energies, and human competencies to build on the new global infrastructure, which we will examine shortly, to overcome the structural lag with world order structures commensurate to the new global realities.

An important preliminary step to such mobilization is to

identify the structural *straitjacket* of the present nation-state system that underlies the powerlessness of leaders and people to use humanistic, life-respecting, and environmental-protecting values as criteria for public policy.

REDEFINING SECURITY AND SOVEREIGNTY

We are at a transitional point in history when traditional concepts and methods for providing security are inadequate. This transition presents a profound challenge to longstanding assumptions and strategies of the peace and justice movements. To *redefine security and sovereignty within the context of global interdependence and world order* is the challenge for both the political and the religious communities.

1. *Rethinking Security*

As nonmilitary threats grow more formidable, the traditional military concept of security is increasingly inadequate. Global interdependence requires a concept that includes economic, monetary, and environmental security as well as security against military attack. These four dimensions of security are interrelated. Each impacts upon, and is impacted by, the others. Indeed, in a world that is economically and environmentally interdependent, the concept of "national" security itself is no longer adequate. *National security is becoming synonymous with global security.*

National economics are ever more deeply dependent upon foreign resources, foreign markets, and foreign currency. This dependency has become a central security concern. The arms race is inexorably linked to it. *For no nation can be expected to radically reduce its armaments as long as that nation is dependent upon a global marketplace that continues to operate in a premise of the survival of the fittest.*

The greater the monetary-economic strains—e.g., the closer the burden of a trillion dollar debt crisis brings global monetary processes to a breaking point or destabilizes national economics—the more likely that competition over global markets will lead to military confrontation and the less likely that nations will move toward disarmament. Conversely, the greater the escalation of the global arms race, the more acute become the monetary-economic crises.

Threats to security are also rising from the deterioration of the ecological foundations upon which viable economies depend. (Threats to security will increasingly arise more from the relationship between nation and nature than from nation-to-nation relations.) Dwindling reserves of nonrenewable resources and the deterioration of the earth's biological systems—both crises being acerbated and accelerated by the mobilization for military, balance-of-payments, and scarce resource goals—now threaten the security of nations everywhere.

2. Rethinking Sovereignty

The issue of sovereignty has long been a major obstacle to advancing disarmament and national security. The irony and paradox is that the reluctance to share sovereignty in a common security system means national sovereignty is left more vulnerable. As global interdependencies increase, and as more dangerous weapons systems proliferate, sovereignty will become ever more a fiction.

We need to rethink sovereignty not only because missiles make the concept of impenetrability obsolete but also because economic interdependence is a reality that will grow rather than go away. Growing dependency on other nations for markets and for resources such as oil, bauxite, aluminum, copper, tin, and chrome, make national self-sufficiency a present and future impossibility. Decisions made in one part of the world dramatically affect the economic well-being of all other nations. Sovereignty is something we presently lack and can gain only through a willingness to share it.

The historical thrust toward ever-greater interdependence requires that we redefine sovereignty. A truly sovereign nation is one in which the citizens are secure from foreign attack, can meet their basic needs, and can participate equitably in the decision-making processes and institutions that affect their lives.

The time available to address these economic, monetary, and environmental threats to national security has been shortened by analytical failures, errors in judgment, and a lack of political leadership in the principal industrial countries. Analyzing and understanding the nature and scale of the new threats will challenge the information-gathering and analytical skills of gov-

ernments. Unfortunately the present decision-making appara-
tus of governments is not organized to balance threats of a
traditional military nature with threats of economic, monetary,
and/or ecological origins.

Most political leaders are only peripherally aware of the new
threats to security. Lester Brown points to some examples. In-
telligence agencies are organized to alert political leaders to
potential military threats, but no counterpart network exists for
warning of the rapid deterioration of biological systems. Military strategists understand the nature of military threats. Economic and monetary analysts are beginning to recognize a
need for international strategies and structures for coping with
the international debt crisis and the radical restructuring of the
global marketplace. Energy analysts understand the need to
shift from oil to alternative energy sources, and ecologists understand the need to arrest ecological deterioration. However,
only a few individuals, whether they be policymakers or leaders of the peace movement, are trained or able to weigh and
evaluate such a diversity of interrelated threats and then translate such assessments into the coordinated strategies and allo-
cation of resources needed to handle them.

Nonmilitary threats to a nation's security are much less clearly defined than military ones. They are often the result of cum-
mulative processes that, if not changed, ultimately lead to the
depletion of a country's scarce reserves or to the collapse of
biological or monetary systems. These processes in themselves
are seldom given much thought until they pass a critical thresh-
old.

In his book, *Stable Peace*, Kenneth Boulding wrote about the
"strength-stress equation" in war and peace.[1] Simply put, when
a stress on a system is greater than its strengths for managing
conflict or preventing war, conflict is more likely to spill over
into war. When the strengths of a system are greater than the
stresses placed on it, peace is more possible to sustain. A stress
in the world community needs to be balanced by a strength
both equal to or greater than the stress and capable of managing the related conflict. As the world becomes increasingly
interdependent, there will be *more*, not less, conflict and tension. We will need, therefore to *strengthen*, not weaken, sys-

tems of global conflict management and security.

Although immediate concern about the prevention of nuclear war must remain paramount, long-range concern about reducing fundamental causes of war and other dimensions of security must also receive major attention. Indeed, myopic concern with only the most urgent, immediate problems might well mean that the underlying preconditions for war and militarization would flourish, rather than diminish. Thus, in the long run—and it might not be very long—a narrow, short-range approach to war prevention and disarmament would prove self-defeating.

Short-term responses to the arms race and to other crises are usually only "catch-up" reactions to initiatives of national security policymakers. Also essential are research, strategies, and transitional steps toward the longer-term structural change at the global level that are needed to end the arms race and to achieve other closely-related security goals. Rather than an either/or choice, short and long-term approaches are *both* needed at the *same* time. For, at this critical juncture of history, leadership is not only the capacity to solve immediate problems; leadership includes the ability to formulate the right questions and, perhaps most importantly, to accurately *frame* those questions.

The National Security Straitjacket

One of the central questions relates to powerlessness. Much has been said over the past twenty-five years about the powerlessness of the people, of rule by self-serving elites. But too little has been said about the powerlessness of their leaders. Too often the assumption has been that citizen powerlessness was rooted simply in class structures and unregulated corporate power. Liberation was thus a struggle between the "oppressor" and the "oppressed." A reading of the signs of the times within a crisis-of-growth context, however, reveals that the oppressor/oppressed analysis is inadequate as the only explanation in that it fails to identify the structural powerlessness inherent in our present world system.

Even in those isolated instances when a grassroot revolutionary movement has succeeded in gaining political power (whether by force or by popular processes), national leaders logically become a new class of isolated elites. Lacking a world security system, that is, functional institutions capable of dealing with the multidimensional threats to security outlined above, the new leaders immediately find themselves confronted by three interrelated national security imperatives: 1) Mobilization for military security; 2) Mobilization for balance of payments and trade security; 3) Mobilization for scarce resources.

This threefold security mobilization results in a growing powerlessness of national leaders and institutions to reorder priorities according to basic human needs. The result is a straitjacket that transcends ideology and economic differences, a set of structures which immobilizes leaders of all nations: rich and poor, capitalist and socialist.

The logical commitment to security priorities underlies much of the social and societal deterioration that we are witnessing around the world. This commitment is at the core of the growing alienation in "developed" and "developing" worlds alike. All nations are logically ruled by national security elites capable of providing the technological, monetary, and economic powers demanded by the security imperatives of multinational markets operating without legal and juridical restraints.

An example of the structural impact of this triple security mobilization is its devastating effect on *land*. In the United States, the struggle over who does or should own the land is between large corporate farmers and those striving to preserve family-size farms and to prevent the destruction of topsoil and contamination of the crops. In many Third World countries, the struggle over "who owns the land" is escalating into armed conflict as pressures from peasant farmers for land reform are resisted by individual and agribusiness owners of large tracts of land. Often missing in these debates and struggles, however, is an adequate understanding of how much, given the present global economy, land and food have become *logical instruments of national security goals*. Exports or cash crops have become a primary national goal of even the poorest nations who may be without food to feed their own people. Agribusiness has become a logical partner of the national security establishment for achieving these goals.

Consider the interrelated crises of food, hunger, environment, and land ownership. A major factor underlying each of the interrelated crises of food, hunger, environment, and land ownership, is that the exportation of agricultural products has become a prime means of dealing with chronic trade and balance-of-payments deficits. Such deficits are threats to a nation's security. They threaten its currency, undermine its ability to compete in international trade, and erode the domestic foundations of its economy. Because agribusiness has the means and capacity to mobilize the capital-intensive mechanization, the large economies-of-scale, and the international logistical support needed to facilitate such exports, its environmentally and socially destructive characteristics are tolerated by leaders responsible for economic and monetary security and well-being.

Driven by pressures from massive foreign debt obligations and/or trade deficits, as well as by economic development goals in markets that have become global, most countries around the world are now giving priority to mobilizing their economics and educational institutions for *export* markets rather than for basic domestic needs.

As we have said earlier, the nation-state is *too large* a unit to solve many of today's problems; and *too small* to solve others. The decentralists' "small is beautiful" movement, concerned about the sovereignty of the individual person, of the family, of the local community, and of the province, is a response to the too-largeness. The movement for world order structures is a response to the too-smallness.

The need is to bring these two movements together. On one hand, some decentralists recognize only the too-largeness of the nation-state. Accordingly, their goals and strategies focus too exclusively on small-scale local responses to problems. They assume that a reorganization of the world's political and economic systems according to decentralized socio-economic-political units is the key resolving today's major problems. On the other hand, some world order advocates recognize only the too-smallness of the present nation-state system. Accordingly, their goals and strategies focus too exclusively on global scale response to problems. Their assumption is that the solution to all problems will flow from the establishment of global institutions.

The question is not one of choosing either of these approaches. Both approaches must be used simultaneously. Most relevant to our discussion is that without global security structures efforts toward a small-is-beautiful, human-scaled, decentralized, and environmentally respectful society will be forced to remain at the periphery of national agendas.

We are confronted here with a *structural* powerlessness— rooted in the present nation-state system. It is a powerlessness of leaders as well as "the people."

This is not to say that national leaders have *no* power. Indeed, they have unprecedented power. They may have the power to make war and to institute monetary and economic policies that oppress and deprive millions of their own citizens and citizens in other countries. They may even have the power to ravage the earth's environment and plunder its scarce resources. Yet, caught in the structural straitjacket of the national security state, the same national leaders seem to be powerless to implement person-centered, social justice values as central criteria for public policy.

Humanistic/Religious/Feminine Values Are Subversive

In our present world system, values such as social justice, human solidarity, primacy of conscience, ecological responsibility, and the centrality and inviolability of the human person are seen by national policymakers—even by those who personally embrace such values—as "subversive." If implemented as the *primary* criteria for public policy, such values would undercut the security of national societies. They would subvert the ability of national societies to survive in today's survival-of-the-fittest global economic and monetary arena.

In the present lawless world system, the national state could not survive the implementation of these values as primary criteria for dealing with a whole range of security issues, e.g., trade deficits, the debt crisis, lack of international credit, loss of jobs in a global marketplace floundering with productive overcapacity, terrorism. The nation's economic and monetary institutions would collapse in a relatively short time—that is, before it had

time to radically reconstruct its society to become a self-suffi-
cient, self-reliant society (presuming that such a reconstruction
was politically and economically feasible). Thus these values,
which are at the core of humanist and authentic religious commitment, will not be permitted to have more than token influence on national policies.

This straitjacket on values is not new. Since the beginning of
recorded history, humanistic, authentically religious, and feminine values have been locked out of "sovereign" decision making. Such values have been traditionally acceptable in one's
personal life, in the family, in the monastery or parish rectory, in
an academic ivory tower, and perhaps even in an enlightened
national marketplace. But this attitude changes radically when
sovereign tribes, kingdoms, city-states, and the modern nation-
states compete for military, economic, and resource security. In
the realpolitik by which our presently fragmented nation-state
system operates, human values will not be allowed to become
criteria for public policy.

The only way in which present national security priorities
could be substantially reordered is to establish a world order
that would include global institutions with authority to share
with individual nations the burden for their military, monetary,
and resource security. Such a world security institution would
not only substantially lower the threat of war and economic
disaster, it would also permit a loosening of the dependency of
nations on defense spending that could be accompanied also
by a corresponding reordering of domestic priorities.

By reducing, and eventually eliminating, the logic for constant mobilization for military, monetary, and resource security,
strengthened international governance would loosen the security straitjacket. No longer could the "haves" within the national
borders have the national security logic to *manipulate* to preserve their power and privilege, as they presently do. Few
banners in history have been so effectively waved to retain the
status quo as the powerful, virtually irresistible banner of "national security." History is replete with examples of tyrannical
rule, social injustice, and dehumanization that were rationalized under the enormous emotional appeal of this banner. Even
before the advent of the modern National Security State, de-

fenders of the status quo have successfully argued for power and armies to defend their self-interest, usually under the guise of the nation's security. A world security system based on strengthened United Nation's agencies could eliminate the logic for these arguments.

Proposals for world security structures are not based on a naive concept that human nature is good and can be depended upon to serve the common good. On the contrary, they are based on a recognition that human beings are *not* perfect and that social controls are necessary for a new world order.

Within national borders the need is for moral constraints on human behavior—individual and corporate—at local, state, and national levels. Public sector structures are seen as necessary not only for providing a basic social order but also for providing services and initiating processes for common good goals which cannot be accomplished by the private structures.

Strong disagreements exist, of course. But they are not about *whether* there should be national public sector structures. Rather, the debate concerns for *what* areas they should have responsibility and *how* much authority they should have in their prescribed areas. Consensus exists over some areas. These consensus areas include national defense, preservation of public order, regulation of money and banking, taxation, consumer protection, and protection of the environment.

So-called "liberals" generally tend to back a relatively active role for public institutions in promoting public welfare and in regulating powerful corporate interests where they impact negatively on the public. "Conservatives" tend toward more minimal legal structures and constraints and would argue strongly for privatization of many areas for which public institutions have major responsibility. But only extremist libertarians or anarchists would argue for abandonment of all public sector institutions and responsibilities.

Now, with history thrusting beyond national boundaries, this public-private discussion is beginning to move into the forum of our global village. Energizing this thrust is an awareness of the growing powerlessness of national institutions to adequately cope with the multiple, interrelated crises of this global village. Visitors from another planet would be amazed by the irrationality of an ethic based on the "survival-of-the-fittest." They would be even more amazed if told by national leaders and economic/monetary "experts" that they had no plans to construct international public sector structures capable of *effective* response to the growing breakdown of viable national and international processes and structures.

The task, then, is not to turn back to the past. Nor is the task to dismantle or bypass the nation-state, or to centralize power at a global level. Rather, the task is to recognize that, in today's interdependent world, both *private* and *public* sector institutions are needed at every level. The functional institutions that are required at the international level should be structured according to the principle of *subsidiarity*. With subsidiarity as the criterion for world order, decision making would be made at the lowest possible level. Only when problems cannot be managed and justice cannot be achieved at municipal, provincial, or national levels are juridical institutions necessary at the global level.

The need now is to strengthen and develop international institutions that would preserve basic sovereignty and cultural diversity and, at the same time, have the functional authority needed to cope with those global problems which nations cannot handle by themselves. The goal is for a world order that would provide a structural framework for nations to achieve economic, monetary, and military security. Such a world order is not a quantum jump into the unknown. With infrastructure already in place, it is, rather, the next logical step in societal development.

Benefits for the Here and Now

The benefits that would accrue from the evolutionary movement toward a new world order are not all in the future. Some benefits from such a movement are immediate and have strategic meaning at the local level.

1. The analysis of the present structural rigidity transcends
   the polarization of diverse issue constituencies which too

often find explanations for their powerlessness in demon-ologies. Blacks and whites, women and men, young and old, rich nations and poor nations—all can rise above mutual recriminations to a shared victimhood and plan together a shared future. Such commonality can modify previous facile judgments. As polarization is thereby miti-gated, coalitions on local, as well as national and global issues become more possible.

2. A world order framed around human and inclusive value can provide hope for the future. Such hope, in turn, fos-ters belief: in human nature, in the ability of humankind to resolve its problems, and in the reality of a Ground of All Being, present and dynamic in history and in the affairs of all people regardless of how they may name their God.

3. Such hope and belief provides a basis for perseverence, for the staying power needed to successfully deal with the complexities of local issues. Such hope and belief will also provide a basis for initiative in seeking new responses and alternatives to local and national problems, as well as to global crises. Local problems and issues will take on new understanding when viewed from a world order perspec-tive. A new human solidarity may prevail.

4. A world order framework provides a perspective for ana-lyzing each problem in a macro frame that identifies all the forces impinging upon it, assuring a more accurate and complete analysis, and therefore more effective problem solving.

A truly just and human world order will be developed to the degree that openness and truth-seeking characterize the efforts of those involved in the formulation and transformation pro-cesses. Such truth-seeking will lead us to a new understanding of the complexity of forming international structures and will be aware of none of the forces that get in the way of world unity. Rather than a view of a world based on demonology, they will have a doctrine that would understand all of life, including human life, as interrelated and that this life has in-deed a hopeful future.

Premises of a World Security System

I would like to propose seven premises of a world order system capable of providing true security to nations and peoples.

1. *We can choose a preferred world.* We need not be passive observers of history. Being able to imagine and choose from a variety of alternatives, human beings have the capacity to explore and initiate action toward the realization of a preferred future.

2. *A more human world order will be built upon foundations that already exist.* Much infrastructure for a preferred world order future already exists, e.g., the specialized agencies of the United Nations. These infrastructures should be strengthened and transformed according to values of social justice, participation, and full human development. These values will increase in effectiveness as more nations come to be full partners in this life.

3. *A nonideological, problem-solving framework provides a practical realism for transitional steps to a world security system.* Building upon existing global infrastructure, functional institutions can be established with adequate means and the authority of effective law to deal with problems beyond the capability of individual nations. Examples of such world order institutions would be a world food authority, an ocean regime, a world monetary and development authority, a disarmament authority, and a world environmental authority. Central to such a system, and adjudicated within a world court system, would be the principles of public accountability and participation through effective citizen representation.

4. *The principle of subsidiary should be a central principle in developing a world legal framework and authority lines for the management of global problems.* Subsidiary begins with the proposition that decision making should be done at the lowest possible level. Only when problems cannot be managed and justice cannot be achieved at the local, municipal, provincial, or national levels is decision making necessary at the global level. A world order based on func-

tional institutions and established to function according to the principle of subsidiarity is not a quantum jump into the unknown; it is, rather, the next logical step in social evolution.

5. *Some sovereignty would be shared with global authorities for dealing with the global agenda.* This does not mean that nation-states would lose all autonomy. On the contrary, one result of an effective world security system would be that individual nations could achieve greater true sovereignty as the loosening of the security straitjacket enables them to overcome their powerlessness and to place domestic priorities at the top of their agenda and permits them to participate equitably in decision making at the global level.

6. *Actors in the shaping and administration of a more human world order must include more than nation-states.* National and transnational networks of religious, trade, industrial, and professional associations can also become major world order actors. The growing internationalization of the women's movement is a good example of how grassroots movements can both transcend and impact national policies and practices.

7. *The participatory development of a new world order must be a transnational and transcultural process.* Existing international structures and processes have been largely products of Western thought and experience. A more just and human world future requires the wisdom and experiences of all the world's cultures. Full human development—and the creation of the structures capable of promoting such development—depends upon an integration of social, economic, political, and spiritual insights of East and West, North and South, masculine and feminine.

Decentralization and World Order

Some fear that a world security system would lead to a global Big Brother. In fact the functional institutions of a world security system would enable a move toward greater decentralization. Rather, it is the mobilization for national security that has led inexorably to the concentration of power in the hands of a centralized, national-security elite in all countries, whether capitalist or communist, rich or poor. Without effective international systems, nations have no other way to respond to unregulated global forces that threaten their security except by investing considerable power in the hands of the military, economic, and monetary elites with a strong central authority.

Such centralized mobilization would not be required with a world security system that has eliminated competition over armaments and has the machinery to effectively mediate and manage international economic, monetary, and environmental conflicts. Resources, talents, and leadership commitments now tied up in national security goals could become available for resolving local and regional problems according to local and regional criteria and control. The more fear and conflict can be reduced between nations the more freedom at the local level will be experienced and realized.

Providing framework for the functional public sector structures needed at the global level should be a broad, flexible set of global standards and values—based on justice, acceptance of diversity, and respect of all life and providing a general sense of compatibility. Although a significant body of such values does exist, as articulated in the United Nations Declaration of Human Rights, much more remains to be done in this area.

Many of the preliminary steps related to a people's movement for peace are already underway. None of the confidence-building steps or world security structures that are needed are beyond our present capabilities, although they may exceed our present political will. Most would utilize or build on the existing infrastructure of the United Nations, especially the specialized agencies. None would require technology beyond our present capabilities.

The fact is that incredible international systems already exist and have played a significant part in contributing to global cooperation, global public-policy development, and greater peace and security. Although not perfect and rather weak because they were established that way (with minimal or no authority), the international systems in existence nevertheless represent an amazing trend in this century toward the development of global-level public policy and global systems to manage global problems.

These structures have not yet been given the authority needed to adequately deal with their respective areas of responsibility. Nor do they yet incorporate the world order values which Global Education Associates and other world order advocates propose as criteria for policy—war prevention, economic and social justice, ecological balance, and participating in decision making. But these international systems do provide impressive interim foundations upon which to construct the global security system required.

World order institutions capable of dealing with today's global crises will not eliminate conflict. Conflict will always be with us. But the legal, structural machinery for dealing with, and negotiating resolutions to, major conflicts will be in place. The global sector structures sought by these world order strategies are seen as building upon the natural, evolutionary thrust of human history. The gradual, incremental, and relentless evolution of ever-widening circles of interdependence—from tribal societies to city states, kingdoms, nation-states, and now toward effective world institutions—constitutes the major thrust of history.

Three Strategies for World Order

Three practical strategies for realizing within a realistic time frame some of the elements of a new world order as envisioned in this chapter are outlined below:

1. *Consciousness-Raising.* The main objective in this strategy is to develop widespread public consciousness. The first effort is to enable citizens and leaders to recognize that true national interest and security, as well as true personal interest and security, lie in a world security structure. A central focus here is on the rigid limitations of the present National Security State system and the powerlessness it engenders. Once this is grasped, the concern more easily moves on to an inquiry about alternative world order possibilities and strategies for achieving them.
2. *Politicization.* In this strategy the question of world order is

Gerald F. Mische

a public issue that has national implications and which will require strategies of political action. Building on the general consciousness raised in the first phase, the main strategy effort here is to mobilize grassroots issue constituencies into effective movements for political change. The political task is a double one: to demonstrate to political leaders that "the people" are ready for world order; and to enable the people to "own" the world order movement through personal involvement in multi-issue coalitions which endeavor to move their national leaders toward the development of an effective global public sector.

3. *Transformation*. This is the strategy in which the various components of a world security system are developed in concrete form. The major work here would be on adoption of an effective global charter and accountability system, on strengthening or structuring the functional agencies of a world order system (based on strengthened United Nations structures), and on gathering globally the authority and resources needed by these agencies to accomplish their function.

These three phases are not mutually exclusive. The processes of consciousness-raising, politicization, and transformation are all already in evidence, to varying degrees, and will continue to be operative throughout the next quarter of a century.

The main immediate need, however, is to strengthen and broaden the base of support and involvement in a widespread, multi-issue movement for world order. Only a relatively small number of people are presently involved in political and transformation processes. The major effort in these next years, therefore, must be to bring the urgent need and possibilities for world order into the consciousness of the world's peoples and to enlist their active involvement.

A key to developing readiness is to identify the linkages between a new world order and local personal concerns. Consciousness-raising begins with specifics. World consciousness begins when the linkages between our present nation-state system and a specific area of concern and powerlessness can be articulated. As these linkages are understood, alternative world order structures become an issue of personal self-interest.

One approach in assisting individuals and groups to identify these linkages is to research and prepare locally special monographs and media materials. These can be strategic tools for local, national, and transnational constituencies to become actors in the issues that will enhance the world order movement.

Networking

Traditional international affairs experts have considered the nation-state as the sole actor on the world stage. More recently, attention has also been given to multinational corporations. A growing number of analysts in the world order movement, however, consider a wider range of actors, that is, persons, organizations, or institutions that can play a significant role in the process of creating and/or strengthening world order institutions.

Four types of networks can be identified that have considerable potential for becoming effective world order actors:

1. Issue networks: Organizations committed to a particular issue, e.g., health, environment, women's rights, etc.
2. Educational networks: secular and faith-related associations of schools, colleges, and universities, institutes and teacher associations.
3. Occupational networks: associations of engineers, educators, medical personnel, lawyers, etc.
4. Religious networks: Catholic, Protestant, Jewish, and other world religious organizations that have national and global networks of individuals, institutions, and local faith communities.

Each of these networks has its own vehicles for exchanging ideas and promoting action initiatives through its respective constituents. Indeed, some are "networks of networks," and many are global networks. The overlap among these four types of networks is positive. Each type of network has constituents who are also members of one or more of the other three. This overlap has positive strategic multiplier ramifications.

Issue Networks

One can take any important issue in most countries and find at least one national organization devoted to that issue, frequently several. These single-issue networks can be important participants in the world order movement. They usually have the power to influence national dialogue and programing related to their issue. They also have the experience and competence needed to generate new insights and new initiatives.

This is true not only in countries where democratic processes permit the citizens to have a voice in public policy but also in those more closed societies where isolated elites and their technocrats largely determine policy. These elites—also confronted with national security priorities and unmet domestic needs—have their own networks with corresponding journals, newsletters, and conferences.

A listing of these issues for which world order has strategic relevance would include the following: hunger, women's equality, housing, war prevention, employment, population, health, the aged, environment, urban renewal, racial justice, democratic participation, education, penal reform, human rights, alienation, and energy.

Each of these issues has local and national organizational networks. Many have transnational networks. Most networks, however, are presently seeking their issue goals within the narrow framework of national boundaries. The challenge is to help these networks place their respective issues within the macro context of global interdependence so that their own issue-interest and social responsibility can be better served.

As leaders of these issues constituencies identify the strait-jacket of our present world system, they begin to comprehend how their particular goals are increasingly dependent upon building a world security system that can loosen that strait-jacket. These constituency leaders can then translate this understanding into a context, a mind-set, and an action process appropriate for their constituents. This is a pivotal step. A great deal depends upon who endorses a world security system alternative.

Educational Networks

Global consciousness and world order are not extracurricular activities. They are at the core of relevant education. If youth are to be prepared for the real world of escalating interdependence and enabled to make a contribution to a more just world order, their educational experience must help them develop the necessary attitudes, concepts, and skills.

Education for interdependence and world order is a question of justice, for students have a right to be adequately prepared to handle the complexities of an interdependent planet. Education for interdependence and world order is also a question of security, for the future security of nations depends upon citizens prepared to build the transnational institutions commensurate with an interdependent planet. Further, education for interdependence and world order is a question of life and hope, for these can be guaranteed only in a world where human development is a priority that can be implemented. To be relevant today, education needs to have curricula designed within a global framework. Education requires the commensurate preparation of educators to effectively deal with such an expanded framework.

Richard Falk speaks of the role of formal education in consciousness-raising. His call for a reorientation in education goes beyond new materials and methods. He believes that the implicit symbol and belief systems behind the educational system must be reformed and that the whole national motivation for education must be reexamined.

Another important group of actors in the world order movement are the national associations of professional persons, e.g., engineers, educators, medical personnel, physical or social scientists, journalists, et al. These networks provide opportunities for communication with thousands of persons who share a common concern about particular issues. Most such networks also have some type of connection with parallel associations in other countries.

Members of such professional networks have a built-in answer to the question, "How can I get involved?" Every profession has at least one major membership association that carries on a continual dialogue through conferences, workshops, and publications about problems, methods, and strategies related to achieving the common goals that bind its membership together. As the connection between the resolution of particular problems and a restructured world order system is seen, these professional networks become natural vehicles for bringing their constituencies into an effective world order movement.

Religious Networks

It is becoming increasingly clear, to many secular as well as religious observers, that a viable world future may well depend upon whether faith-related networks will recognize their unique potential as world order actors. Authentic religion is based upon values fundamental to a viable world order. These include the solidarity of the human family, justice, love, compassion, primacy of conscience, full human development, and reverence for life. Authentic religion is not culture-bound; rather, authentic religion transcends differences, embracing the richness and truths that can be freely interchanged in a world community not fettered by the straitjacket of national security myopia.

Faith-related networks incorporate individuals and institutions that encircle the planet. They provide a global fiber for developing the grassroot awareness and commitment that could make the goal of a world security system based on justice and participation an actuality. Through their organization and widespread membership, these global networks are in touch with grassroots people as well as with people and institutions that influence policy. This "intouchness" is growing as many men and women from these networks move into full-time work with social justice and human needs programs.

The growing focus on world justice and peace by both Catholic and Protestant church networks is impressive. In many other countries, they constitute the only credible voice for the rights of the poor and oppressed. Fortunately, the traditional identification of Christianity exclusively with Western culture is fading. Also diminishing is a too-exclusive preoccupation with proselytizing. There is also a recent emphasis on full human development and on the creation of social institutions which will permit all persons to live in dignity in accord with their own cultural heritage.

Some missiologists are beginning to understand that rather than the unity of humankind being the result of live religious values, a certain political unity may well be the precondition for the living of these values. The analysis of the National Security State as a straitjacket on religious values helps make this point. Thus, "world mission" becomes a mission to build the world security system which would enable the values of love, justice, and freedom of personal conscience to be operative criteria for public policy.

The tasks related to realizing the world order potential of their global networks provide religious organizations a historic opportunity to move to a broad ecumenism. "World order values", e.g., war prevention, economic equity, social justice, and ecological balance, resonate with the inherent values of Christianity, Judaism, Hinduism, Buddhism, Islam, and other religions.

A Framework for Hope

A summary word about the importance of correctly "reading the signs of the times" is in order. One can hardly overstate that the importance of doing this lies in the essential role which hope plays in building an effective world order movement. Any reading of the signs of the times, that is, interpreting contemporary trends and crises, involves some aspect of a self-fulfilling prophecy. If we read today's crises as signs of imminent breakdown, we act in one way—usually with passive despair and immobility. But if we read these crises as evidence of the crisis of growth outlined at the beginning of this chapter, we can be energized to act with bold, faith-filled initiatives to achieve the world order alternatives needed to overcome the structural lag that underlies the crisis.

History is not closed! The human community is experiencing the growth pains of a historical transformation. Both the creating spirit of humankind and the Spirit of Life are straining to break out of the security straitjacket that has constrained all of recorded human history. For the first time in history, the global infrastructure needed for the transnational security system that is essential to peace and human solidarity is in place. Awareness of the global dimension of unmet local needs and of the powerlessness of national leaders to cope with the new global interdependencies is growing. Growing also is a spirituality rooted in a holistic embrace of the whole earth as well as the total human community.

A reading of the signs of the times that identifies this transformational moment and recognizes that history is open to bold, faith-filled initiatives provides a context for the reconciliation. World order offers a conceptual and strategy framework to reconcile much of the emotional conflict between nations, cultures, and ideologies. World order provides the only path to loosen the security straitjacket that constrains all nations, races, and issue constituencies and pits each against all—a straitjacket that reinforces ethnocentrism and hardens ideologies as nationalistic tools.

Notes

1. Kenneth Boulding, *Stable Peace* (Austin, Tex.: University of Texas Press, 1978).

5

Politics and the Religious Consciousness

James M. Wall

Religion and the Common Good

Two moments in twentieth-century American life stand out as examples of the impact of the nation's religious consciousness on its politics. One was a disastrous failure; the other a profound step forward in the well-being of the national community. Religious forces, largely Protestant, played a major role in the passage of the 18th Amendment to the United States Constitution, ratified in 1920. This amendment, which prohibited "the manufacture, sale, or transportation of intoxicating liquors" within the United States led to wide-spread criminal activity as the consumption of alcohol continued. The belief that by legal fiat the drinking of alcohol would be stopped proved to be an impossible dream. In 1933, the 21st Amendment repealed the 18th. Prohibition, began as a religious crusade, ended as a failure.

A Supreme Court ruling in 1954, *Brown v. Board of Education*, was the turning point in another crusade in American life, the effort to overturn decades of tradition and law which left black citizens in an inferior status. The 1954 ruling involved public school education, just one segment of American life that was segregated, especially in the Old South. By the 1960s, a religious crusade, led by Martin Luther King Jr., a black Southern clergyman, swept through the nation, leading to passage of federal laws that, legally at least, eradicated the separation of races. King was serving as pastor of a Montgomery, Alabama, church when the crusade moved forward. Because of his non-violent philosophy, rooted in the Baptist church and drawing from the thought of India's Mahatma Gandhi, the integration campaign was peaceful. Though this changed in the late 1960s, the spiritual dimension of the crusade was largely responsible for keeping the effort to eliminate segregation on a moral, rather than a political plane.

These two moments in American life suggest that a moral fervor behind social causes can have an impact on the political process. In more recent history, conservative forces, inspired by a Christian fundamentalist perspective, have sought to change American cultural practices believed by them to be immoral and detrimental to the social health of the public. These efforts have also had about them the nature of a "crusade," the belief that an evil resides in some specific locale and must be eradicated by action of the people.

The "crusades" of the Middle Ages led kings and knights of the European continent to travel to the Middle Eastern areas of the world to "eradicate" what for them was an evil, the presence of Muslim rulers in the land of Israel, land "holy" to the Christian faith. Crusades in twentieth-century United States are less violent; instead they involve political activity, designed to change laws and impose the will of a religious consciousness on an entire population.

As the Prohibition effort would suggest, morality imposed by law will not be successful unless there is sufficient public support for the issue involved. The legal elimination of segregation, on the other hand, while initially meeting considerable opposition, is now believed to be a positive step, one that was in the best interest not only of black citizens, but of all citizens. When a religious consciousness of individual believers moves into the public arena the outcome will be determined by the willingness of the public to accept that consciousness as not only morally correct but also in the best interest of the common good.

A frequent response to moral principles put forth in public

debate coming from opponents of the cause involved is that the 1st Amendment to the United States Constitution forbids the Congress from making any laws "respecting the establishment of religion, or prohibiting the free exercise thereof." The concept of the separation between church and state derives from that amendment. Supreme Court rulings over the years have struggled with a definition of where a religious consciousness influences public policy and where it imposes itself to such an extent that it becomes an "establishment" of religion. But that is only one side of the religion and politics issue. The courts keep the structural institutions apart. But they do not touch the right of the religious consciousness to impact public life. That right, unfortunately, is being eroded through a failure of the "keepers" of the religious consciousness—the religious communities—to insist upon the importance of a link between religion and the political process.

The Religious Influence on Public Policy

Influencing public policy, then, is the commonly accepted role of a religious consciousness, so long as that influence does not lead lawmakers to impose sectarian religious beliefs on the general public in such a manner that the imposition becomes a form of "establishment" of religion. The larger problem today may be the absence of a religious consciousness in the public to work its will on policy for the common good.

If our public arena is available for input from religion, the question becomes, what is the consciousness that is available to participate in public policy decision making? In recent years observers of American culture have noted a serious decline in "religiousness" among the public. Plato's *Republic* described the important connection between "the moral character of a people and the nature of its political community, the way it organizes and governs itself." When the French social philosopher Alexis de Tocqueville traveled through the United States in the 1830s, he found a people who possessed what he called "habits of the heart," mores that formed the character of the nation. Those mores, he felt, were shaped largely by family life, religious traditions, and voluntary organizations, which included local political groups.

In a book entitled *Habits of the Heart*, taken from de Tocqueville's phrase, five co-authors, headed by Robert Bellah, of the University of California, Berkeley, surveyed a number of Americans to find out to what extent individualism, which this new nation felt was so important to its own freedom, was now affecting the culture. De Tocqueville had concluded that one aspect of American character, the belief that each individual must be free to pursue his or her own good, could become a danger to the larger common good. The French visitor's belief was that families, religion, and voluntary groups would have to make sure this individualism did not corrode the American spirit; they, in short, had to sustain and maintain the "habits of the heart" so essential to the survival of a republic.

"We are concerned that this individualism may have grown cancerous—that it may be destroying those social integuments that de Tocqueville saw as moderating its more destructive potentialities, that it may be threatening the survival of freedom itself."[1] The metaphor of "cancer," used by the researchers, is appropriate, for it suggests the growth of cells in the healthy body which, if allowed to spread, could lead to death. De Tocqueville's original assumption that religion and the family would have major roles in holding back this "cancer" is crucial to our understanding of the importance of the religious consciousness in the political process. In his insightful study, The Lost Soul of American Politics, John Diggins notes that it was de Tocqueville's judgment that this nation was founded by a group of leaders who believed that "freedom is preserved not by the forms and structures of political institutions but instead by the peculiar habits, attitudes, and values of a people, by the moeurs that have been inculcated by society itself."[2]

What came to be known as "religious education" thus became that effort by religious bodies to assume responsibility not only to inculcate members in the principles of the faith as they interpret it but also to play a role in shaping the "habits, attitudes, and values of a people." A particular religious consciousness does not pervade the land, but a diversity of experience and beliefs does. This diversity provides the mosaic of faith which contributes to the strength of a republic.

This is not to suggest that the American democracy was created and sustained by a highly moral people. On the contrary, the founders and their successors are as self-centered and pre-occupied with their own individual needs as are any other peoples on the earth. De Tocqueville put it succinctly, "Americans are not a virtuous people."[3] However, the Constitution itself has been written to take this into account. Restraint of unbridled passion is a centerpiece of that classic document of freedom. Diggins has written that "in America de Tocqueville saw, as did the Founders . . . that the citizen had little of the inner strength needed to discipline his desires and to lead a virtuous life of simplicity and austerity."[4]

This understanding of the human condition is consistent with the realistic assessment of humankind's sinful condition found in the classic understanding of the Christian faith. Reinhold Niebuhr, the American theologian who did so much to correct the illogical liberal belief that goodness is the naturally superior part of the human condition, put it succintly: "Thus the moral urge to establish order in life is mixed with the ambition to make oneself the center of that order; and devotion to every transcendent value is corrupted by the effort to insert the interests of the self into that value. . . . Man is destined, both by the imperfection of his knowledge and by his desire to overcome his finiteness, to make absolute claims for his partial and finite values. He tries, in short, to make himself God."[5]

Tension has been a centerpiece of the American experience from the outset, tension between claims to virtue by the populace and denials of that virtue by religious teaching. But, at the same time, that same teaching has insisted that through responsible behavior toward one's fellow humans a republic may survive precisely because its members live under a Constitution that restrains the damage of unvirtuous acts while permitting the development of a society that aspires to virtuous behavior. Religion thus plays an important part in holding back the "cancerous" growth which individualism encourages. Without the presence of religious groups, teaching succeeding generations the importance of virtuous behavior and the reliance upon an ultimate source of values, the republic could not survive.

Diggins describes the basic conflict that existed among our founding parents. Our nation, Diggins asserts, was a unique creation, brought into existence by a conservative people who created liberal political institutions. We employed radical activity— a violent revolution—to achieve conservative ends, the creation of a society which was designed to protect property and create institutions which would protect individual groups and interests through a "mosaic of mechanisms known as checks and balances."[6]

Religion and Individualism

Liberal individualism, championed through the writings of Thomas Jefferson and Thomas Paine, sought the reduction of the authority of government and the elevation of the will of the people. In contrast, such figures as Alexander Hamilton and James Madison wanted a constitution which would celebrate liberal pluralism, a system which would pit special interests against one another but, through checks and balances, would protect all interests from one another.

At the heart of this new republic were economic interests, the right to hold and acquire more property. But individualism was also crucial to the new nation. Diggins cites Richard Hofstadter's *The American Political Tradition* (1957) in which Hofstadter describes "a kind of mute organic consistency" in the thinking of these early American leaders. And the thinking has remained consistent, from Jefferson to Herbert Hoover, leaders believing in the values of competitive capitalism to such an extent that America has become a "democracy of cupidity rather that a democracy of fraternity."[7]

To this cupidity religious teaching must speak. It is Diggins' contention that neither the liberal individualism nor pluralism "committed America to political ideals that appealed to man's higher nature. Individualism provided the means by which Americans could pursue their interests, pluralism the means by which they could protect them."[8]

Whether our national leadership is "liberal" or "conservative," the pattern is the same. The political conflict between the various segments of political thought in the nation is not over the validity of individualism versus pluralism but over how our nation will act to maintain the existence of an economic system which permits both individualism and pluralism to function with maximum efficiency and benefit for all.

A religious consciousness recognizes the inherent human need to protect oneself, but at the same time that consciousness calls for a higher purpose, the need to serve the common good, the entire community. Operating in an atmosphere of absolute greed, a counter force is needed to educate the public as to alternative visions. The need for religious training in a society which is geared to the laws of the jungle, win-lose, survive-perish, should be obvious. What should also be obvious is that this religious consciousness has done more than keep the peace between warring greedy factions. This religious consciousness has also inspired creative individuals to rise above the economic conflicts and search for self-interest, to call for a higher purpose, to point to a moral vision that transcends the human enterprise.

Reinhold Niebuhr's contribution to this call came at a time when the religious enterprise had drifted into a self-satisfied belief that the sinfulness of the human condition was a misreading of the biblical story and of human history. Niebuhr was an optimistic pessimist, recognizing both the cupidity and goodness inherent in humankind. "Man's capacity for justice makes democracy possible, but man's inclination to injustice makes democracy necessary."[9]

Since the nation was settled primarily by persons of either no uniform belief system, or of the Christian faith, we have been a people who relied heavily on the Christian interpretation of God and human sinfulness. But other religious traditions have contributed to this call for a higher moral vision, including Judaism, with which the Christian faith is so closely linked.

Two "case" studies should be helpful at this point. Consider the situation in Iran, where that nation has entered a phase in its history in which Islamic fundamentalism controls the government. This did not happen in a void. The Shah of Iran sought to bring his people into modernity, dragging them from cherished and ancient traditions into an acceptance of the benefits of Western civilization. This move is a good example of ambiguity in action. Modernity had much to offer the people of Iran. But secularization brought more than a higher standard of living; it also brushed aside dependence on a divine dimension. Ancient traditions were leveled by the rush to build new patterns for living in the modern era. The transition did not succeed. Fearful of change and still resentful at the oppressive style of the Shah's government, the people of Iran turned to yet another dictator, the Ayatollah Khomeini. Under his leadership, Islamic fundamentalism offered the people of Iran a sense of security through the belief that a religious state would rescue them from the uncertanties of modernity. The tension between freedom and faith collapsed in a loss of freedom.

The state of Israel is another example of a nation attempting to function within the tension of a traditional religion honored in the context of a thoroughly secular modernity. Committed to a religious consciousness dating back to the era of Abraham, Isaac, and Jacob, Israel is a relatively new state, created in 1946 out of ancient Palestine.

Dan Segre, a professor of political science at Haifa University in Tel Aviv, Israel, writes in his *Memoirs of a Fortunate Jew: An Italian Story* of his experience as a young Italian immigrant to Palestine in 1939. He recalls the intense debate in his agricultural kibbutz on the future state of Israel. A leader of the kibbutz, Enzo Sereni, was greatly troubled by the inherent ambiguity of a Jewish secular state, clearly a contradiction in terms, if one is to take "Jewish" in its religious meaning.

Segre recalls that Sereni feared the "creation of ghettos, of Indian-type reservations for the religious Jews in a Hebrew Palestine, in which people would be the object of ethnological curiosity, rather than the guardian of the most ancient national identities."[10]

Retaining the vitality of a basic faith of a nation without allowing that faith to become a harsh theocracy was the challenge the modern state of Israel faced at its beginning, and it is the challenge that continues to confront the state today.

How is a state to maintain respect for a diversity of religious or nonreligious opinion among its people and still allow its religious values to affect how it functions as a state? In light of the importance of religion to the basic principles of nations as different as Iran, Israel, and the United States, the option of turning away entirely from a "founding" faith is not realistic. The answer lies in a constant search for a balance between religious values and secular freedom.

Religion and the Public Order

In light of this history of religion's involvement with the political process, it makes no sense to argue that "religion and politics" should remain separate. The Constitution certainly does not mandate such a separation, and tradition indicates that no separation has ever really existed. That "separation" argument invariably comes from persons who use it as a political handle to argue against a particular position espoused from a religious perspective. This is an invalid argument, for a quest for a higher moral vision in the nation is not only permitted but is essential, as de Tocqueville points out, if we are to continue the development of those "habits of the heart" which keep the tension between justice and injustice, which Niebuhr identified.

How does religious education address this arena without falling into the moralism of political self-pleading? We have seen that a political agenda that is adopted first and then bolstered by religious terminology seldom derives from an authentic religious search. The Prohibition experience is just such an example. Imposing a moral structure on the public without making sure that position has a solid base in religious tradition shared by the general public is a fatal political error. Tradition in this country has left Sunday as a "day of rest." That tradition obviously came from Christian practice setting aside that day as a sacred time when "worldly" activities ceased and believers concentrated on spiritual matters. Where the local communities earlier in our history shared that specific belief in the "sacredness" of the Christian Sabbath, laws were implemented to enforce that observance. Gradually, as the tradition shifted, the laws were removed, but the tradition has continued. What is different is that people use Sunday as a day set aside for their own purposes, and people of faith also use the day for worship. But tradition, and not legal requirements, are behind Sunday "closings" of the workplace.

Some smaller religious bodies still adhere to the practice of "closing down" all activities on Sunday, as was illustrated in the motion picture *Chariots of Fire*. A Scottish layman, deeply committed to protecting the Christian Sabbath, refused to run in an Olympic race scheduled for Sunday even after his king asked him to do so. The public can respect this strong stand without wanting it implemented for the entire community.

Some of the more controversial religious positions of the Roman Catholic church—abortion and artificial birth control, for example—are strongly opposed by other church bodies.

The American public will respect the belief that the Sabbath is sacred for some and honor their desire not to work on that day, but there is no sentiment to translate that into laws. The old "blue laws," which did incorporate Sunday closing into law, have gone. In the same manner, even many Roman Catholics who feel that abortion and birth control are morally wrong would nonetheless be against implementing that position into statutes. In short, the American public appears to have strong convictions against imposing morality by fiat.

Religion teaching is intended to shape opinion, and thus to influence public decision making, but it is not meant in this republic to impose the will of a religious minority on the majority of the public. The difference between influence and imposition is basic to the principles which have kept this republic from becoming a religious state. Yet, as the nation has grown into a world power, and as its small original population has expanded into a pluralistic society, there are concerns that even the power to influence public policy has waned.

Henry Adams, the grandson of a president and one of the most influential authors of the late nineteenth and early twentieth centuries, struggled with what he perceived as the loss of virtue in the nation. Living in post-Civil War America, he despaired of finding a key to a moral authority to which one could point without succumbing to parochial domination. Adams felt that mediocrity had taken over in the halls of leadership in the country in which his family had played such an important role.

Alfred Kazin suggests that in his writings Adams was really looking for a meaningful national identity.

The famous Adams family was his tradition; as was the centripetal thinking of the two Adams presidents, father and son united by a prickly sense of superiority but dedicated to America as a new proposition among the nations of the world. But where in this nation's own capital was there a

sense, except in wartime, of this special purpose and authority?[11]

The quest for authority is a quest for ultimate meaning. The
Israelites once expressed this longing for meaning which they
felt could only be found if Yahweh would give them a king.
They got their king, but they also received enormous problems
because the greatness of the nation became dependent upon
the greatness of fallible kings, at times inferior, at other times
better than average. The message in this biblical passage rests
in the mistaken belief that ultimate meaning could be located
in a human ruler. Writing to a friend in 1869, Adams lamented
that the nation he loved so deeply was sinking into such depths
that "I suspect that our people may properly be divided into
two classes, one which steals, the other which is stole from. . . .
The whole root of the evil is *political* corruption; theory has
really not much to do with it."[12]

Adams is expressing a feeling a hundred years after this nation's founding that the spiritual dimension is absent from public life, that the motive of seeking the common good is earth-
bound, well-intentioned, but feeding only on itself. Adams is in
despair, a modern prophet who cries out that without a religious consciousness to lift the people to a higher moral plane,
the nation will sink deeper into political corruption. Like de
Tocqueville, Adams calls for something outside the political
structure to restore the nation's greatness. He is seeking for
what a character in his novel, *Democracy*, describes as the
"great American mystery," something that would restore virture
to the public order.

John Diggins points to another American writer of the nineteenth century, Herman Melville, as one who is also seeking to
identify that "great American mystery." In his final short story,
"Billy Budd," published some years after his death in 1924
(though it was written in 1891), Melville suggests why "political
thought must be informed by ideas and values outside the
domain of politics."[13]

What Melville and Adams are both seeking is some understanding of the "mystery" at the heart of the American experience, that transcendent note which makes sense of the ambi-

guity of the human condition. In a nation founded with that ambiguity written into its original Constitution, it is clear that ambiguity would always plague the citizens living under that document. A religious sensibility, which informs individual and group consciousness, is required to address that ambiguity. It would permit these activities to be followed by the portion of the public which prefers them but would not enforce them on the public.

The "mystery" being sought by both Melville and Adams has more to do with ambiguity than it does with moralism. Religious education that addresses public policy issues must do so with the same kind of cautious hope that characterized the search of these two nineteenth-century authors, a hope that just maybe the "mystery" is there, even though they seem to despair of finding it.

Melville is such an important thinker in this process because he fully appreciated the natural depravity of humankind. He recognized, as he illustrates so well in "Billy Budd," that purity and innocence in a fallen world will always suffer. He also pointed to the response of a "mysterious dimension" to human existence which transcends depravity, innocence and ambiguity, sin, and guilt. To face this reality is to peer into the abyss, as Paul Tillich put it so well, and that experience drives one either to utter despair or faith in the mysterious dimension we call God.

The political process is symbolized by the *Indomitable*, the British warship on which Billy Budd serves. In that real world we must confront evil choices, not good *or* bad, but *both* good and bad in the same choice. Budd is the center of the story, the "embodiment of moral innocence and physical beauty."[14] As James Pickering summarizes the plot, it contains three main characters:

> Billy Budd, the Handsome Sailor; John Claggart, the Master-at-Arms; and Edward Fairfax Vere, the captain of the *Indomitable*. Billy's innocence is no blessing, for it only leaves him exposed and vulnerable. Unable to perceive evil, he is highly susceptible to the practiced deception and natural depravity of men like Claggart, and the tragic confrontation that results is an almost inevitable one.[15]

A careful reading of this story "educates" the modern reader as to Melville's artistic rendering of ambiguity in the political process. The author does not tell his story to be didactic *about* ambiguity, but as an artist he provides this insight into the human condition and the result "educates" us at a level different from the discursive. In the story, Billy is presented as the embodiment of perfection, the "good, innocent man." He has one imperfection, however, and that is a tendency to stutter when under pressure. That flaw proves his downfall when he is provoked by John Claggart. Unable to respond verbally, Billy lashes out in frustration and the blow proves fatal to his tormentor.

As captain of the ship, Edward Vere must render a verdict on this action, described by Melville as "an impulsive act of self-justification." The larger political problem facing the captain affects his judgment. His ship is at war (England against France), and there have been occasions of rebellion in the ranks of sailors. Vere fears that if he does not act with a show of strength in this incident, he will leave the impression that such attacks on a ship's officer could be repeated and go unpunished. He could postpone his decision until the ship reached shore, but he decides that "his private sentiment must yield to the dictates of the naval law under which he serves.[16] As Melville puts it, Captain Vere decides that "the angel must hang."

Ideals clash with reality and there is no easy solution; indeed, the only reasonable solution is to be made for the good of the larger order even though "an angel" dies. Critics have differed over what led Melville to write his story of the young sailor. It is clear that Melville wanted to establish Billy Budd as "the jewel of 'em," the sort of person who is perceived as above reproach and undeserving of punishment. When Billy is transferred to the *Indomitable* his former captain complains over his loss:

> Before I shipped that young fellow, my forecastle was a ratpit of quarrels. It was black times, I tell you, aboard the *Rights* here. I was worried to that degree my pipe had no comfort for me. But Billy came; and it was like a Catholic priest striking peace in an Irish shindy. Not that he preached to them or said or did anything in particular; but a virtue went out of him, sugaring the sour ones.[17]

Billy Budd's death is particularly sad because of his "innocence," and his entrapment in a societal situation that rendered
his verdict of death as "just" under the law and wartime circumstances. Why did Melville present the story in this manner?
"Some [critics] insist that *Billy Budd* marks Melville's final recognition that man must come to terms with his ideals in order to
preserve the stability of the social order and the 'true welfare of
mankind.' For others, the story is to be read ironically as an
indictment of a narrow and rigid Captain Vere, who, lacking the
wisdom to see through his own doctrine of expedience, tacitly
becomes an accomplice to the moral injustice of an inscrutable
universe."[18]

Whichever interpretation one follows, Melville does indicate
that human existence is torn with ambiguity. Fallible humans
are forced to make "political" decisions in that environment.
The meaning he finds in the narrative is clearly not to be located within the single dimension of the observable world but is to
be found in a dimension other than the facticity of a world at
war and a sailor condemned to die on a sailing vessel.

In this he is consistent with the view of Abraham Lincoln, an
American president who faced moments of anguish as a national leader. John Diggins contrasts Lincoln with Niccolo Machiavelli, the Italian political theorist of the sixteenth century, who
contributed to modern political thought by insisting that the
task of the ruler was to hold power in order to rule, regardless
of the tactics required to maintain leadership. "Machiavelli ex-
ploits appearances and deception; Lincoln values honesty and
truth. Machiavelli envisions the greatness of the state; Lincoln
hopes for the goodness of the soul. [Machiavelli] conceives
politics and civic activity as the highest form of human association; Lincoln always distinguishes politics and especially 'the
politician' from 'the people.' "[19]

Abraham Lincoln functioned in public office with a religious
"sensibility," which is to say, his dominant worldview was
of a person convinced of the ultimate power of God, and his
own concern for his co-humans was informed by the necessity
of caring for, and seeking justice for, all others. Lincoln is a
classic example of the "politician" who took a religious sensibility into office with him and employed it even as he made

decisions that were less than perfect. In this he shared the agony of Captain Vere who made a decision for the political order even as he regretted having to make the decision from a personal standpoint. Unlike Machiavelli, Captain Vere did not relish his choice as a "civic activity," but he anguished over it because of the damage it rendered to his "soul."

To Lincoln, or to the writings of Melville, then, we must look on our search for the social order that ensures us of a future with a vision of hope. The Christian tradition mandates our involvement in the political process, but it does not agree with the Machiavellian position that success in politics is essential. With Lincoln the classical Christian tradition acknowledges that a higher justice may at times be reached only through lower injustices, as in the case of Billy Budd.

Political Decisions As Moral Acts

Politicians make political decisions from a moral perspective; they do not make moral decisions from a political perspective. At least that is the appropriate stance for the Christian to take.

To live in a political environment in which we know we must make choices that are ambiguous leaves the decision maker with a sense of unease. But this unease is tolerable only if, as a believer, he or she knows that, as Diggins describes Lincoln's view, "The meaning of history is found beyond history itself, outside time and space and inhering within the inscrutable mysteries of providence."[20]

That statement, which from all available evidence appears to be an accurate assessment of Lincoln's worldview, is difficult for the twentieth-century reader to accept. The reason for this difficulty lies not in Lincoln's willingness to acknowledge the existence of a divine power, but rather in his acceptance of a meaning that lies "beyond history itself, outside time and space." So accustomed are we in modern times to viewing the world as manageable under our own measurable machinations that the suggestion that final answers are beyond our scope is intolerable.

"Religious" people involved in politics often describe themselves as carrying out the dictates of God. Too often they appear to be quite certain as to what those dictates actually are, whether in the halting of the sale of alcohol or the ban on the sale of contraceptives. Lincoln's theology would not have tolerated this certainty. Speaking of the "awful calamity of Civil War" which was then desolating the land, Lincoln suggested that the war "may be but a punishment, inflicted on us, for our presumptuous sins, to the needful end of our national reformation as a whole people."[21]

To understand the depths of Lincoln's realistic appraisal of the human condition, compare what he said about the nation he was then leading in a war with what contemporary presidents say about our own twentieth-century endeavors.

> We have been the recipients of the choicest bounties of Heaven. We have been preserved, these many years, in peace and prosperity. We have grown in numbers, wealth, and power as no other nation has grown. But we have forgotten God. We have forgotten the gracious hand which preserved us in peace, and multiplied and enriched and strengthened us; and we have vainly imagined, in the deceitfulness of our hearts, that all these blessings were produced by some superior wisdom and virtue of our own. Intoxicated with unbroken success, we have become too self-sufficient to feel the necessity of redeeming and preserving grace, too proud to pray to the God that made us.[22]

An authentic part of our American history is to look for divine guidance. Such guidance does not come as a blessing on our successes; rather it comes only as we acknowledge the ambiguity of our actions and confess the need to search for and follow a higher moral vision. Our social order moves forward only as we acknowledge that we are morally ambivalent in our actions. In Perry Miller's essay, "Errand into the Wilderness," he stresses that the early settlers who came to these shores envisioned themselves as undertaking a mission to create a "New Jerusalem." But that mission was always a dream, never realized. And, Miller records, the dream was soon lost because of the very ambiguity of the nature of the "errand" itself.

For, as Sacvan Bercovitch reminds us, an errand "may be either a venture on another's behalf or a venture of one's own."[23] The errand for the Puritans shifted on them in the seventeenth century. First, they failed to establish the divine community in this land, and then they were unable to keep even the religious community itself free of unbelief. Hence, the compromise of the halfway covenant for those children of the original settler-believers who could not profess their belief in the divine God, but who were still needed as part of the religious community. The glorious venture, begun to establish the "New Jerusalem," became a venture on behalf of the people themselves.

Nor may we look to the famous sermon by John Winthrop, "A Model of Christian Charity," as a paean to the glories of this nation. That Puritan divine preached his sermon to Pilgrims who had reached the new land on the ship the *Arbella* and gave them the harsh task that lay ahead: "For we must consider that we shall be as a city upon a hill," a phrase taken from Jesus' Sermon on the Mount. But that "city" was not to be a success story which would be the envy of the world; rather, it was a call to the fortunate ones who had reached these promising shores bearing a mandate from their Maker to accept that "God almighty in his most holy and wise providence hath so disposed of the condition of mankind, as in all times some must be rich, some poor, some high and eminent in power and dignity, others mean and in subjection." There is no egalitarianism in this sermon. But there is the call to all those who had sailed on the *Arbella* to recall that as a "city upon a hill" they had a responsibility to be his witnesses to the errand before them." If we shall deal falsely with our God in this work we have undertaken, and so cause him to withdraw his present help from us, we shall be made a story and a byword through the world . . . we shall surely perish out of the good land whither we pass over this vast sea to possess it."[24]

The social vision that energizes the American experience, dating from Winthrop's sermon, is a vision of responsibility to others under the overarching hand of an almighty God. A religious sensibility in the political process must be mindful of that responsibility and also of the consequences of a failure to live up to that responsibility. At the same time, as Lincoln so clearly perceived it, knowing that political leaders would fall short, it

was reassuring to know that "the almighty" forgives the ambiguous choices we made, provided we confess that they are
ambiguous. If we must condemn Billy Budd to the gallows it
would violate our social vision as a people to argue that the
decision was correct and that we have no regrets over the
downside of the choice, namely, that his innocent bearing
could have no effect on the ultimate decision.

To believe God cares for a people and that in God's own
inscrutable wisdom God expects nations to perform what is
best for the common good is not to claim divine superiority
over others. Rather it is to acknowledge that we have a task to
perform in order to provide the best possible care for citizens
in the state without insisting that we know that our every action
on their behalf is morally justified. We can only seek the right
choice; we are never sure we have made it. There will always
be a "mystery" in our attempt to connect human action with
the will of the "almighty." Not to seek the connection would be
a violation of our social vision as a people. To claim that we
have made the connection would be equally in violation of our
vision.

Herbert Butterfield, the British historian, was an active member of the Methodist church throughout his career and he was
a leading proponent of interpreting history with a belief in God
that did not pretend to know God's actual will in every event.
Butterfield's own personal religious sensibility led him to write:

> We may say at the first level (of analysis) that our actions
> make history—and we have free will—so that we are re-
> sponsible for the kind of history that we make. But then,
> secondly, at a different level, we find that history, like nature
> itself, represents a realm of law—its events are in a certain
> sense reducible to laws. However unpredictable history may
> be before it has happened it is capable of rational explana-
> tion once it has happened. . . .There is a futher factor that is
> operative in life and in the story of the centuries—one which
> in a sense includes these other two things—namely, the
> providence of God. God, in whom we live and move and
> have our being.[25]

In the introduction to this book of Butterfield essays, C. T. McIntyre says that analysis has several levels, the first is biographic, the second is scientific and statistical, and the third approach is faith.

Persons like Butterfield and Reinhold Niebuhr could think of politics and religion in dimensions or perspectives, rather than in spatial terms. With his three "levels" of analysis, Butterfield could do justice to responsible historical scholarship without doing an injustice to his own personal faith. His religious consciousness not only permitted but required that he function in secular society with the best understanding of how that society worked. But at the same time, that religion be an integral part of his thought process was essential.

In this way religious consciousness informs and shapes a worldview without dictating the categories or the final answers to problems posed by, and questions raised by, secular society. Louis Halle, in an essay in which he discussed his career in civil service, writes that in examining his experience in a foreign office

> generally close to where decisions of policy, on which everything depended, were being made with considerable anguish of conscience . . . . I came to one simple and transcendent conclusion which seems to be at the heart of the human plight and the human tragedy.

> It is that the great questions for decision all arise out of what are ethical dilemmas in the literal sense of the word. There are choices among alternative evils only. This is quite different from the picture one gets from the popular press and popular commentary generally, where all choices tend to be presented in Manichean terms as choices between a good course and an evil one, even as choices between what is righteous and what is wicked.[26]

The perspective represents a humility before complex decisions but does not suggest a turning away from having to make those decisions. To function within the political process as a person with a religious sensibility means that decisions are made between given sets of options and made from a set of values informed by the "mystery" of one's religious faith. "Mystery," in this sense, does not refer to an unknown awaiting solution, as in a detective story, but rather speaks of a dimension of existence which transcends the human equation and as such cannot be handled or manipulated as can things in our more precise and objective world.

The "popular press," as Halle terms the media that interprets decision making and events for society, finds it virtually impossible to comprehend the sort of three levels of life that Butterfield outlines. The first two, concrete and analytical, are objective enough to warrant serious attention in the popular press, but the third, the level of functioning from a faith perspective, eludes not only the press but the general public as well.

Many observers of former President Jimmy Carter's campaigns and four years in the White House could not understand his occasional reference to his personal faith. Since they assumed that religion for public officials was an area of life trotted out for display to convince the public of the piety or seriousness of the persons involved, they did not want to believe that Carter actually meant that prayer was an important part of his life.

As his Illinois 1976 campaign chairman, I spent considerable time with the former governor of Georgia as he campaigned in that state. On one occasion we were traveling from one event to another in the backseat of his limousine. To make conversation I talked to him about the recent primary in the state of Massachusetts, which he had lost, a loss which threatened to end his drive for the White House. Carter recovered from that setback and began to win other states, including an unexpected large share of the Illinois delegation. But as we were talking about Massachusetts, he made an observation that is not political wisdom but a religious faith: "Rosalyn and I have talked about it and we have agreed that it was for the best." My first thought was to hope that he would never repeat that remark in hearing of the busload of media personnel then traveling behind our limousine. I could imagine the headlines; "Carter glad he lost in Massachusetts"; or "Candidate enjoys losing." Neither, of course, would have accurately reflected what he actually meant. For Carter was speaking in religious terms, recalling the New Testament admonition that "all things" work for the best for those who "love the Lord." He was speaking out of a worldview that would not make sense to the journalists covering the campaign.

Later on, in a well-publicized interview with *Playboy* magazine, candidate Carter did make public a Sunday school phrase that was misunderstood by the media and subsequently by the public. Answering a question about "lust," he "admitted" that he had indeed felt "lust in his heart." Since most Americans are accustomed to seeing "lust" only on the marquee of a movie theater, it seemed shocking that a public official would openly confess to such a feeling. What he was actually saying, of course, was a reiteration of Jesus' reminder that part of the human condition is to "lust" after others. This interview, and the fact that it appeared in a magazine that featured nudity, was a setback to the 1976 general election campaign. The former president did survive the slip, however, and subsequently was more cautious in how he used "religious" language in the public arena.

What Carter's experience suggests, however, is that our society does not comprehend the language or value system of the religious consciousness. How is this possible, since various polls continue to suggest that ours is a "religious" nation because most people believe in God and a large percentage of people polled say they pray and attend religious services? Why shouldn't a "religious" people accept religious language from public officials?

The Value Basis for Political Action

The answer appears to lie in the governing mindset of the public, a mindset that fixes the common value system in areas other than in religion. David Tracy offers a helpful model when he suggests that our society draws its values from three major "realms," areas in which we place our effort and from which we derive meanings. His three realms are techno-economic, governmental, and religion/arts.[27] Each of these realms generates values for the consideration and adoption of the public. Each realm operates with its own value system and the public is free to choose which will be its major source of value.

In Tracy's model the techno-economic realm is clearly dominant, not only in the United States but in the Western world and, increasingly, in the developing world. The governmental world is a more restrictive part of the model, providing values that relate to justice, determining the values that belong to the institutions that actually govern us in our corporate lives. The techno-economic realm, however, is the major source of meaning, value, and a measure of what is important in life. Will it work? Will I succeed? Can I exercise power? These are questions that are behind the value system of the dominant variety in our society.

The religion/art realm—and Tracy's reason for linking the two shall be addressed in a moment—is envisioned in this model as over to the side, spatially removed from the center of society. In Tracy's provocative phrase, religion/art is confined to the "reservation of the spirit" in much the same manner American Indians were confined to reservations to get them out of sight in the nineteenth century.

A secular society, as ours most certainly is, does not want to lose the religion/arts realm and periodically returns to it with pomp and ceremony, at times like Christmas or Easter or through events like the funeral of a public official or the visit of a pope. But we only have to consider just how removed from actual decision making and value orientation the "sacred spaces" actually are to appreciate to what an extent the religion/arts realm is not considered central to public life and policy decision making.

Many fundamentalist Christians have been active in the political arena since the mid-1970s, and their presence is confusing and frustrating to the rest of society. They have, in effect, left the reservation and are plying their trade on the open market. The fact that in doing so they have largely confined their efforts to a narrow agenda, centered on a few issues, doesn't alter the fact that their presence in the public arena is both consistent with their faith and with the tradition of American politics.

A valid criticism of these fundamentalist Christian politicians and activitists is that they have brought a particular political agenda, which looks suspiciously like the agenda of the conservative wing of the Republican party, to the public state. In some cases, however, they have gone beyond the anticommunism and promilitary bias of the political conservatives and have introduced family life issues, centered largely on sexual matters—abortion, homosexuality, sex education, and pornography.

They are not the first religionists in the post-World War II era to get off the reservation, however. The American "liberal" churches were actively involved in support of the civil rights movement and in opposition to the war in Vietnam. And Jerry Falwell, a leader in the fundamentalist Christian political movement, readily admits that the success of the liberal left churches helped him to see that there was a place for fundamentalist Christians in the public arena.

The argument can be made, of course, and I would do so, that in many instances in which religionists have left the "reservation," they have done so armed, not with the religion/arts value system, but with the value system of the techno-economic realm, the belief in power politics, success, history, and, in short, a Machiavellian worldview. The religious consciousness which will most effectively inform the public debate and affect our social order in the future will be the one that functions with authenticity from its own "realm."

David Tracy has wisely linked religion with art in speaking of the three realms in our society. He does this because in describing values he is speaking of a source, not any particular content. The Christian religious sensibility, for example, is rooted in a specific understanding of history in which (it is felt) that God has acted through history in order to save the world. Salvation, in this sense, refers to a restoration of unity lost in the "fallenness" of the human condition, and, while restoration is always sought, it is not completely found. As such, the Christian sensibility remains open to the "gift of grace," the unexpected, undeserved invasion of the human condition. Something other than the accumulated human experience is involved in this story of salvation and grace. That something is celebrated in the Christian sensibility as the God who redeems in this concrete world even as that God is not confined to this concrete world.

That something of this sort is a "mystery" is acknowledged by the Christian sensibility; but that something is witnessed to in various ways by classical expressions of the Christian faith. The world of the "arts" derives also from a "mystery," the creative dimension of existence which cannot be explained in rational categories any more than religion finally yields to rational, measurable patterns. In this sense, then, the two, religion and the arts, may be said to inhabit the realm of the creative, mysterious dimension of life which infuses society with a worldview and a value system.

This value system is ignored by modern society in society's absolute devotion to the techno-economic realm's value system. As we have aready seen, Abraham Lincoln and Herman Melville, speaking in a political context and in a literary context, both spoke of a value system which relied on something other than the natural world. That these two stand out in history is a further indication that they are, sad to say, exceptions. The reason they are exceptions is that the modern mind-set is largely committed to a one-dimensional view of reality.

Modernity has given us the gift of insisting that reality is real only if it is observable, measurable, and, finally, can be proved. In Huston Smith's phrase, modernity, which he describes as functioning with a "modern Western mind-set," puts its trust in "the quantitative, material domain that the methods of modern science have brought into view."[28]

There is no way modern religious education can develop a moral vision and still function entirely within that "modern Western mind-set." At the same time, since we do live in the period of modernity, we must acknowledge that modernity is the primary way society functions.

Our task, therefore, is to be as wise as foxes in the secular society in which we function but at the same time to proclaim without hesitation that our source is not limited to the wisdom of this world. This is a more difficult assignment than it appears to be. For a mind-set is an established pattern of viewing reality; secular education is designed to guide its students in the world of the "one-dimensional. " Any suggestion as to another dimension either is denied outright or, as Douglas Sloan puts it, "is called into question, if only by neglect."[29]

The Task of Religious Education

Our task in relating religious education to the political process is to first of all recapture the high ground, to redefine the issues so that we are not locked entirely into the worldview that blocks input from the realm of the arts. "The most immovable . . . of all the assumptions of the modern mind-set is that which holds that the qualities of experience reflect only subjective preferences and emotional states. The tendency of the past four hundred years has been to regard only that which can be dealt with by science—quantity—as objective and real, and all else—qualities—as purely subjective and thus, ultimately, nonexistent."[30]

Further, the modern Western mind-set has, since the secularization of the world, beginning at least in a symbolic sense with the trial of Galileo Galilei in the early 1600s. Galileo's clash with religious and secular authorities of his time was over the scientific method; he insisted that truth should be measured, they maintained that only the church could declare truth. Though the Italian scientist was forced to recant, his position eventually prevailed and modernity was born. Galileo's position was a positive force in Western society because it released thought from shackles of superstition and clergy authoritarianism. But the downside was that Galileo's stand led not just to a triumph of reason but also to a narrowing of reason. "Reason itself has been cut off from its own deep sources of imagination, intuition, and insight in the mind of the knower."[31] In addition, "a reason that is limited to dealing only with sense experience and the logical relations among observed phenomena cannot speak of any nonempirical dimensions of structures in reality."[32]

Since modern media shape our perception of reality by the manner in which all events are reported and since the traditional journalistic questions of Who-What-When-Where seldom add the needed "Why," our understanding of all that happens to us and around us remains locked in a narrow band of reason without imagination. There is no place, for example, for the third level of analysis that Herbert Butterfield describes as "faith," the interpretation of events at a level other than the objective and tangible.

A religious sensibility frees the modern thinker from the trap of narrow reason. This releases us to perceive the world from a vantage point other than the scientifically provable, reasonable, measurable dimension. Yet a religious sensibility does not free the thinker from being responsible in the proper use of reason; hence if one uses his or her imagination to insist that hot is not hot, a severe burn can result. There are some segments of life which modernity has clarified and continues to clarify for us. But "a total reliance on a narrow conception of reason abolishes wonder and mystery and leads to the thinning and flattening out of the actual richness and complexity of life. A sense of wonder and mystery comes to be viewed as a source of confusion and obfuscation, an obstacle to clear thinking and efficient implementation of policy."[33]

But just as we have noted that political processes must be conducted within the framework of the given political structures—if someone loses an election, no amount of imagination can change the outcome—nevertheless, imaginative use of reason in the political process breaks the user out of the realm of the techno-economic realm of values and makes way for the fresher, deeper realm of arts/religion. There is no way, of course, as classical Christian thought would quickly point out, for superiority to be claimed for a political candidate or office holder because of a prior religious commitment. The important point here is that a religious consciousness permits the political practitioner to at least function with a full deck and not be limited to the half of the deck found in the modern Western mind-set.

Clearly, to argue for an involvement in the political process which employs the language and strategies of the process itself is realistic. But further, a religious education program that did not at the same time insist on preparing the practitioner to function with resources beyond the modern Western mind-set is an education that loses the claim to be "religious." In short, we must acknowledge that we operate in a hostile environment; the secular world does not take kindly to the claim that politics, like every other segment of life, can be practiced from a religious base. And we must train in religious education to live in that environment.

Religious practitioners who use their faith to push liberal or conservative agendas "in the name of God" miss the point altogether. In addition, they make the task more difficult because they increase the credibility gap between secular and religious. Novelist John Updike, in his novel *Roger's Version*, displays the sensibility of a "religious artist" with his treatment of the ultimate absurdity of modernity's attempt to corral God.

In the novel a young man comes to a seminary professor with a request for a financial grant so that he can pursue his theory that God can be located through the computer. He believes that the ultimate proof of God's existence will finally be grasped through technology. Updike, who has often indicated an appreciation for the theology of Karl Barth, presents this situation with irony, for he writes that the seminary grants the request for funds. The result is disastrous; the project fails, of course, because the proper number of keyboard punches will not lift a graduate student into the heavens, but for Updike, Roger's request, and the approval by the faculty, is a symbol of the empty end of the human quest for absolute control over God.

Which is what the modern mind-set is finally all about— control. In Francis Bacon's understanding of modernity, the purpose of science was to "put nature to the rack, to torture her secrets from her."

The holder of the secret is the holder of power.

The saga of Adam and Eve in Genesis has usually been seen as a story of sin, which it finally is. But the sin is that of seeking to control God, to know what God knew. All that the God of the Garden expected of these first humans was that they trust their creator, and this they could not do; thus they were thrust from the garden into the real world where they and their descendents to this day continue to repeat that original sin. The environment in which we seek to be religious educators is an environment which has made such enormous strides in technology that the conquest of God always seems just around the corner. Religion is seen, in its limited sacred spaces, as the place for subjective feelings and personal thought to be expressed. But the real "religion" of this modern Western mind-set is technology.

As Douglas Sloan sums it up:

Technology (now) elicits feelings of awe and veneration once associated with a sense of the sacred. Technology has its own priesthood and initiates—the scientific-technological elite—and its own temples and cathedrals—research institutes and universities. And it is to technology that millions in the world look for ultimate salvation—a kind of "second coming" in the next breakthrough of medical science, genetic engineering, or space colonization.[34]

Flannery O'Connor was another modern artist who worked against the limitations of the *one-dimensional* scientific world-view. She deliberately employed the outrageous and the grotesque to prepare the reader for the gift that came only from another dimension, the gift of grace. Describing what she calls "serious fiction," O'Connor observed that any story "that can be entirely explained by the adequate motivation of the characters or by a believable imitation of a way of life, or by a proper theology, will not be large enough."[35]

The writer does have to be concerned with matters of facticity but only, she insists, because "the meaning of [the] story does not begin except at a depth where these things have been exhausted."

And then O'Connor adds, "the fiction writer presents mystery through manners, grace through nature, but when she/he finishes, there always has to be left over that sense of mystery which cannot be accounted for by any human formula."[36]

In this search for a vision of the world which is appropriate for religious education, the scientist should not be cast as the villain. Nor should the artist be the heroine. Rather the villain is the religious educator who fails to recognize the limitations of the modern Western mind-set. Breaking out of the limitation involves an openness to the mysterious dimension of reality we know as God. We must pursue in religious education what E. M. Forster describes as appropriate for literature. Writing of the novel, Forster, the author of *Passage to India* and other novels and short stories, wrote of the difference between a novel which is good, but not great, and a novel that is great. The good novel, he maintains, has as its underlying theme the fact "that we grow old and die." "But a great book must rest on something more than 'of course.' "[37]

The task of the religious educator is to go beyond the "of course." "Of course" we should train students in the basics of the faith, its history, its literature, its basic application to living. But that is only "good" education. To develop "great" education, we must seize what is uniquely ours, access to the ultimate dimension, to that beyond in the midst of reality which lays claim upon us. To be open to the mysteries of that which is more than the accumulation of all that we know is to be open to the source of what can give us a "greatness" for the future of religious education.

Armed with that base, we will venture with confidence into the swamplands of political activity, never claiming superiority, but always confident that we are functioning in a crucial area of society with a mandate from the power that will not be conquered.

NOTES

1. Robert N. Bellah, Richard Madsen, William Sullivan, Ann Swidler, Steven M. Tipton, *Habits of the Heart: Individualism and Commitment in American Life* (Berkeley: University of California Press, 1985), p. viii.

2. John P. Diggins, *The Lost Soul of American Politics: Virtue, Self-Interest, and the Foundations of Liberalism* (Lake Station, Ind.: Basic Books, 1984), p. 232.

3. Quoted in Diggins, *The Lost Soul of American Politics.*

4. Ibid., p. 233.

5. Reinhold Niebuhr, *An Interpretation of Christian Ethics* (New York: Harpers, 1935), p. 85.

6. Diggins, *The Lost Soul of American Politics,* p. 5.

7. Ibid.

8. Ibid.

9. Reinhold Niebuhr, *The Children of Light, the Children of Darkness* (New York: Scribner, 1944).

10. Dan Segre, *Memoirs of a Fortunate Jew: An Italian Story* (Bethesda: Adler and Adler, 1986), p. 130.

11. Alfred Kazin, *New York Review of Books,* May 29, 1986.

12. Ibid.

13. Diggins, *The Lost Soul of American Politics,* p. 286.

14. James Pickering, *Five Tales by Herman Melville* (New York: Dodd Mead, 1967), Introduction.

15. Ibid., p. xi.

16. Herman Melville in *Five Tales by Herman Melville*.

17. Herman Melville, *Billy Budd, Sailor, and Other Stories* (New York: Penguin, 1985), p. 325.

18. Pickering, *Five Tales*, p. xii.

19. Diggins, *The Lost Soul of American Politics*, p. 322.

20. Ibid., p. 329.

21. Lincoln's *Works*, Vol. I, p. 382, quoted in Diggins, *The Lost Soul of American Politics*, p. 330.

22. Ibid.

23. Sacvan Bercovitch, *The American Jeremiad* (Madison, Wis.: University of Wisconsin Press, 1978).

24. Perry Miller and Thomas H. Johnson, eds., *The Puritans: A Sourcebook of Their Writings* (New York: Harper & Row, 1963), p. 199.

25. "God Is History," in *Herbert Butterfield's Writings in Christianity and History*, ed. C. T. McIntyre (New York: Oxford University Press, 1979).

26. Cited in *Herbert Butterfield: The Ethics of History and Politics*, Kenneth W. Thompson, ed. (Lanham, Md.: University Press of America, 1980), p.11

27. David Tracy, *The Analogical Imagination* (New York: Crossroad, 1981).

28. Huston Smith, *Beyond the Post-Modern Mind* (New York: Crossroad, 1982).

29. Douglas Sloan, *Insight-Imagination: The Emancipation of Thought and the Modern World* (Westport, Conn.: Greenwood, 1983), p. 10.

30. Ibid.

31. Ibid., p. 16.

32. Ibid.

33. Ibid., p. 21.

34. Ibid., p. 29.

35. *Flannery O'Connor*, ed. Harold Bloom (New York: Chelsea House, 1986), p. 32.

36. Ibid.

37. James Gindin, in *Forms of Modern British Fiction*, ed. Alan Warren Friedman (Austin, Tex.: University of Texas Press, 1975), p. 18.

6

Transformation At Work

William Johnson Everett

INTRODUCTION

Religious education seeks to transform people. It leads us out of our old selves into new selves. It leads us out of old social structures into new ones. It is not merely a communication of ideas but a transformation in faith. It seeks to transform institutions as well as persons and groups. Key figures in our history of religious education—Bushnell and Coe—have all emphasized this manifold character of religious education as a work of social as well as personal transformation.[1] In this chapter I want to focus this concern on the world of work.

As soon as we examine the process by which people are transformed we see that this conversion results not only through the impact of religious ideas and institutions but also through the impact of all the institutions in which we invest our loyalties and lives. Not only are we called to transform our workplaces, we are also deeply formed and transformed by the organization and conditions of work itself. How we work shapes our faith and ethics. Thus the relation of religious education to work is reciprocal. Work shapes religious education even as religious education seeks to shape work. Work is not only a target of conversion, it is also a partner in the process of human transformation.

To explore this complex dynamic I shall first expose the theory of human transformation underlying my own approach. This theory will already orient us to the important relationships we need to examine in the relation of religion and work.

We shall then examine the relationship between these two partner institutions. In this case we find a history marked by professed concern and practical estrangement. The relations between the two spheres have been hidden and indirect. We need to lift them up so we can face new patterns of relationship more intentionally.

In seeking a more dynamic and intentional relation between these two arenas of transformation we must then proceed to an indentification of the central changes that are going on in the world of work. This analysis should lift up not only key partners for the process of human transformation but also identify targets of the church's concern.

We can then explore the impact of these changes in the workplace on the process of religious transformation, especially as this is advanced by churches themselves.

In turn we need to identify important alternative strategies pursued by Christians in shaping the workplace. Here we need to exercise our critical judgment to evaluate approaches showing more promise in light of the changes going on around us.

The need to choose among alternative responses forces us to clarify our underlying theological commitments. I shall therefore direct us to some theological issues requiring reformulation in our present circumstances. I shall sketch some elements in the move from individual asceticism to covenant publicity as the guiding concept for moving us forward in the dialectic between work and religious education. On this basis we can then conclude by highlighting some emerging church responses to the changing workplace.

The Process of Human Transformation

In this examination of the relation between work and faith I presuppose a particular theory about human transformation; namely, that we are transformed through the ways we are emotionally bonded to others and to significant beings and objects in our world. We can only hear information along the charged lines of our relationships. Information that comes in to us along lines that are emotionally dead never reaches us.

These emotional bonds are established not only in families, as Martin Lang and others have pointed out, but also in our work.[2] Sometimes work and family are very closely associated and resonate with each other, as in the family farm, family firm, or in homemaking and child rearing. Other times work and family are so distant from one another that they compete, even to the extent that one sphere loses all emotional significance to one's life, as with monotonous factory drudgery or the isolated home life of the overtime executive. In any case, no effort at education and transformation, whether in church, school, or clinic, can overlook the power of the emotional structures we gain in our work and family life.

The emotional bonds of marriage, parenthood, kinship, and work create a charged grid or filter through which we can assimilate new relationships, new ways of acting, and new objects of loyalty. In computer jargon, our basic emotional patterns are an operating program which receives some commands but not others. Our emotional bonds are patterns of love as well as faith. They are patterns of love in that they dispose us to embrace certain kinds of commands and demands but not others. They are patterns of faith in that they establish an adherence to a net of relationships we take as ultimately trustworthy, whether it is our relationships with our parents in childhood or our relationships in school, church, work, or even sports. Our basic faith is rooted in an internalized pattern of relationships we can take into all areas of life. Faith is a network of fidelity. Our life is a continual effort to give public form to our covenant of trustworthy relationships. It always contains an effort to make this faith public enough that it can be shared with others. Here we find some roots of the concept of covenant publicity which shall guide this analysis.

Transformation in our faith structures, that is, conversion, occurs not merely because of some ideas we have, but because the structures of our world change and force us to respond. Changes in our work, whether personal or institutional, dissolve old faith patterns and open us up to new ones. We can see this clearly in the typical life path of men and women: first career entry, reentry after child rearing, shift in career, and retirement. We can also see it in the collapse of old industries and the rise of new ones, the death of farms and the birth of new firms. We also know it in the devastating impact of unemployment. These are social changes which also entail personal transformation. They are transformations in work, but also transformations in faith. It is the church's task to enter into this dynamic in its own way. Engagement with transformations in the workplace is central to the task of religious education.

This chapter is too brief to spell out a refined theory of educative transformation along these lines. My main concern is to lift up the powerful way our basic emotional bonds shape learning and faith. Because of its primacy in our daily life, work is one of the most powerful workshops of the heart. It is one of the forges of faith.

The Estrangement of Work and Religion

If work is so central to faith, why has it not occupied a central place in religious education? Religious educators have traditionally looked to the family and the school as the key partner institutions in the overall work of religious education. They are the most important shapers of religious education as well as the key institutions to be transformed by it. After that, some attention has been paid to political institutions, primarily in their legislative functions. The workplace, now often displaced by leisure institutions, comes in a distant third or fourth if it is mentioned at all.

Why has this pattern existed? First of all, religious education has typically focused on childhood education. Religious education was seen as preparation for work rather than reflection on work. This focus on the child can be seen as one effect of the separation between work and family life that became normative in the nineteenth century. In that situation, the home no longer effectively mediated work skills to the next generation. The child, independent of kinship bonds, went to school to gain the requisite skills and certification for work. This reliance on one's own self and on value-free knowledge gained from experts in the school nourished the rise of "personality" as a value. Or, to put it more precisely, these economic conditions cultivated a particular kind of acquisitive individualism whose "positive" side was a deep belief in the importance of "personality." Individuals each had to have and find their special talent (how many people were raised on that parable?) in order to negotiate the many decisions and take the many risks necessary to enter into their own occupation.

In this situation the school emerged as a partner to the factory and tried to cultivate virtues compatible with industrial organization—punctuality, efficiency, deference to scientific experts, and a mechanical division of knowledge and work.[3] This ascetic individualism was nurtured in self-control through moral injunctions voiced in family, church, and home—sexual restraint, teetotalism, self-denial, thrift, and self-examination. The churches supported this model with the development of the Sunday school—a little factory of religious values to fit this new structure of work and family life. Schooling, that is, a controlled progression ("grades") in the acquisition of discrete specialized skills and concepts, came to dominate our approach to education just as the factory dominated the world of work.

In the culture of schooling, occupation was seen as a lifelong commitment—a secularized version of monastic profession. The occupations people were schooled for were not seen as flexible and changing. Once educated for that work, one no longer engaged in education. Education was not a lifelong pattern of reflection for the sake of transformation and change— both in the self and in the workplace. It was the achievement of a fixed vocation in which God's eternal call crystalized in the occupational order.

This emphasis on cultivating the individual personality characterized the strong idealistic strand in religion generally. Personality was a spiritual matter emanating from God. Work and the economic sphere were materialistic. The church stressed personality over materialistic determinism, voluntary association over the involuntary bonds of work, democracy over the hierarchies characteristic of the factory and business. Within this appoach it was all too easy to contrast and oppose the realm of work and that of the spirit, in spite of the many strands of Christian utopias, communalism, and socialism that wove through the fabric of the times. Factory work was characteristically dull, repetitive, brutalizing, and mechanical. Being so opposed to the spiritual aims of religious education it could not even be examined for its reciprocal interplay with the church.

Of course, the personalism and democratic idealism embedded in the thought of people like George Albert Coe could fuel a zeal for reform of work. Coe wanted to pursue some kind of industrial democracy but was unable to engage that task with any rigor. We need to ask, then, why religious educators did not pursue this challenge more vigorously?

Responses to this question lead us to other factors in the separation of work from religious education. In the nineteenth century we see the domestication of religion under the impact of its institutional separation from government and the development of an autonomous economic sphere. Both politics and economics were seen as spheres primarily of conflict rather than cooperation. Only the church and home could lift up alternative, spiritual ideals of love, cooperation, and emotional commitment.[4] The public sphere was seen as an arena of combat among free citizens, free entrepreneurs, and, most ironically, "free" laborers.

According to this "two-spheres doctrine" work and politics were reserved for men, the raising of children for women. While the church continued to be governed by men, its actual work was carried on by women as one facet of child-rearing and homemaking. Religious education, likewise, became women's work—an activity rigidly cut off from public life and the realm of work.

However, this rigid separation of work from religion and the home did not mean the absence of reciprocal influences. Inspection reveals a powerful and contradictory dynamic between work and religion, especially in Protestantism. The idealistic belief in free personality could provide a powerful critique of work life, but it also reinforced the individualism characteristic of its ideology. Free personality was also an ideal underpinning the freedom of the entrepreneur to do what he wished with his property and of laborers to enter repressive contracts even if they violated traditional claims of home, religion, and the common good. In short, the Protestant ethic of enterprising individualism legitimated the very economy it could also critique. In cultivating honesty, sincerity, promise-keeping, punctuality, literacy (and often literalism), efficiency, and thrift among the emerging middle classes it reinforced an economy rapidly sundering the common bonds of humanity between owner and worker, between corporation and its environment, among work, family, and faith.

In addition to cultivating these ideals of the Protestant ethic outlined by Max Weber in his classic essay, the churches also reinforced patriarchal order through their repristination of the home as a kind of castle ruled by the male and managed by the female. This emotionally grounded image of right order was reinforced in worship as well as church order, further legitimating hierarchies of obedience in other spheres.

The historical scene was of course richer than this brief sketch of major elements can convey. There were always countercurrents and lone voices with singular insight. However, these four factors operated generally to divorce the church and religious educators from attention to the workplace as an institution of central concern for the transformation sought through religious education.

Transformations in Work

With this preliminary grasp of the dialectic between work and religion in our own culture we turn to an analysis of the workplace itself. First, what is being meant by work? My primary concern, in light of my approach to transformation as a process of covenant publicity, is the human relationships in the workplace; that is, how work is organized. Within the field of economics I am concerned first of all with the firm. This is the basic structure of work in our society, whether it is a small family business or IBM. It is the point of identification for people. It is their emotionally significant frame of activity.[5]

The way our national economy is shaped both internally and in its profound connections with global markets and industries also conditions the shape of individual firms but is not my central focus here.[6] While concerned with these wider forces I want to focus here on the network of human relationships they shape in the workplace. Moreover, it is this web of organization, rather than its statistical face which primarily concerns me. The bottom line of a work organization is not found in its quarterly statement but in the relationships of love, respect, cooperation, faith, and trust that enable people to work together in the first place.

Work in this perspective is the public expression of a certain set of covenants defining our life in relation to people, natural resources, land, and to God. It is a complex pattern of expectations among actors playing such roles as consumers, producers, organizers, clients, and coordinators. The entire network of work relations articulates a web of public trust. In this sense it expresses a particular faith binding people together in a process of transformation—not only of their environment but of themselves. It is an arena of covenant and public interchange.

Since World War II dramatic changes in the workplace have ruptured the industrial era's interplay of work and religion. Not only has the pattern of organization shifted, but the two-spheres division of labor has dissolved. The workplace has been undergoing great transformations which demand changes in our patterns of religious education. These changes also demand new challenges from our faith traditions. First, let us review the salient changes that have occurred in work before moving to the religious impact and response.

One of the most heralded developments is the rise of women in the workplace at increasing levels of authority. By 1986, 60 percent of all women between sixteen and sixty-five held jobs outside the home. Though most of these were not stepping into a lifelong career, they still have produced enormous changes in the way we raise children (at day care centers), feed the family (at the drive thru), and maintain households (call the service professionals). In short, we have moved from the doctrine of the two spheres to a life in two jobs if not two careers.[7]

Two-earner and two-career couples have begun to bring about some changes in the way work and career are envisaged. While senior management is still permeated by expectations of unlimited devotion to the firm, people are beginning to accept the importance of family and community within a sense of vocation broader than occupation. People almost expect to change occupation, often drastically, once or twice in their lifetime. Education is a continuing expectation in developing one's work life.

This expectation of continuing reeducation is augmented by the rapid technological changes in work. Computerization and robotization are still working their way through the economy, with the outcome profound but still unclear. In addition, the global expansion of economic organization introduces greater complexity into these processes of change. Work requires increasing skills in communication, problem solving, adaptation to organizational change, and cultural (not to mention gender) pluralism. Technological change is joined by rapid financial movements to restructure organizations constantly. Not only does this require that people repeatedly change the way they work, but also increases the chance they will be out of work, not only in their robust years but in the form of retirement. Men and women are faced with many years of active life beyond their expected devotion to work and rearing children. We have hardly begun to assimilate the impact of these changes in our institutions and in church life.

As a result of this constantly changing work environment businesses have become major educators. The corporate classroom reaches as many people each year as are enrolled in higher education—at an expense of over $50 billion.[8] This education is both preparative and reflective. It has become a dimension of work itself.

All of these changes bring to sharper contrast the tension between the political and the technical-scientific character of work. While many people try to reduce work and work relationships to "objective" rules, formulas, and statistics, the actual fact of organizational complexity and change requires a heightened attention to its political character. Not only must people in an organization counsel together more frequently and openly, they must also recognize the rights and claims of co-workers and the many outside "stakeholders"—neighborhoods, consumers, suppliers, governments, natural environments, and future generations.[9] Thus work becomes a crucial arena for people's efforts to make their lives public—to find expression, recognition, and confirmation through the formation of dependable covenants with each other. It becomes even more clearly a place where people can forge and remold covenants of public trust. This is not only the religious theme I am pursuing here; it is also a crucial development in work life today.

Transformations in Religion

What impacts are these changes having on people's basic patterns of relationships, that is, their faith—both in work and in the church? The movement of women into the workplace demands that people transform their basic instincts about the relation of men and women. People have to move from relations of master and mistress to those of colleague and collaborator. The intimacy of the home as the structure for relations of men and women yields to the civility of the public as the model of interaction.

Both men and women begin operating out of patterns of rational problem solving and civility learned in the workplace. We start living in terms of contracts for domestic as well as church relationships. Discrete and specified obligations and rights replace the diffuse and totalistic embrace of the traditional home and parish.

It is already clear that lifelong learning patterns have become general expectations in our society. This has always been a strand in the Sunday school movement and the CCD. To this is added an awareness that the focus of this process lies in the crises and junctures where people must deal with the end of old relationships and the beginning of new ones—divorce, job loss, job change, work force reentry, retirement, and the like. Religious education, whether conducted through classes, workshops, retreats, or programs of counseling and spiritual direction, engages people where they face changes in the way they put together their work and family life. Here is where the structure of fidelity upholding our lives is tested, broken, and converted. Here is where integrity must be fed by the communion of the saints.

Work changes have also drastically affected the availability of women for traditional volunteer work in the church. While most of us may not lament the passing of women's circles and luncheons, we all feel the pinch when no one can devote extra time and energy to Sunday school, outreach, and maintenance.

We have yet to figure out whether and how to replace these women volunteers with older retired people, for our society has not conditioned us to expect their contributions. In any event they would differ from those previously tendered by mothers and housewives.

This loss of volunteers in the face of changed work patterns leads to a renewed professionalism in church staffs. While great lip service is paid to the volunteer aspect of church life, mainline churches have become increasingly specialized and professionalized. Work relationships at church also have become more contractual, specific, and monetary. While some churches, especially those trying to resist these changes, use this professionalism to construct more schools based on the old model, there is considerable question whether a schooling model can help people cope with the actual challenges of a new economy and family life.

At the same time that church work and religious education in particular loses its volunteer character, it loses its label as "women's work." It becomes first of all everyone's work and then the work of the professional. Indeed, to sum up one strand of this argument here we could say that religious education is shifting from being an expression of women's work to being an engagement with the quality of work. The heart of our transformation moves from the old alliance of home and church to include a new nexus of work and church. Religious education is now challenged to take seriously this new center of gravity in our lives.

All of these transformations in work have therefore effected changes in family life and church, the two primordial molders of our deepest emotional bonds. This change presents challenges and dilemmas to a church that would seek to be about the work of human transformation.

The church's dilemma lies in the fact that the workplace has become increasingly important as a separate arena of deep human loyalty, commitment, suffering, and transformation. Work life is profoundly important for both men and women. It must be lived out religiously through its many calls, transitions, and corruptions. It has enormous impact on the way people organize their family, church, and community life.

However, in the face of this the churches remain deeply estranged from work. Even entertainment is more closely allied to the church than are the ordinary processes of work. The place needing religious response the most is furthest from the church's ambit.

Moreover, the church's traditional way of affecting work through family life and the school has been greatly attenuated. The loss of the family farm and the family firm as dominant patterns even within middle-class Protestantism cut one nerve. The gap between work and ordinary schooling, whether in public, private, Sunday, or parochial schools, severs another. Since people can no longer be prepared for a lifetime of work, the kind of schooling based on lifetime specializations is no longer relevant for the student. Not only do the emotional bonds of the family not carry over into school, but those of the school do not carry over into the workplace.

Religious Responses to Work Issues

These are some of the reverberations from the workplace revolutions we are undergoing. They confront the church with two questions: How will it bridge the gap between religious and workplace processes of transformation? Moreover, with what critical edge, with what definition of its faith, will it respond to workplace changes in a faithful manner? Contemporary church responses generally take three forms: *reactive,* *adaptive,* and *reformist.* Each of these offers handholds for entering the work-based dialectic of faith transformation.

Reactive responses seek to recover a nineteenth-century (so-called "traditional") pattern of work, with its attendant connections with family and church, typical of an earlier time. Some Christians seek to foster and preserve Christian business whose ethos resembles that of the Christian home and church community. The Fellowship of Companies for Christ (Atlanta), for example, comprised almost wholly of family-owned private companies, typifies this response. Here we find an effort to maintain a close relation of church, family, and work that was widespread in the last century but is very hard to preserve in publically owned corporations in a pluralistic world.

A very different type of reactive response is the Christian

commune or cooperative. These have been a regular though marginal phenomenon throughout American history, from the Puritan experiment to the Shakers and Owenites and the counterculture Christians of the 1960s.[10] These experiments do not accept the estrangement among work, family, and church. Communes seek to rejoin them, usually on an agrarian or artisan base. Cooperatives generally tolerate greater differentiation of these three spheres. In all of them, however, there is a tight relationship among the domestic, religious, and economic arenas.

In this context it is also important to remind ourselves of the radical Christian responses to industrial capitalism. In addition to Christian utopias and communes, we have also seen the way Christian faith informed the populism of people like William Jennings Bryan and the great twentieth-century socialist leader Norman Thomas. From Henry Demarest Lloyd we have a pithy summary of evangelical populism: "The proof that an individual has been regenerated is that he proceeds to regenerate things around him—and that's Democracy and that's the Religion of Labor."[11] More recently groups such as American Christians Toward Socialism (ACTS) carried this banner in response to the emergence of United States globalism and multinational corporations.

While these quite varied responses lift up alternatives to our present fragmentation or hostility, they both require a pattern of work life increasingly marginated in our own society. They are for the few. They remind us of the critical edge necessary in every Christian stance, but make that stance dependent on a particular form of economic organization. This selection of a specific organizational form over against the mainstream of economic developments helps us remember that faith transformation demands larger structural as well as interpersonal expression.

Adaptive responses generally accept the new economic forms but help people cope better with them. Here we find first of all the many programs in lay ministry, faith, and life, and Christian leadership. Drawing on religious themes, theories, and values, they assist people with business decisions, cultivation of religiously grounded leadership styles, and problems in work life transitions. For instance, the Institute for Servant Leadership at Emory University draws on the writings of Robert Greenleaf to try to reshape executive leadership along religious lines.[12] The Center for the Ministry of the Laity at Andover Newton Theological School seeks to help people in all areas of organizational life exert a relevant Christian influence through their work. There are also many workshop seminars sponsored by business organizations, independent consultants, churches, and universities seeking to bridge the gap between faith and work, though often in disguised ways.

The positive contribution of these efforts is that they probe deeply into the many interrelationships of work and faith, sometimes also picking up some family themes. Their weakness is twofold: They tend to miss union employees and working-class people, especially blacks and Hispanics, and they tend to skirt issues of structural change. Many union employees and most hourly wage people have a very different orientation to work than do middle-class and managerial Christians. For them work often does not have vocational importance in the religious sense. It doesn't carry the same kind of emotional weight. It is a means for maintaining the family rather than securing the central worth of the individual. In short these people demand different responses. The quandary here is that the church and labor union connections once forged primarily by the Roman Catholic church have lost their momentum. We are confronted by a very different economic situation requiring a recasting of those old alliances.

The second kind of adaptive response is more practical in an immediate sense. It involves the de facto cooperation between churches and businesses through church-sponsored day care centers for children.[13] While the relationship may not be a formal one, churches and businesses have a symbiotic relationship in which businesses need quality day care for their employees and churches need a creative use for their space. Many of these programs seek to enhance child development and even religious growth. In turn, the work day creates the structure governing the interaction if not the very culture being transmitted to the child. While the day care center may provide for an encounter of parent, child, and church, it is not at all clear that churches have found ways to go beyond the facade to deal with deeper issues. Moreover, churches need to ask more critically whether they should even be filling this role in the economy.

Churches also seek to assist individuals and families in dealing with problems which often have origins in the organization of work.[14] They provide or support counseling centers dealing with work-related problems or support pastoral counselors active in industrial chaplaincies and Employee Assistance Programs. EAPs began as industry efforts to deal with alcoholism and addiction but have now developed a whole range of services from financial advice to family life. Here again there exists an opportunity to help people shape more adequately the transformations they are undergoing at work in the light of Christian faith. Here too we find the tension between making a profound impact on the lives of individuals and attending to transformation of the structures that create family problems, personal self-destruction, and spiritual alienation.

For reformist responses to the need for structural changes we turn to the many church statements on economic matters that have emerged from the Roman Catholic, Methodist, Lutheran, Presbyterian, and other mainline denominations.[15] While rarely calling for wholesale overhaul of the economy or an outright rejection of the trends I have lifted up, they often focus in a critical manner on the ruthless exploitation of land and natural resources, the mistreatment of part-time, seasonal, and hourly wage workers, the misallocation of resources through the market system and the link between militarism and economic growth.

These statements can and do serve to bring people into argument and even mutual education. Ministers, business people, union leaders, and academics are forced to come to the table together because they all share moral concerns but disagree on the best structures for advancing them. These pronouncements have generated a good deal of publicity about economic issues and have become a part of the educational diet in churches themselves. They are a hopeful sign that we are beginning to redress the estrangement that has characterized church/workplace relations for some time.

For more activist manifestations of reform we can look not only to church support for migrant farm worker movements but also to efforts to resist the massive dislocations in the steel industry through boycotts and employee buyouts in Pennsylvania and Ohio.[16] Churches have also maintained numerous quiet engagements to reform economic structures. They have been involved in creating urban and rural land trusts, producer and consumer cooperatives, credit unions, low-income housing, and community development organizations. Religious organizations have also been leaders in shareholder actions to reshape corporate policies toward greater justice and environmental responsibility.

Here we see a focus not only on corporate change but also on the very conditions necessary for work to exist at all—basic necessities, land, housing, and community infrastructure. Sometimes these may operate with a rather radical stance toward our present economic organization. Other times they are simply trying to help people survive an economy that has no room for them.

The human transformation needed in the face of the deformation of land, communities, and people by our economic revolutions requires concerted attention not only from religious educators but from the entire church. Religious educators, however, have to lead in helping people understand and think through how faith should speak in the midst of these transformations. This demands not only appropriatetanalyses of economic change but also a clear articulation of a faith vision. We move now to the final part of this chapter—clarification of the challenges before us.

Reworking Religion

As a first step we need to refashion key theological concepts in the light of a changed economy. Without theological clarity we will simply imitate the language, thought patterns, and practices of the workplace without a prophetic edge. Moreover, many traditional Christian concepts have, often unwittingly, become embedded in reinforcing an older pattern of work. We need now to disengage them from those older uses and recast them in the light of contemporary theological argument as well as social circumstance.

Every theory of religious education, and therefore of its relation to work, operates under some master concept. George Albert Coe and Walter Rauschenbusch cast religious transformation in terms of democracy and urged us to democratize the workplace.[17] Paulo Freire and Ivan Illich called for conscientization, humanization, and de-schooling. More recently, Thomas Groome has advanced themes of liberation and freedom. My own thrust uses the concept of covenant publicity.

I have already pointed out how the long heritage of Christian asceticism came to reinforce the industrial obedience and entrepreneurial acquisitiveness central to the industrial revolution of the eighteenth and nineteenth centuries. It is a revolution still reverberating throughout the world. In our own time, however, another religious theme reemerges with new force. I call it the theme of covenant publicity.[18] It has the possibility of being the contemporary theological bridge between church and work.

Briefly stated, covenant publicity points to people's need and capacity for joining others in public expression of their life. Publicity highlights people's need to participate in the decisions affecting their lives. Covenant lifts up the need that people be joined in enduring bonds of trust that bring together their work, family, and faith in relationship to the land. This expansive embrace of covenant making is rooted in ancient scripture and finds renewed validity in the light of our modern ecological awareness of human life.

Both of these themes find points of resonance in contemporary work developments, though they also find much challenge and resistance. In nurturing persons who seek to live out lives of covenant publicity, churches can foster an appropriate spirituality for the workplace. In developing and supporting pilot projects exemplifying these ideals, whether in cooperatives, community development, or in internal church life, churches can sharpen their dialogue with the world of work.

Moving to a new religious orientation enables us to reinterpret numerous aspects of our faith tradition. For instance, we can reexamine the concept of vocation so that we can move from the individualistic view of vocation as job and occupation to one which captures the original biblical view that vocation is God's call to a whole people. To respond to God's call was originally not an individual selection of a career but a response by a whole community to reshape its common life around a higher standard of justice.

Similarly, we can reexamine the notion of stewardship to overcome a fixation on its monetary aspects.[19] Taking the parable of the talents (Matthew 25: 13-45) as an example, we can see that the "talents" given to the various stewards were not personal properties, as our culture typically views it, but representations of the gospel itself. The "talent" Jesus was talking about symbolized the good news of God's transformation of creation. We are called to be stewards of that good news as members of the church, multiplying it by our very sharing of it. What does this original meaning of the parable mean for an economic culture that prizes talents as individual abilities to be marketed to the highest bidder? What does it mean to our society to reinterpret this parable, which has been used to legitimate its occupational structure and market economy?

Moreover, we need to recover the lasting meaning of Sabbath in a time when it no longer sets limits to the dynamics of work. Sabbath means that there are and must be boundaries to the demands people can place on each other—whether in the exploitation of workers by managers and owners or the exploitation of self by the workaholic. The idea of the Sabbath as a day set apart also means that it is not simply a day of rest for an individual. It is a time when all can refrain from work together and remember their covenant as a people dedicated to higher purposes. Work must honor these other relations of life and the transcendence of a God who speaks and listens to all people as citizens of a divine republic. We are not simply producers and consumers. We are not simply workers. We are actors in the theater of God's drama, players in a wider story of redemption.

The Sabbath can thus be seen as that moment when we remember that we are partners in covenant, a concept which goes far beyond the individual contractual relations typical of the modern marketplace. A life in covenant involves the whole range of biblical concerns: God's relation with our history, with all of creation, with other peoples, and with each person as a partner in world transformation.

In drawing on such theological resources we can develop

further the concepts of covenant, which bespeak the deep relational character of existence, and publicity, which bespeaks our yearning for a life in which God is fully revealed to us and we to each other. These themes, present in our work lives, need to be drawn out by the church to help transform the workplace as an arena of faithfulness.

These themes must also find practical expression in our society. What must be done in light of this transformed faith? First, churches need to attend to the creation and improvement of the bridge structures between churches and workplaces. Adult education centers, day care centers, employee counseling programs, alternative economic structures—all these are places where faith concerns can be nurtured. They are as important as the home in shaping our patterns of faithfulness. Religious education must reflect this importance, and resources for dealing with the issues of work need to be developed for those points of intersection.

Second, the schooling paradigm in religious education needs to be subordinated to the kinds of educational processes present in workplaces that have moved beyond a slavish devotion to the old factory model. In these contexts group relationships of open consultation and negotiated goal commitments replace a bureaucratic command structure which isolates individuals in rigid job descriptions. The mentoring and consultation emerging in those arenas need appropriate reinforcement in churches. The move toward spiritual guides and directors in Christian circles needs to be evaluated as a model for religious education generally. Relationships based on a common trust and commitment can then move to the center of educative transformation. The priority of reflective process reminds us that no curricular foundation of information, whether it be Bible stories or catechisms, is ever secure but must be redone continually in the light of new experience—especially transition experiences in our working lives.

Third, to grasp these transitions we need to investigate the way work is organized and how it affects people, families, churches, community organizations, and politics. Work is transforming people—enabling more women to have a public life, power in family relations, and greater citizenship in the church.

Workplace changes often train people with new skills at communication and problem solving that enhance the rest of their lives.

Work also continues to deform people. It can subordinate them to market dynamics and imprison them in the hierarchies of firms unable to develop more pliable structures. It often narrows human vision and aspiration. It deprives people of energy, time, and access necessary for public as well as private life. Religious educators need to know both effects of the workplace so they can fashion appropriate responses to enable people to be active agents of the transformations their lives need before God.

Fourth, to fashion this critical knowledge of the workplace, churches constantly need to be engaged in actions affecting the workplace, whether they are constructing alternative housing markets, pushing for corporate responsibility as shareholders, or conducting seminars in business ethics. Only within this engagement can we experience the processes of transformation where God is calling us to exercise our capacities for public profession and covenant. In the struggle to understand what we are doing and to recast it in terms of faith, religious educators can play a crucial role.

Fifth, to augment these external engagements religious educators need to take serious account of the way the church itself is a work institution. As a workplace it educates its members just like any other business. Many times church organizations compare very poorly with businesses in their attention to the dignity of employees, their rights, compensation packages, and environment, not to mention management methods. They smother with love and good intentions the deformations produced by patriarchal command or simple disorganization. Not only the staff but the members of the church internalize a model of human relationships through participating in the church. Religious education must lead in the task of helping us become more aware of what we are doing in church administration and organization. Management educates and shapes faith. It should be a central concern of educators.

In becoming more aware of the transformative impact of management methods churches need to be critical of the patterns they take up from the workplace, whether it is in achieving goals through contracts, programing with marketing models, or computerizing office procedures. Just as every baptism must be preceded by a catechumenate, so must organizational patterns and methods be subjected to theological scrutiny and refinement. In this way the church is always a critic as well as a partner in the process of human transformation.

NOTES

1. George Albert Coe, *A Social Theory of Religious Education* (New York: Arno, [1917] 1979). For a history, discussion, and proposals for recovering this thrust see Jack L. Seymour, Robert T. O'Gorman, and Charles R. Foster, *The Church in the Education of the Public: Refocusing the Task of Religious Education* (Nashville: Abingdon, 1984).

2. Martin Lang, *Acquiring our Image of God: The Emotional Basis for Religious Education* (New York: Paulist, 1983), and William Johnson Everett, *Blessed Be the Bond: Christian Perspectives on Marriage and Family* (Philadelphia: Fortress, 1985). Parker Palmer develops a relational approach to learning in *To Know As We Are Known: A Spirituality of Education* (San Francisco: Harper & Row, 1983).

3. For a prominent example of the theological centrality of the idea of personality at the turn of the century see Ernst Troeltsch, *The Social Teachings of the Christian Churches,* trans. Olive Wyon (New York: Harper and Brothers, 1960), pp. 51-68.

Max Weber set the agenda for this approach to industrial virtues in *The Protestant Ethic and the Spirit of Capitalism,* trans. Talcott Parsons (New York: Charles Scribner's Sons, 1958). For an analysis of the American history see James B. Gilbert, *Work Without Salvation: America's Intellectuals and Industrial Alienation, 1880-1910* (Baltimore: Johns Hopkins University Press, 1977) and Daniel T. Rodgers, *The Work Ethic in Industrial America, 1850-1920* (Chicago: University of Chicago Press, 1978). C.B. Macpherson traces the Puritan roots of acquisitive individualism in *The Political Theory of Possessive Individualism: Hobbes to Locke* (New York: Oxford University Press, 1964). Samuel Bowles and Herbert Gintis present a radical critique in *Schooling in Capitalist America: Educational Reform and the Contradictions of Capitalism* (New York: Basic Books, 1976).

4. Carl Degler offers a fulsome description of the two-spheres doctrine in *At Odds: Women and the Family in America from the Revolution to the Present* (New York: Oxford University Press, 1980). Christopher Lasch provides a contemporary psychoanalytical perspective on the dissolution of this structure in *Haven in a Heartless World: The Family Besieged* (New York: Basic Books, 1977). Ann Douglas portrays the turning away from practical reform to literary endeavor in *The*

Feminization of American Culture (New York: Knopf, 1977). For a historical examination of the interaction between Protestantism and industrial era labor movements see Herbert Gutman, *Work, Culture and Society in Industrializing America* (New York: Knopf, 1976), ch. 2.

5. To begin an inquiry into the literature on work see Elliott Richardson, *Work in America: Report of a Special Task Force to the Secretary of Health, Education, and Welfare* (Cambridge, Mass.: MIT Press, 1978), Eli Ginzberg, *Good Jobs, Bad Jobs, No Jobs* (Cambridge, Mass.: Harvard University Press, 1979), and Rosabeth Moss Kanter and Barry Stein, *Life in Organizations: Workplaces as People Experience Them* (New York: Basic Books, 1979).

For religious perspectives see John Raines and Donna Day-Lower, *Modern Work and Human Meaning* (Philadelphia: Westminster, 1986) and Richard Gillett, *The Human Enterprise: A Christian Perspective on Work* (Kansas City, Mo.: Leaven, 1985).

6. Contemporary discussion on the globalization of economic life begins with Richard Barnett and Ronald Mueller, *Global Reach* (New York: Simon and Schuster, 1975), Louis Turner, ed., *Multinational Companies and the Third World* (New York: Hill and Wang, 1974), and Raymond Vernon, *Storm Over the Multinationals: The Real Issues* (Cambridge, Mass.: Harvard University Press, 1977).

7. Jane C. Hood, *Becoming A Two-Job Family* (New York: Praeger, 1983), and Rosabeth Moss Kanter, *Men and Women of the Corporation* (New York: Basic Books, 1977).

8. Nell P. Eurich, *Corporate Classroom: The Learning Business* (Princeton: Carnegie Foundation for the Advancement of Teaching, 1985), pp. 6-12.

9. Thornton Bradshaw and David Vogel, eds., *Corporations and their Critics: Issues and Answers to the Problem of Corporate Social Responsibility* (New York: McGraw-Hill, 1980); Donald J. Kirby, *Prophecy vs. Profits: An Ethical Investment Dilemma for Churches* (Maryknoll: Orbis-Probe, 1980). For a good business text survey see Richard N. Farmer and W. Dickerson Hogue, *Corporate Social Responsibility*, 2d ed. (Lexington: Lexington Books, 1985).

10. For classic histories of the commune movement in America see William A. Hinds, *American Communities and Co-operative Colonies,* 2d rev. ed. (Philadelphia: Porcupine Press, [1908] 1975) and Mark Holloway, *Heavens on Earth: Utopian Communities in America, 1680-1880,* 2d ed. rev. (New York: Dover, 1966). Contemporary developments are discussed in Sallie TeSelle, ed., *The Family, Communes, and Utopian Societies* (San Francisco: Harper & Row, 1973).

11. Quoted in Gilbert, *Work Without Salvation,* p. 104. For Thomas see Bernard K. Johnpoll, *Pacifist's Progress: Norman Thomas and the Decline of American Socialism* (Chicago: Quadrangle Books, 1970).

12. Robert K. Greenleaf, *Servant Leadership: A Journey into the*

Nature of Legitimate Power and Greatness (New York: Paulist, 1977). Other centers include the Trinity Center for Ethics and Corporate Policy (New York), the Center for Ethics and Corporate Policy (Chicago), and the Center for Ethics and Social Policy (Berkeley). For a critical reflection on earlier efforts see Henry Clark, *Ministries of Dialogue* (New York: Association Press, 1971).

13. The church involvement in day care is surveyed by Eileen Lindner, Carol Mattis, and June Rogers in *When Churches Mind the Children: A Study of Day Care in Local Parishes* (Ypsilanti, Mich.: High/ Scope Press, 1983). Sheila Kamerman and Alfred Kahn investigate numerous workplace developments in *The Responsive Workplace* (New York: Columbia University Press, 1987).

See also Rosabeth Moss Kanter's penetrating analysis of nursery dynamics in "The Organization Child: Experience Management in a Nursery School," *Sociology of Education* 45 (Spring 1972), pp. 186-212.

14. For a practical entree see Henry Haskell Rightor, *Pastoral Counseling in Work Crises: An Introduction for both Lay and Ordained Ministers* (Valley Forge, Pa.: Judson, 1979).

15. "Catholic Social Teaching and the United States Economy," National Conference of Catholic Bishops, *Origins* 14:32-33 (1984), pp. 338-83; Gregory Baum, *The Priority of Labor* (New York: Paulist, 1982) (including the Encyclical Letter of Pope John Paul II, "Laborem Exercens"); Audrey Chapman Smock, ed., *Christian Faith and Economic Life* (New York: United Church of Christ Board for World Ministries, 1987); General Assembly of the Presbyterian Church in the United States, "International Economic Justice" (1980).

16. Roger T. Wolcott, "The Church and Social Action: Steelworkers and Bishops in Youngstown," *Journal for the Scientific Study of Religion* 21:1 (March 1982), pp. 71-79.

17. In addition to Coe, cited above, see Walter Rauschenbusch, *Christianity and the Social Crisis* (New York: Harper Brothers, 1964) and *A Theology for the Social Gospel* (New York: Abingdon, 1945); Paulo Freire, *Pedagogy of the Oppressed*, trans. Myra B. Ramos (New York: Herder and Herder, 1972); Ivan Illich, *De-Schooling Society* (New York: Harper & Row, 1972), and Thomas Groome, *Christian Religious Education* (San Francisco: Harper & Row, 1980).

18. For a much fuller discussion of the implications of covenant publicity see my volume *God's Federal Republic: Reconstructing our Governing Symbol* (New York: Paulist, 1988). M. Douglas Meeks presents a theology based in an expansive notion of economy in *God the Economist* (Philadelphia: Fortress, 1987). See also the essays in *Christianity and Capitalism: Perspective on Religion, Liberalism and the Economy*, ed. David Krueger and Bruce Grelle (Chicago: Center for the Scientific Study of Religion, 1986).

19. Max L. Stackhouse offers a critical theological view of stewardship in *Public Theology and Political Economy: Christian Stewardship in Modern Society* (Grand Rapids, Mich.: Eerdmans, 1987). See also Douglas J. Hall, *Imaging God: Dominion as Stewardship* (Grand Rapids, Mich.: Eerdmans, 1986).

7

The Ecology of Human Existence: Living within the Natural Order

C. Dean Freudenberger

Although we continue to try to deceive ourselves, we humans now know that we are part of the web of life on planet earth. Our Native American sisters and brothers have tried to fix this fact into our heads since the arrival of our ancestors upon this continent. We now know, as crew members of space-ship earth, that we are not set apart, but, to the contrary, we are part of this fragile spacecraft. Our survival as a species, like the survival of all species, depends upon the health of the lines of our interdependences with all life, in life's full, unfathomable, delicate, and intricate pattern of sustenance. We now know that the planet is a "living planet." To within a radius of at least one thousand light years distance (186,000 miles x 60 seconds x 60 minutes x 24 hours x 365 days) we now know that life is a cosmic miracle. Our astronomers inform us that, thus far, except for planet earth, life has yet to be detected within this region of the cosmos. We now know that we are made of the same stuff as the grass about our feet, the trees above our heads, the spiders, salamanders, and whales, the creatures of the land and the birds of the air. We now know that no organism can exist for long if, in its lifestyle, it consumes resources essential for its sustenance at a rate that exceeds the capacities of its ecosystem to renew or recycle those resources and produces wastes at a rate beyond the absorption capacity of its surroundings. We now know that to continue to work for the development of the quality of human life independent of these relationships and fundamental limits places us on a collision course with extinction. Although we search for every means to deny it, we now know that we are reaching the end of the age of enlightenment during which time we learned to observe life in its most reduced and detached form. This form of observation gave rise to a narrow human centeredness which, consequently, excluded fundamental concerns for the welfare of other life forms. We now know that an ecological understanding of human existence is essential for the survival of life . . . all life, at least as we observe it during the time of human existence. We now know that to try to live as though we are set outside the natural order, or above it (in order to conquer and manipulate it), is a formula for disaster. We now know that our survival, like the survival and development of all life forms, is dependent upon the maintenance of the health of the relationships of dependency of all life. We now know, once again, that all life is sacred. Life cannot be reduced to least common denominators in order to be understood. Understanding and wisdom come only in the perception of the necessity of maintaining a high level of integrity toward the relationships of dependency.

That a book on religious education includes a chapter on the ecology of human existence is significant. Contemporary writings in religious education, at least in the Christian tradition, generally have neglected this subject. Religious education should begin to recognize the interdependency between the family, sexuality, global, technological, economic and political order, and the quality of human life, as being interdependent with the quality of life of the whole biosphere on which we are so intimately dependent and to which we must demonstrate a constant commitment with respect to the maintenance of its integrity. Such books will define in new ways the meaning of *noblesse oblige*.

The problem is simply this: The goodness of God's creation is being diminished as a consequence of abusive human behavior. The vision of our ancient Hebrew-Christian heritage is threatened by modern humanity. The vision of the opening chapter of Genesis, that unsurpassed literary marvel which functions as the prelude to the scriptures, is being shattered.[1] As intelligent beings this we must recognize, otherwise we will resemble the ostrich. Humanity is not being faithful to its mandate to be fruitful (imaginative), to cultivate (nurture), and to multiply (restore). Humanity is not living up to its potential of being an image of God (compassionate, inventive, empathetic). Humanity is not fulfilling its covenant to have dominion. Domination is what we practice! Dominion (the maintenance of justice and righteousness in God's domain, as representatives of God's reign) is what is intended. The problem being addressed in this chapter, and by the religious community almost everywhere in the world, is the problem of the denial, by our actions, of the spiritual foundations of our faith. By this is meant the denial of our sense of self-identity and our self-understanding of what being created in love and in the image of the creator means. What is the impact of all this? The impact is "an impoverished humanity and a threatened biosphere."[2] The United Nations document used in preparation for the world conference on the human environment stated it this way:

> In short, the two worlds of man—the biosphere of his inheritance, the technosphere of his creation—are out of balance and in deep conflict. . . . This is the hinge of history at which we stand, the door of the future opening onto a crisis more sudden, more global, more inescapable and more bewildering than any ever encountered by the human species.[3]

A parallel observation comes out of the Christian community just a few years later:

> The responsibility that now confronts humanity is to make a deliberate transition to a sustainable global society in which science and technology will be mobilized to meet the basic physical and spiritual needs of people, to minimize human suffering and to create an environment which can sustain a decent quality of life for all people. This will involve a radical transformation of civilization, new technologies, new uses of

technology and new global, economic and political systems. The new situation in which humanity now finds itself has been created in less than a generation. There is even less time to create the transition to a sustainable global society if humanity is to survive.[4]

The problem being addressed involves historically unprecedented concerns of nearly unimaginable magnitude which, until very recently, never entered the human imagination. With this problem reality as a working context, one can suggest that never before has there been such an urgency, within the churches' sense of responsibility, for renewed theory in religious education. Never before has the church experienced such a priority to witness to that vision which Jesus called his disciples to pursue—the vision which is at the center of the Lord's prayer and which points to the essence of the mission of the church in our time and into the long future . . . that God's kingdom might come.

Now that we are a human species numbering more than five billion persons and destined (before we can predictably conquer the injustices of poverty, which is the breeding ground of human population growth, in all of its violent forms) to number nearly seven billion by the turn of the century, the human impact upon the welfare of the planet is threatening.[5] "The biosphere of our inheritance and technosphere of our creation are out of balance and in deep conflict."[6] Do we really understand what this means?

As a worker in global agriculture and an observer of the new phenomenon of desertification (desert encroachment as a consequence of enviromentally abusive human behavior), I have some feelings for the magnitude of the problem being addressed. I have observed on every continent that our human endeavors to feed and clothe ourselves over the past few centuries have resulted in the irrevocable loss of half the soil resources which were in existence ten thousand years ago (a flash of a moment in geological time). Given present trends in abusive agricultural systems and the conversion of prime agricultural land to non-food producing uses, by the year 2000 C.E., 50 percent of our remaining soil will be lost, leaving only 4 percent of the earth's surface arable to feed and clothe seven billion persons.[7] The international appetite for forest products has, and continues, to reduce many regions of the planet to raw desert. Atmospheric oxygen is not being generated in these places. Since forest and grassland cover has been reduced drastically and atmospheric carbon dioxide is not being reabsorbed adequately because of the diminished process of photosynthesis in forest and grassland systems, the planet no longer "breathes" as it did in the very recent past. This puts the stability of life in question. With the loss of vegetative cover, there are fewer roots. Rainfall and snow melt is not adequately reabsorbed into the living organism called soil. The continents are drying up.[8] With this phenomenon called desertification at loose across the world, climates change, growing numbers of people (nearly two-thirds of humanity) are impoverished, species of life are going into extinction at rates beyond comprehension, and the chemistry of the air, having evolved over countless of millions of years to be the right material for our lungs and thus our lives, is changing significantly.[9] We are also deeply concerned by the growing evidence that (due to upper atmospheric exhausts from transport systems, oxides of nitrogen, and the oxidization of more than one hundred million tons of nitrogen fertilizers applied annually in our food systems) the protective shield of ozone, some thirty to fifty kilometers above the surface of the earth, is being threatened.[10] We have as yet no knowledge of the time-span involved in the feedback loops of these new phenomena.

Beyond this basic litany of issues to be faced in our time and into the foreseeable future are the impacts of overharvesting the fisheries of the seas and of the growing toxicity of our environment as a consequence of the dumping of more than 60,000 toxic chemicals, in massive quantities, across the face of, and within this living planet. Military expenditures are draining the resource (human and economic) capabilities of the nations to deal with these awesome issues. Of course, the prospect of a nuclear winter is the ultimate ecological offense.

This is the problem dimension of this chapter: "The Ecology of Human Existence: Living within the Natural Order." The following questions emerge. Where is to be found our sense of the sacredness of creation? What is the shape of the churches' witness to the ancient Hebrew convenant about the gift of land and life? Where is to be found a more inclusive spirituality in the contemporary concept of Shalom? Where lies our security? What is the nature of the human trust? How do we understand priority and strategy in our acts of witness and service, as individuals and as religious people with our religious education for today and into the future? We live in a radically changed world now that we are so numerous and abusive as a species within the community of species of this living planet. How do we begin to understand the magnitude and shape of change (social, technological, and economic) essential for the continuation of life on our planet . . . of God's creation?

For religious education for social transformation and the renewal of natural systems (rehabilitation) to be relevant, these questions have to be faced, as ill-prepared as we are because of a lack of experience with these matters which were not in the human imagination less than thirty years ago. By religious education the writer refers to teaching of faith traditions across the entire spectrum of the great world religions. The ecology of human existence involves all of us. But, being more specific for the audience which this book addresses, religious education refers to the teachings of the Judeo-Christian traditions with reference to ecological matters. The author writes out of the religious heritage of the Protestant ecumenical world of Western Europe and the United States. Religious education must begin to address the issues which compose the subject of the ecology of human existence. In the case of this chapter, ecology references the complex lines of relationships that exist between life forms and their surroundings. Specifically, ecology refers to the study of relationships; usually relations of interdependency. The subtitle of this chapter, "Living within the Natural Order," is an attempt to remind us all that the challenge is not to manage natural systems nor to manipulate them for our use. Rather, the challenge is to find ways to live symbiotically, within the fine-tuned and highly evolved biosphere of our inheritance. As we are called by the necessity of our time to ponder these definitions, immediately we begin to sense the need for entirely new ways of self-understanding and more encompassing criteria for moral and ethical behavior.

Moral Issues and Ethical Criteria for the Renewal of the Social and Natural Order.

What is needed is a recapturing of the sense of the sacredness of all life. Basic to this orientation is a needed shift in the human understanding of morality from its human centeredness (the idea that humanity is the measure of all things, an idea leftover from ancient Roman culture) to an inclusive, holistic orientation of life and creation. This is to say, the value foundation of a new morality, or a postmodern morality, is that all things are of intrinsic value and all things are of instrumental value. An ecological understanding of human existence acknowledges the fact of the interdependency of life and the integrity of life's uncountable patterns of dependency. We now know that global security, in a full ecological sense, is dependent on the maximization of biological diversity. We understand this, even though we have yet to take this fact seriously, during a time when the human species is placing into extinction nearly 100 species of life per day during the closing decades of this century. This rate of species loss over the course of one year equates the estimated rates in prehistoric times which would take about one hundred million years.[11] The biosphere has never before experienced such a magnitude of change.

The most basic of moral issues involves this shift in value orientation from a narrow anthropocentrism to a full biological, ecological, and theological orientation about the interdependence and sacredness of all life. James Gustafson, in his two volume work *Ethics from a Theocentric Perspective*, illustrates a fresh attempt to move us beyond human preoccupations.[12] His thesis is that we ought to relate to all things as all things relate and have meaning to the creator of all things. Gustafson acknowledges the fact that we hardly know how to deal with the implications of such moral and ethical positions. But, is this not what the writer of Psalm 104 was acknowledging where it is written: " . . . and let not these foundations be shaken." There is a recognition that much more than immediate human welfare considerations are involved in moral behavior and decision making.[13]

A shift in moral understanding, and therefore new perceptions about moral issues, involves a modification of our prevailing and dominating worldview, or paradigm. In our modern world we have placed ourselves outside of creation. We have established a self-serving hierarchy of value which emerges in patterns of domination, use, and manipulation. This is quite the opposite of an ecological understanding of existence. We have placed God above creation. We have made the self-serving claim that creation is subordinate to humanity. Man dominates woman. The rich dominate the poor. White dominates black. In modern times, modern humanity has set out to dominate, control, and change the natural systems. The earth is understood as existing for the human use.[14] The earth is that which gives us pleasure. Unless elements of the "natural world" are of use from the perspective of meeting perceived human need, then whatever is considered nonutilitarian is understood to be "wasteland." We refer to life and patterns of sustenance of life as "natural resource." This is a very reductionistic and mechanistic point of view; it is abusive. Yet we continue to use these language forms without sensitivity, just as, prior to the feminist movement, many of us thoughtlessly and abusively used masculine word forms. We recognize today, all too well, that language reveals insensitivity. We need to remind ourselves that the word "nature" does not appear in the Bible. Rather, only the word "creation" is referenced. This tells us something of the foci of past paradigms.[15] Today, relationships are lost to a mechanistic and reductionistic worldview. The contemporary church in its urban and industrial cultural setting (including its leadership in religious education) is also caught in this mechanistic and reductionistic paradigm. Theological education has been urbanized. The question emerges: Can the church transcend this predicament? The fundamental moral issue for us to consider in making judgments about whether an action is right or wrong involves the health and integrity of relationships of life in every sphere. The soil conservation agent of the early 1920s, Aldo Leopold, was correct when he said: "A thing is right when it contributes to the integrity, beauty and harmony of the biotic community. It is wrong if it goes the other way."[16]

Until there is a shift in moral perception to embrace the whole of existence, and a concomitant shift in value orientation to look at things as having both instrumental as well as intrinsic value (i.e., all things having meaning and purpose from the perspective of the creator of all things), we shall continue to fail in the process of moral maturation. Without this shift, morality continues to be self-serving. The ancient Hebrew concept of the gift of land in covenant (trusteeship) still stands firm as a fundamental moral and spiritual principle of human existence.

The church has a moral vision for a renewed humanity and a renewed earth. The church has established some working (tentative) goals and ethical guidelines for its contemporary vision of peace, justice, and the integrity of creation. If we are looking at the relationships and goals of religious education in social transformation, then to be exposed to the insights coming *out* of the ecumenical struggle for over sixty years and to fathom the meaning of responsible society and responsible freedom are important.

Out of the ashes of the first and second world wars, the churches perceived society to be caught in the tides of rapid social and technological change . . . changes of magnitude and swiftness unprecedented in human existence.[17] In the midst of social and economic injustice and dictatorships of individuals and groups of individuals, the church began to ponder the nature of responsible society.[18] The question, "Where lies responsibility?" was being pondered. How do we understand the limits of human and social freedom? Theologically, how is freedom to be understood? In the process of the rehabilitation of wartorn nations, questions about the goals of the social, economic, and technological order were raised. What are the goals of social transformation . . . from a war footing to a world beyond war? These were the questions of the 1940s and 1950s. By the beginning of the decade of the sixties, eighty-five new nations were born . . . former Western colonial possessions. The question of how to overcome global poverty began to emerge.[19] Development of the quality of human life was then understood to involve economic and industrial development. The issues of human injustice in their international form were yet to be recognized. Marshall Plan development mentality for the reconstruction of a war-torn Western Europe were thought to be relevant for the so-called Third World.[20] But this approach turned out to be a false start. By the time of the Fourth

Assembly of the World Council of Churches (1968), insights emerged about social justice as being foundational for development. Then, following the five-year ecumenical study on "The Future of Man and Society in a World of Science Based Technology,"[21] which unfolded during the United Nations Second Development Decade, the churches began to confront, for the first time, the issues of the so-called ecological movement. In 1979, at the Massachusetts Institute of Technology, the Commission on Church and Society brought together 2,400 scientists, industrialists, theologians, and ethicists from around the world to ponder the conference theme: "Faith, Science and the Future."[22] The main task of the consultation was to challenge science and technology to give attention to basic human and biospheric needs rather than needs in the field of military strength and economic advantage for wealth accumulation. New moral issues emerged at this time which related questions of human justice to ecological stress. Out of these many years of ecumenical conversation has emerged an ecologically inclusive understanding of our common unity. The dichotomies of the modern era have been identified as dysfunctional at best. The concern to move to new moral and ethical insights was carried to the Sixth Assembly (1983) at Vancouver: "We need ethical guidelines for a participatory society which will be both ecologically responsible and economically just, and can effectively struggle with the powers which threaten life and endanger our future."[23]

Following the Sixth Assembly, the World Council of Churches Commission on Faith and Order, and the Commission on Church and Society, with official Catholic participation, began working on an ecumenical study theme: "Justice, Peace, and the Integrity of Creation."[24] This work parallels the Third United Nations Development Decade entitled: "Development Without Destruction." The reference here is ecological in terms of development processes (social and economic) which contribute to the rehabilitation of environmental and resource conditions as an essential part of the process for overcoming human poverty and injustice. A vision of a new moral order is beginning to take shape.

In ecumenical social thought, tentative goal and guideline

concepts about responsible society have taken on new and concrete form. The challenge to meet these standards of responsible freedom for responsible global society are being considered seriously in many places.[25] At the present stage of the evolution of these ethical criteria, the meaning of *justice* refers to fairness in human relationships; it refers to fairness between men and women, persons and their societies, fairness (equity) in economic relationships, education, and health services. The concept of justice evolving at this time also refers to fairness in relationships between the human species and other species of life and their patterns of sustenance. The concept of justice is shifting from an anthropocentrism to full theocentrism . . . a concept which is so central to much of the creation theology found in the Old Testament.[26] Justice is emerging as a concept having ecological dimensions. New ecumenical social thought clearly makes reference to the great creation themes which are seen vividly in the opening sections of Genesis, the Deuteronomic codes, Proverbs, many of the Psalms, and the writings of the major prophets about right relationships with the land . . . with the gift of life and the gift of creation itself.[27]

The ecumenical concept of the *participatory society* which emerged at the MIT consultations has similar meaning. The question was asked: "How shall the poor and socially marginated have an effective voice in the decision-making process of society?" In addition to this critically important question, the ecumenical world is asking: "How shall the human species participate with other species of life in making a contribution to the health of the evolutionary process of creation?"[28] In other words, how shall technology and the economy serve the health of the land and the welfare of human life and its future?

The third element of a responsible society is that the structure of the society be *sustainable* or *regenerative*. At MIT the question also emerged: "How can a society, even a global society, so organize itself that its lifestyle (science and technology and economic order) and support systems are engineered to be sustainable? How can a nation's agriculture for example, be designed so that it does not exhaust the human and natural resource base essential for its existence, nurture and productivity and future?"

At the Fifth Assembly of the World Council of Churches in Nairobi, the Commission of Church and Society was mandated to proceed with the growing vision of a responsible global order. The mandate was born out of a sense of urgency. The closing prayer was, in part, as follows:

> Warned anew of the threats to human survival, we confess that the way we live and order society sets us against one another and alienates us from your creation, exploiting as though dead, things to which you have given life.[29]

The prayer continued:

> Help us struggle to conserve the earth for future generations and free us to share together, that we all may be free. . . Help us struggle for your own justice against all principalities and powers and to persevere with faith and humor in the tasks that you have given to us.[30]

So, being heirs of an urgent mandate within the ecumenical movement and its work to better define the meaning of responsible society, the Sixth Assembly at Vancouver (July 24 to August 10, 1983) issued the following recommendation to the member churches and their constituencies:

> The churches can adequately face the threats to human survival today only if they take up the problems and promises of science and technology for the human future. The dialogue initiated by the World Council of Churches with scientists, and the technologists, which found its fullest expression in the Conference on Faith, Science and the Future at MIT, needs to be continued and deepened.[31]

Today, religious education needs to be, and often is, an expression of commitment to the mandates of the ecumenical community of churches of every nation. The foundational values of the task of religious education are the values of faithfulness to justice, meaningfulness in our relationships of life and work, commitment (with reverence and a sense of the sacred) to the renewal and preservation of life in all its forms, and commitment to the welfare of uncountable generations that yet can be born. Religious education, in our time and into the foreseeable future, ought to be an expression of gratitude to God for life and for our experience of covenant responsibilities during our moment of its ongoing history and to the renewal and preservation of all life in its intended fullness.

I am hopeful about the future prospects of humanity living in ecological harmony. This hope is founded upon our common observations over the past fifteen to twenty years. We observe that entirely new sets of questions about human and biospheric existence are being asked. We observe global discussions about the limits of the carrying capacity (resource base and absorption capacity of toxic wastes) of the biosphere.[32] We are unsure of where the limits are, but there is a recognition of limits. The frontier mentality in our own nation is changing. We have begun the shift from a Wild West ethos to that of riders on a fragile spacecraft whirling in the vastness of space. In significant places new questions are being raised that acknowledge a postmodern orientation to the world. Even though answers are still beyond our reach, we know that questions are prerequisites for social and technological transformation. I am hopeful due to the growing discontent with the spectacle of social and ecological injustice. Today there is growing distrust of science and technology—not of its potential for good but of its narrow fields of present concern. Science and technology are not, at this time, serving the welfare of life on the planet any more than they serve to guarantee the integrity of the earth's future. In many ways one can interpret the growing phenomenon of a new religious conservatism as due to the frustration with the social order that provides everything but comfort, security, hope, or significant sense of purpose. There is a growing moral outrage over the way society invests its talents and resources in activities of destruction and social privilege. In this outrage is to be found new energy which has potential for creative change. We witnessed creative social upheaval in the Philippines with reference to political oppression. Is it too much of an exaggeration to suggest that in the wealthy, seemingly complacent Western nations, that social demand for overcoming technological oppressions is beyond reach? The phenomenal growth of the ecological movement (Greenpeace, The Greens of W. Germany, the Greenies of Australia, the growth of the World Wildlife Fund, the emergence of environmental protection agencies across this land and elsewhere, the reality of the United Nations Environmental Program, The International Union for the Conservation of Nature and Natural Resources, etc.) gives us reason to hope for significant change for renewal. These are all indicators of progress toward the building of a postmodern and sustainable global community. The challenge to the religious community is to deepen the insights and motivations of these many activities with a renewed and well-articulated theological understanding of human relationship to the gift of land in covenant. In my own work covering the past thirty-five years in rural community and agricultural development for a just, domestic, self-reliant, and regenerative food system, I have found, particularly in my work in tropical agricultural ecology and recently in church response to the U.S. farm crisis, that when issues are clarified, humans respond positively with renewed imagination and determination. Nevertheless, the task before us is enormous.

One should point out that biologically (ecologically) speaking, time is running short: If an ecosystem is overly stressed, it has a tendency to collapse, and oftentimes, irrevocably. This we experience in observing desertification. But given the massive momentum of new efforts over a relatively short period of time (twenty-five to thirty-five years), I am cautiously optimistic. The task is to maintain this momentum. The connection between arms proliferation, human poverty, deforestation, exhaustion of the fisheries of the sea, climate shifts, and the precarious supply of the most basic of all essentials for the substance of civilizations—soil—is being more widely understood. At this time we have to ask: How do we evaluate the contribution (and its potential contribution) of efforts in religious education for social and environmental transformation toward the achievement of regenerative and just futures? In the context of this discussion about the ecology of human existence, how do workers in the field of religious education begin to understand new challenges for making a contribution to global efforts for social and biospherical renewal? How does the problem being addressed broaden the scope of consideration in religious education, including more inclusive approaches in Bible, theology, and ethics? Is there a way to overcome the ecological ambiguity in contemporary Christian thought?

The words of E. F. Schumacher are appropriate for those of us in religous education. He wrote: "I cannot myself raise the winds that might blow us to a safe harbor, but I can a least raise the sails so that when the wind does come I can catch it."[33]

In terms of how to live within the natural order, the winds are rising. This is quite apparent. The question is, can we, as members of the religious education community, enable societies to catch the wind so that we, in our lifestyles (the science and technology that enables us to support ourselves) contribute to the beauty, integrity, and harmony of the whole community of life of the biosphere for its renewal and preservation? Any lessening of this scope of consideration in religious education will leave us in a position of irrelevancy, for our time and the decades of the centuries beyond our time, for contributing to the healing and restoration of the planet.

The Role of Religious Education in Addressing the Ecology of Human Existence.

To explore the role of religious education in addressing the ecology of human existence is to take on a new responsibility and to enter into a new, and oftentimes lonely, frontier. Such work has yet to be done in an extensive way. All that is intended in this chapter is to suggest why the work should be done and to encourage its undertaking as soon as possible. I have tried to point to the sense of urgency in the first section of this chapter. Describing our problem context and arguing the necessity for giving primary consideration has been one of the purposes of this chapter. We have no immediate answers to the questions thus far raised. However, the questions about the shape of religious education in dealing with the ecology of human existence are now before our generation. We can no longer ignore the necessity to give serious consideration to this situation. Our ecological existence, as previously stated, is much more complicated today than ever before, due to our number as a species, and to the impact of our present technologies upon the planet. The magnitude of the problem of human and biospheric existence should leave us with a sense of urgency. Necessary shifts in human self-understanding in relation to the biosphere and in value orientations and responsibilities are pushing us into new moral and ethical territory. These issues have been identified in the previous section. The challenge for making a shift from our present mechanistic and reductionistic worldview, and consequent lifestyle with its supporting science and technology, to an ecological worldview is enormous and complex. Such is the case because the task is filled with bewilderment as well as with high expectation. We are bewildered due to the fact that we have no experience in dealing with the problem in its contemporary form. We are challenged with the expectation that the so-called "postmodern world" will be fulfilling in ways that far exceed what we value in our culture at this time, particularly as we are witnesses to the worldwide spector of environmental degeneration and resource loss in soil, water, and species. To be able to measure the human contribution to the health and welfare of future generations of life and to be witnesses to renewal and preservation of the miracle and beauty of life is a thought that kindles the human imagination in such ways that we can once again rejoice in the words of the ancient psalmist: "How wonderful are thy works . . . in wisdom thou hast made them all" (Psalm 104:24).

The role of religious education is foundational in opening up for the churches the subject of the ecology of human existence. Upon immediate reflection, this is really an inadequate statement. The ecology of existence, as defined at the beginning of this chapter, is more than subject. The ecology of existence is object, process, human spirituality, identity, relationship, and cognizance of the sacred. We need new terms to get at this "subject." The use of the word "subject" is a left-over usage about land, the biosphere, an attitude born during the age of the enlightenment. The use of the word "subject" connotes a very destructive and dehumanizing dichotomy because the usage separates our species from the creation. In our time and culture we perceive ourselves as subject, the creation is object, an object available for our own use and satisfaction. This, of course, runs through our entire set of human relationships and of relationships with the earth itself. We obviously need new terms to get at this "subject" of the ecology of human existence. Perhaps to suggest that the role of religious education is to enable the emergence of a greatly expanded sense of human identity, of what it means and what is required to be human, is more useful. Foundational to this process is the necessity to make a massive shift in the contemporary Christian preoccupation with self, personal redemption, salvation, even in their full social configuration. Religious education has to return to the basic biblical and theological task of regaining our roots in ancient Hebrew theology of creation and to work as best as we can in identifying the ecological assumption, based in Christian scriptural thought, about human relationships to the gift of land in covenant.[34] Christian scriptural material is preoccupied with the following questions: Who is Jesus? What is required for Christian discipleship? What are the implications for the Christian way of living? Given the apocalyptic ethos of the intertestamental and the early post-Christian scriptural period, questions about endtimes were paramount in relation to personal and community behavior and to eternal life. Preoccupation with these critical faith issues preempted ancient Hebrew history and the struggle to understand right human relationships with the creation (and live by the understandings), as referenced in the creation metaphors of Genesis, the Deuteronomic Codes, the Psalms, Proverbs, and many aspects of the prophetic writings, particularly in Isaiah, Jeremiah, and Amos. The New Testament preoccupation has been dominating Christian thinking through the centuries at the expense of maintaining the insights about creation and our relation to it as found in the more ancient writings of the Christian heritage. We see this shortcoming in the neo-conservative movement of recent years.[35]

The Gnostics presented a message of an alien God and an evil earth. In Irenaeus nature was affirmed. In Origen the emphasis was on cultural environment, and the idea of human alienation from nature emerged once again. Origen also suggested the hierarchy of being that is very much with us today. Augustine spoke of the overflowing goodness of God and of creation. But by the time of Thomas Aquinas (twelfth century) humanity was once again described as being alienated from nature, and nature was placed in a subordinate position. St. Francis of Assisi embraced creation, trying to correct the ethos of earlier times. The reformation theology of Calvin and Luther laid the foundations for modern secularization. The ambiguity in the Christian scriptures influences us all, leaving us in an uncomfortable and ambiguous position as the circumstances of the closing years of the twentieth century force the ecological question once again. We are unprepared to deal with the most primary of all human concerns in our new world of massive numbers and technological forces which are undermining the ecology of human existence. Our religious training and cultural orientation have been responsible for this insensitivity. Until the advent of the so-called environmental movement, we have had little stimulation to cause us to give time and thought to the ancient tradition in Hebrew scriptural creation theology.

At this time it is important that religious education engage the churches and their wider constituents in pondering the ecology of human existence. This is not a simple task. The "subject" is new and complex. The constituency of our efforts in religious education is largely unaware of the "subject." A great deal of experimental work for the development of educational theory in this field awaits to be done.

For many years, the author of this chapter has been engaged, through the churches, in educating the U.S. public concerning the problem of world hunger and personal and social responses to it.[36] Scores of community and ecumenically sponsored lectures have been given, along with workshops, consultations, seminars, and "hunger events." During recent years, focus has been placed upon the tragedy of the U.S. farm crisis, which is itself an outgrowth of the world food crisis. Perhaps the approach that was taken to address these above mentioned issues is useful for looking at the incorporation of the ecology of human existence into religious education.

We worked with this simple but effective matrix of interconnected components of the problem and approach to world hunger:

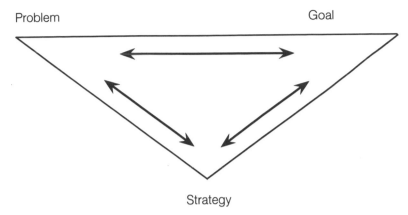

We (many co-workers across the United States) identified the three components: the problem, the goal, and the strategy. We worked very hard through the years to do an adequate analysis of the problem: its causality, magnitude, and impact. This in itself was a very difficult task. When we began in the early 1970s, following the United Nations World Food Conference held in Rome (1973), very few teaching materials were available. But now we find that keeping up with the new literature in the field is very difficult! The more we worked on problem analysis, the more we began to think about a world without hunger, of what a world would look like if each and every nation would be able to feed itself on a sustainable basis. Pondering the question of strategy (of how we get from where we are to where we want to be), we began to develop new ideas for action. The three components under consideration became mutually informing. This is the reason for using the arrows in the matrix design. Our understanding of these matters matured during these years to the place where significant research and development, by many persons and in many institutions all across the world, have been initiated in envisioning what we as agronomists call a regenerative, or sustainable, domestic and self-reliant food system. A broad-based analysis of the problem pushed us to the recognition that prevailing capital and petro-chemically intensive agricultural technologies, with the accompanying emphasis on breeding for high yielding plant varieties of mono-cropping systems, is a critical part of the problem. We began to recognize that totally new approaches in national and world agriculture must be taken. During the time of the writing of this chapter there were a significant number of land grant colleges searching for new faculty to work upon the new frontier of regenerative, or sustainable, agriculture. But still faculty persons are not yet available in sufficient numbers, even to begin to meet the new demand for workers with the entirely new approaches and skills essential for the needed transformation. It has been a dramatic experience to be a part of this breakthrough. For a decade we struggled to envision new goal concepts that would function as alternative directions in the status quo of agriculture.[37] As we began to think about goals, or new alternatives, ideas about how to get out of the morass of world hunger (farm crises within every nation as a result of nearly 200 years of colonial occupation with resultant rural poverty and desert encroachment) and to stimulate movement toward more promising futures, the question of "how to get from where we are to a better future" began to have an answer. The story is long, complex, exciting, and, of course, unfinished. Obviously, the story has only begun. I simply describe this experience with the hope that it might suggest one possible approach for Christian educators to consider in working through the question of this chapter about the emergence of a social and religious ethos and redemptive human behavior in terms of the ecology of human existence. The obvious needs to be stated again. A great deal of serious work goes into the process of problem identification, goal conceptualization, and strategy for social transformation.

In approaching the task of contemporizing religious education to address the ecology of human existence, the first piece of work appears to be in returning to our ancient religious ecological insights found in the Hebrew scriptures. From this perspective we need to examine how a narrowly defined preoccupation with the central themes of the Christian scriptures has separated us from other important aspects of our religious heritage and to look beyond the themes of human redemptive history and human purpose to insights about creation history and purpose. The normative insights to be found in this research are of critical importance. Christians need to be reminded of their ancient covenants, of the fact that creation is God's and that, in accepting the gift of land in covenant, we accept responsibility to practice dominion and to be stewards in maintaining God's righteousness and justice in God's domain. In rediscovering essential aspects of our Christian faith, rooted in ancient Hebrew thought, we will discover that we are not free to do as we please.[38] This ancient Hebrew understanding, representative of the best in moral and ethical insight that history has thus far produced, leads to fresh opportunities to look at the ecology of human existence from our self-understanding as persons within the Judeo-Christian tradition. We can look at Christ's vision of the reign of God and the meaning of Christian discipleship in this renewed context.

From this kind of a beginning, one's imagination dances when formulating new approaches to, not only studies in biblical literature, but liturgy, worship, the celebration of the great sacraments, youth work, summer camping, counseling for career choice, and spiritual formation. The list can be extended. From these beginnings we can anticipate new work in judicatory pronouncements and advocacy for local, regional, and national legislation. One's imagination begins to soar when thinking about shifts in personal lifestyles, the kinds of food we set on the family table, the new forms of recreation that put us in touch with the sacredness of life and challenge us to work for sustainable and regenerative futures for all aspects of life. The shifts coming out of these experiences—value reorientations, ways of living, and new technologies for our sustenance—are quite different in comparison to the exhaustive ones which have captured our imaginations and energies at this stage of the development of modern global civilization.

As a way to summarize briefly what has been said, I remember a discussion that was held at the Francis Bacon Library on the campus of Pomona College a few years ago following a lecture by Nobel Prize winner, the late professor René Dubos. Someone asked him what has brought him the most joy and satisfaction during his life. Dubos' response: "Planting wild strawberries at the edge of the stream that flows past my little cottage in upstate New York." He added: "It is quite exciting to observe each spring that as the strawberries ripen the turtle eggs hatch!" He continued: "Of all the things that I have accomplished in my lifetime as a biological scientist and writer, nothing gives me more joy than to feel as though I participated, even in this small way, in the ongoing process of life in creation." Dubos then carefully told of the critically important role that the turtles of the streams feeding the Hudson river play in maintaining the health, integrity, and harmony of that river system and of the function of the river in relation to the health of the sea and the sky above the sea.

To the writer of this chapter, the role of religious education appears to be to help unleash this kind of human potential so that we can all become responsible participants within the natural order. To help others is to be part of the process of maintaining the ecology of existence, of which humanity is but one part. To do this will require radical departures in traditions of religious education—both in its theories and its practices.

NOTES

1. To gain a full appreciation of this statement, see Claus Westermann, *Genesis 1-11: A Commentary* (Minneapolis: Augsburg, 1984).

2. See the World Council of Churches' journal *Anticipation* 1-30 (April 1970-July 1983) for articles on the future of humanity in a world of science-based technology.

3. Barbara Ward and René Dubos, eds., *Only One Earth* (New York: Norton, 1972), p. 12.

4. Paul Abrecht, ed., *Faith, Science and the Future* (Geneva: World Council of Churches, 1978), p. 4.

5. For a wide-ranging survey of these issues, see Lester Brown, ed., *The State of the World* (New York: Norton, 1984).

6. See Ward and Dubos, *Only One Earth*, p. 12.

7. For an overview description of the magnitude of the problem and predicted outcome, see Secretariat of the United Nations Conference on Desertification, ed., *Desertification: Its Causes and Consequences* (New York: Pergamon, 1977), pp. 4-10.

8. A thorough description of this phenomenon is presented in Lester Brown and Edward C. Wolf, *Reversing Africa's Decline*, Worldwatch Paper, no. 3 (Washington, D.C.: Worldwatch Institute, 1985).

9. For a vivid account of species extinction during this century, see Norman Myers, *The Sinking Ark* (New York: Pergamon, 1979).

10. For a full analysis of atmospheric stress, see Stephen H. Schneider and Lynne E. Mesirow, *The Genesis Strategy: Climate and Global Survival* (New York: Plenum, 1976).

11. The reader is again referred to Myers, *The Sinking Ark*.

12. James Gustafson, *Ethics from a Theocentric Perspective* (Chicago: University of Chicago Press, 1981-1984).

13. For an ecological focus on Psalm 104, see Odil Hannes Steck, *World and Environment,* Biblical Encounters Series (Nashville: Abingdon, 1978), pp. 78-85.

For an in-depth treatment of this subject, see H. Paul Santmire, *The Travail of Nature: The Ambiguous Ecological Promise of Christian Theology* (Philadelphia: Fortress, 1985).

15. A historical review of the ecological ambiguity in Western history is presented by J. Donald Hughes, *Ecology in Ancient Civilizations* (Albuquerque: University of New Mexico Press, 1975).

16. Aldo Leopold, *A Sand County Almanac, and Sketches Here and There* (New York: Oxford University Press, 1949), p. 217.

17. For a full history of this recognition, see Paul Abrecht, *The Churches and Rapid Social Change* (Garden City, N. Y.: Doubleday, 1961) and Egbert de Vries, *Man in Rapid Social Change* (Garden City, N. Y.: Doubleday, 1961).

18. A brief historical review appears in W. A. Visser 't Hooft, *The Genesis and Formation of the World Council of Churches* (Geneva: World Council of Churches, 1982).

19. See Richard Dickinson, *Line and Plummet: The Churches and Development* (Geneva: World Council of Churches, 1968).

20, See *Partners in Development: The Report of the Commission on International Development,* by Lester B. Pearson, chairman (New York: Praeger, 1969).

21. For the study reports, see *Anticipation* 1-17 (April 1970-May 1975).

22. For a full statement of the purpose of this consultation, see Abrecht, *Faith, Science and the Future,* pp. 11-65.

23. David Gill, ed., *Gathered for Life: Official Report of the VI Assembly of the World Council of Churches* (Geneva: World Council of Churches, 1983), p. 78, paragraph 23.

24. See Marlin VanElderen, "Justice, Peace and the Integrity of Creation," *One World* (May 1987), pp. 12-17.

25. For a full coverage of these questions see the two-volume work, World Council of Churches' Conference on Faith, Science and the Future, *Faith and Science in an Unjust World* (Geneva: World Council of Churches, 1980).

26. To pursue this shift in Old Testament research, see Steck, *World and Environment;* Jürgen Moltmann, *God in Creation: A New Theology of Creation and the Spirit of God* (San Francisco: Harper & Row, 1985); Claus Westermann, *Elements of Old Testament Theology* (Atlanta: John Knox, 1982); and Rolf Knierim, "Cosmos and History in Israel's Theology," *Horizons in Biblical Theology* 3 (1981), pp. 59-123.

27. See Walter Brueggemann, "Land: Fertility and Justice," in *Theology of the Land,* ed. Bernard F. Evans and Gregory D. Cusack (Collegeville, Minn: Liturgical Press, 1987), pp. 41-68.

28. For an extensive discussion of the relations between human

and nonhuman species, see Charles Birch and John Cobb Jr., *The Liberation of Life: From the Cell to the Community* (Cambridge: Cambridge University Press, 1983).

29. David M. Paton, ed., *Breaking Barriers, Nairobi 1975: The Official Report of the Fifth Assembly of the World Council of Churches* (Grand Rapids, Mich.: Eerdmans, 1976), p. xi.

30. Ibid., pp. xi-xii.

31. Gill, *Gathered for Life*, p. 77, paragraph 19.

32. In addition to the annual reports of Brown, ed., *The State of the World*, see Donella H. Meadows and others, *The Limits to Growth: A Report for the Club of Rome's Project on the Predicament of Mankind* (New York: Universe Books, 1972); Mihajlo Mesarovic and Eduard Pestel, *Mankind at the Turning Point: The Second Report to the Club of Rome* (New York: Dutton, 1974); and *The Global 2000 Report to the President—Entering the Twenty-first Century*, Gerald O. Barney, study director (Washington, D.C.: U.S. Government Printing Office, 1980-1981).

33. E. F. Schumacher, *Good Work* (New York: Harper & Row, 1979), p. 65.

34. A provocative study of scriptural thought about human relationships to the land is offered by Vincent Wimbush, "Joining the Debate: The Bible in the Struggle to Make Peace with Creation," in *Proceedings of the Forum on Church and Land*, vol. 2, ed. C. Dean Freudenberger and Carol Ann Seckel (Claremont, Calif.: School of Theology at Claremont, 1987), pp. 79-99.

35. The reader is again referred to Santmire, *The Travail of Nature*.

36. For example, see C. Dean Freudenberger and Paul Minus, *Christian Responsibility in a Hungry World* (Nashville: Abingdon, 1974); and the five-part filmstrip with theological overview and teacher's guides, *A World Hungry: A Resource on Hunger and Hope*, executive producer, Karl Holtsnider, based on the work of C. Dean Freudenberger, Franciscan Communications Center, 1976.

37. See Kenneth A. Dahlberg, ed., *New Directions for Agriculture and Agricultural Research: Neglected Dimensions and Emerging Alternatives* (Totowa, N. J.: Rowman & Allanheld, 1986).

38. See Steck, *World and Environment*; and Brueggemann, "Land."

8

Dangerous Memories: Toward a Pedagogy for Social Transformation

Russell A. Butkus

INTRODUCTION: THE TASK AT HAND

In the last two decades concern for issues of peace, justice, and social responsibility in public life has steadily grown within the boundaries of North America's religious communities: Protestant, Catholic, and Jewish. Within Catholicism in particular there has been somewhat of a "renaissance" of reflection and action on behalf of justice the likes of which the U.S. church has not experienced since the Depression era of the 1930s. The document from the 1971 Synod of Bishops, entitled *Justice in the World,* did a great deal to promote this significant turn to the world. The episcopal statement boldly proclaimed that "action on behalf of justice and participation in the transformation of the world fully appear to us as a constitutive dimension of the preaching of the gospel."[1] Subsequently the decade of the 1970s witnessed a whole range of theological and pedagogical approaches that attempted to address the issues of peace, justice, and liberation. More recently the U.S. Catholic bishops have ratified a new and challenging economic pastoral by which they wish to add their voices to the public debate on the

future direction of the U.S. economy. This action will surely
spawn a renewed proliferation of programs and sourcebooks
on economic justice as U.S. Catholics seek to implement and
teach the views found in the pastoral letter.

We can assume, I believe, that religious education for justice
has been a topic of discussion among religious educators for
some time. While not an entirely new enterprise (for example,
the roots of justice education extend back to the 1930s), the
last several years have witnessed an increased attentiveness to
the centrality and importance of justice and public responsibility in Christian religious education. The current task in a U.S.
Catholic and Protestant context is to develop a strategy for
justice education that is culturally appropriate, educationally
efficacious, and adequately grounded both theologically and
pedagogically. This task has brought principles such as critical
reflection and praxis to the forefront of pedagogical discussion
and practice. However, the task continues. The ongoing challenge in North American Jewish-Christian theology and education is to develop and employ a language and a strategy that
adequately reflects our social, economic, and cultural context. I
would maintain that our socio-cultural context can be largely
defined as a middle-class reality.[2]

A case in point is the U.S. Catholic community which is, at its
roots, an ethnic-immigrant church whose members were often
victimized and exploited both socially and economically. Thus,
a tradition of suffering exists embedded in the formative process of U.S. Catholicism. However, the church has "made it" as
an accepted participant in the social, political, and economic
life of the U.S. A majority of the church's members are the
beneficiaries of middle-class status and socio-economic privilege.

This situation raises two important questions. First, what does
it mean to educate for justice and social transformation in a
land of plenty within a church that has made it socially, politically, and economically? Second, what are the foundational
principles upon which education for justice and social responsibility must take shape within this socio-historical and ecclesial
context?

In response to these questions, the purpose of this chapter is to make a small contribution to the ongoing task of developing foundational theological and pedagogical principles for doing social justice education within a U.S. Christian context. Within this focus special attention is given to "dangerous memory," understood as the remembrance of suffering and freedom.[3] "Dangerous memory" is developed as a pedagogical strategy, defined and interpreted within the unique journey and experience of U.S. Catholicism and Protestantism. While the specific nature of these reflections is conditioned by my U.S. Catholic experience and context, I contend that dangerous memory has potential applications to other religious communities and traditions, especially Protestant and Jewish. I attempt to make this claim explicit later in this chapter by offering some suggestions of dangerous memory within the American Protestant experience. The underlying assumption is that the remembrance of suffering and freedom is deeply embedded in both our historical experience in North America and our biblical-theological tradition, as well as belonging to the structure of practical-critical reason. Dangerous memory is, therefore, a possible category for theological-pedagogical reflection vis-á-vis the magnitude of human suffering and the call to justice and social responsibility in public life.

U.S. CATHOLICS: AMERICANIZED AND MIDDLE-CLASS

Roman Catholic presence in the United States dates back to the prerevolutionary period, and the Catholic journey in this country is in many respects an American success story. An important point, however, for contemporary Catholics to remember is, as Edward Duff states, that "contemporary American Catholicism . . . does not derive from the miniscule prerevolutionary elite of Maryland but from the flood of immigrants that ended in the mid-1920s."[4] In other words, the roots of most American Catholics extend back to the massive waves of foreign immigration during the mid-nineteenth and early twentieth centuries.[5]

Despite the ethnic-immigrant roots of American Catholics, however, a dramatic change has occurred in the U.S. Catholic community in the last 150 years. This dramatic, and oftentimes painful, transformation is succinctly described by David

O'Brien: "American Catholics, traditionally associated with immigrant working-class minorities, are now firmly integrated into
the main currents of American life."[6] The process of integration, commonly called assimilation, began as soon as Catholic
immigrants landed upon these shores. In some respects the
American Catholic journey is a story of their Americanization.[7]
O'Brien claims that "the concept of Americanization provides
an indispensable key to the past, for upward mobility and acceptance into American culture were indeed objectives of immigrant Catholics and their leaders."[8]

There are four consequential factors of the Catholic experience of Americanization which shed considerable light on the
current socio-cultural context of most U.S. Catholics. First, as a
result of the assimilation process, American Catholics can no
longer be considered a foreign church. The era of the immigrant church is definitively over. Closely associated with the
loss of foreignness has been the waning of ethnic loyalties
among U.S. Catholics.

Second, Americanization of immigrant Catholics has resulted
in the attainment of social and economic success and parity
with the dominant American culture. As Catholic immigrants
shed their foreignness and ethnic customs and appeared more
"American," they began to make socio-economic progress. Related to Catholic upward mobility is the third factor: That assimilation also resulted in the adoption of prevailing attitudes
and values by American Catholics. Joseph Fichter contends that
"upwardly mobile middle-class Catholic families tend to have
the same aspirations, belong to the same clubs, have the same
frustrations . . . hold similar political and economic attitudes, as
other upwardly mobile American families in the neighborhood."[9]

Finally, the end result of Americanization has been the attainment of middle-class status by the majority of U.S. Catholics.
Writing about Catholic immigrants, John L. Thomas states, "Using the ample economic and educational opportunities available in our open-class society, their second and third generation descendants gradually achieved middle-class status. This
group now constitutes the bulk of American Catholics."[10]

The point is that U.S. Catholics have fared very well as a

result of being assimilated and Americanized. Socially and economically American Catholics have arrived; they have made it and are now considered full participants in the American, middle-class way of life.[11]

Andrew Greeley's research in *The American Catholic, A Social Portrait* confirms the assertion that U.S. Catholics have made remarkable upwardly mobile progress. His findings suggest that U.S. Catholics are no longer overwhelmingly working-class or blue collar. He writes that "the picture which is part of American mythology, of the children and grandchildren of immigrants struggling upward in American society is generally validated by the research evidence available to us."[12] Greeley contends that Irish and German Catholics achieved success in the U.S. by the turn of the twentieth century, and after World War II, Catholic immigrants from eastern and southern Europe began their dramatic upward climb.[13] In his opinion, "American Catholics are now thoroughly acculturated to American society."[14]

Will Herberg in *Protestant, Catholic, Jew* also corroborates the assertion that U.S. Catholics have attained middle-class status. He states,

> With the emergence of a middle class, the entire body of Catholics became more American—America is preeminently a middle-class country; and with the advancement of large segments of the Catholic community the church advanced, becoming on its part more middle-class and more American.[15]

The process of "bourgeoisification" has allowed U.S. Catholics to become members of what Herberg calls the "American Way of Life."

According to Herberg, the American Way of Life is the "common religion" of the American people which "supplies American society with an overarching sense of unity amid conflict."[16] In other words, the American Way of Life is the civil religion, or the "sacred canopy," of U.S. society; it is a structure of ideas, ideals, aspirations, values, beliefs, and standards. The American Way of Life also influences and is influenced by the three great

religions of U.S. society: Protestantism, Catholicism, and Judaism. Furthermore, the American Way of Life is, according to
Herberg, the "idealized description of the middle-class
ethos,"[17] and is an expression of the middle class and a description of middle-class thinking, believing, and acting.

One must reasonably conclude that Herberg's version of the
American Way of Life as the "common faith" or the "sacred
canopy" of U.S. society contains the earmarks of a middle-class
religious ideology.[18] If the analysis is correct that U.S. Catholics
have become a middle-class people and full participants in the
American Way of Life, then important questions are raised for
Catholic theologians and educators who seek to promote social
responsibility in public life. Specifically what have been the
costs of Catholic assimilation into the American Way of Life? I
suggest that a significant cost of Americanization has been the
consequent process of forgetting. In other words, being Americanized and achieving middle-class status may have contributed to a particular form of social amnesia among contemporary
U.S. Catholics. This social amnesia is particularly directed at the
ethnic-immigrant experience which embodies a tradition of
suffering, injustice, and the quest for freedom.[19] The task of
religious education in a Catholic context is to cultivate the
remembrance of suffering and freedom with the aim of promoting compassionate action and social responsibility.

THE REMEMBRANCE OF SUFFERING AND
THE SEARCH FOR SOCIAL JUSTICE

In *An American Strategic Theology* John Coleman points in the
direction of Catholic social amnesia when he declares that "most
American Catholics are near illiterates in their own history. American Catholic history is conspicuously absent from parochial
schools, church colleges, and even seminaries."[20] If Coleman's assessment is correct, then I would claim that the "con-
spicuous absence" of American Catholic history from Catholic
education is one way in which our social amnesia has become
"institutionalized" (reified) in our educational practice.[21]

With this assessment in mind, the purpose of this section is
to briefly highlight two significant aspects of the U.S. Catholic
journey. First, some historical reflections on the experience of

immigrant suffering embodied in the process of emigration from the "Old Country" and in the experience of immigration to the "New World" are offered. Second, some attempts to alleviate suffering through the church's search for social justice are briefly outlined. The primary interest is to lay the foundation for understanding "dangerous memory" within a U.S. Catholic context.[22]

The Immigrant Experience

The Roman Catholic Church in the United States is, at its roots, an ethnic-immigrant religious community. The church as we know it today was formed through two massive waves of immigration in the nineteenth and early-twentieth centuries. As Herberg points out, the story of Catholicism in the U.S. "is that of a foreign church, or rather a conglomeration of foreign churches, recruited from the successive waves of overseas immigration finally emerging into one of the three great American religions.[23]

However, the Catholic journey does not begin with the arrival of immigrants but with their departure from their native lands. One must return to the "Old Country" and to the nearly cataclysmic political, economic, and social events that created millions of dispossessed and uprooted people. After 1800, European social patterns and structures collapsed under the strain of profound political, social, and economic upheaval. The end result of this social disintegration was the displacement of millions of people, primarily peasants and artisans.[24]

Faced with fewer choices and dwindling alternatives, the dispossessed could either move to rapidly expanding cities and take their place among the urban proletariat or leave Europe altogether and emigrate to Australia, Canada, or the United States. Consequently millions emigrated, wave after wave of the "tired, the poor, and the huddled masses," composed largely of Protestant, Catholic, and Jewish peasants and artisans in search of freedom and some measure of justice.[25]

With few exceptions newly arrived Catholic immigrants were already impoverished. Handicapped by their ignorance of English, except for the Irish, they settled in ethnic enclaves. While many Germans settled on the land, most Catholic immigrants

sought work and shelter in the large industrial centers of the
east and midwest. There, exploited and crammed together in
teeming slums near mine, mill, and slaughterhouse, the newly
arrived immigrants experienced the victimization of social disorganization and economic discrimination. Saul Alinsky captures the experience of immigrant suffering very well when he
writes that the ethnic ghettos were restricted worlds within
which

> lived a people by and large temporarily immobilized by fear
> and suspicion of a strange land; a people subjected to dis-
> crimination and exploitation; a people struggling to learn a
> new language, new customs, and new ways of life, and find-
> ing most of their reassurance from the security of their na-
> tional churches. . . . Overall hung the spectre of firetraps for
> homes, dirt, disease, dependency, delinquency, and a conse-
> quent considerable demoralization.[26]

Common among all Catholic immigrant groups, regardless of
nationality, was the experience of poverty, as demonstrated by
Jay Dolan's research on the Irish and Germans in nineteenth-
century New York and also of Handlin's work on the Irish immigrants in Boston.[27] Dolan writes that "in 1852 the New York
Association for Improving the Conditions of the Poor stated
that half of the people assisted that year were Irish; three out of
four were Catholic. In 1858, 64 percent of the people admitted
to the City's Alms House were Irish."[28]

Combined with the oppressive socio-economic conditions
under which most Catholic immigrants lived, was the recurring
experience of anti-Catholic hostility. Occuring first within the
Nativist period (1830-1860), anti-Catholic hostility reemerged
again in the late 1880s with the American Protective Association and again in the early 1900s with the Ku Klux Klan. Even
as late as 1960 anti-Catholic sentiment surfaced in conjunction
with John F. Kennedy's campaign for president.

The Search for Social Justice

The experience of economic oppression and nativist hostility
forms one side of the Catholic story in the U.S. The other side

includes the church's attempt to side with the immigrant poor in an effort to alleviate suffering by securing some measure of social justice. These efforts began shortly after the Civil War when it became evident to many Catholic leaders that an increasing number of Catholics occupied the ranks of the destitute. This awareness initiated the "Charity Phase" of Catholic social action aimed primarily at the high rate of destitute and homeless children.

After 1875, however, a growing number of socially minded Catholics began to believe that urban charity alone could not alleviate poverty and social discontent. I refer to these as "voices of transition," a transition to a more sophisticated form of socio-economic analysis whereby attempts were made to uncover and understand the systemic causes for poverty. One such voice was Peter Foy, a St. Louis journalist, who delivered a paper called "The New Social Order" at the lay congress in Baltimore in 1889.[29]

Between 1880 and 1918 Catholic involvement in the emerging industrial conflict became more prevalent. The hierarchy entered the fray when in 1887 Cardinal Gibbons succeeded in convincing the Vatican not to condemn Catholic involvement in the Knights of Labor. His efforts prepared the way for full Catholic participation in the labor movement. Other progressive-reformist voices were also heard, such as John A. Ryan who quickly emerged to the forefront of Catholic social thought when he published *A Living Wage* in 1906 in which he argued for a just, living wage for the working classes.

Perhaps one of the most colorful and controversial voices of the period, and an example of an emerging radical Catholic tradition, was Mary Harris Jones also known as Mother Jones, the "Miner's Angel."[30] The daughter and grandaughter of Irish revolutionaries, Mother Jones knew first hand the injustice, suffering, and death of ghetto existence. Because of her commitment to exploited mine workers and her solidarity with the poor, Mother Jones stands as a powerful figure in the church's search for freedom and justice.

The church's search for social justice and the emergence of Catholic radicalism did not, however, become full-blown until after the economic crash of 1929. The decade of the Great

Depression which followed can be described as a vibrant period in the church's involvement in the social, political, and
economic life of the country. There were a multitude of Catholic responses to the massive suffering caused by the Depression. One need only remember the outspokenness of John A.
Ryan who became the major spokesperson of the Catholic
establishment. Others committed themselves to union activities such as Charles Owen Rice, an extraordinary example of
the Depression-era labor priest. And, of course, one cannot
forget the powerful and radical witness of Dorothy Day and the
Catholic Worker Movement.

While no single solution, spokesperson, or program dominated the Catholic scene there was an overriding disillusionment
with capitalism. Generally speaking the political position of the
Catholic leadership shifted to the left. According to Neil Betten,
Catholic social leaders, in response to the Depression, "expanded the church's welfare function, supported national economic reform, and in some cases advocated radical change in
the capitalist system."[31]

Dangerous Memory and the Protestant Experience: Reclaiming a "Usable Past"

In her book *Human Liberation in a Feminist Perspective—A
Theology,* Letty Russell writes of the search for a "usable past."[32]
The search for a usable past refers to the attempt to reclaim
elements of past traditions, once hidden and repressed, for the
purpose of forging new identity and building toward a better
future. Within the context of the feminist experience Russell
writes,

> Awareness of their own history and struggles is frequently
> nonexistent among women as a group. Yet it is toward such a
> search for a usable history that they must turn to build a still
> living and evolving past in order to shape their future as
> partners in society. . . .This attempt to recreate a usable past
> as her-story and not just his-story is part of a widespread
> development in the modern world. All peoples searching for
> new identity and liberation seek out ways to shape the future
> by turning to history as a medium of human liberation.[33]

There is, I believe, important linkage between Russell's language of a usable past and the notion of dangerous memory. The search for a usable past requires, in part, the uncovering and reclaiming of dangerous memories—memories of suffering and freedom that have been repressed or forgotten. The focus of this section is to offer some suggestions on how dangerous memory can be understood within the American Protestant experience.

Quaker Sufferings

Quaker history must be recognized as a primary example of a Protestant religious tradition which embodies the notion of dangerous memory. The experience of suffering and search for freedom lay at the very heart of the Quaker experience, underscored by the fact that Quakers were both the frequent victims of persecution and at the forefront of emancipatory causes. D. Elton Trueblood writes that "thousands of Quakers, both men and women, suffered cruel imprisonment; many were whipped and beaten; and four, including one woman, were hanged on Boston Common."[34] On the other hand, the Quaker record for freedom is well known. For example, according to Trueblood, Quakers were the first people of the Western world to take a stand against the system of slavery and their participation in the American abolitionist movement speaks for itself.[35]

The persecution of Quakers was particularly severe in the "New World," especially in Massachusetts. This experience of suffering became embodied in the American Quaker tradition in two major ways. The first was a special form of Quaker writing called the "literature of suffering," which often included rosters of imprisoned or martyred Friends. From this body of literature we read about the imprisonment and execution of four Quakers: William Robinson, Marmaduke Stephenson, Mary Dyer, and William Leddra in Massachusetts between 1659 and 1661. In a written appeal to the king of England, Edward Burrough provides us with a summary of Quaker suffering in New England. Entitled *A Declaration of the Sad and Great Persecution and Martyrdom*, Burrough wrote in 1661 that

Of the People of God, called Quakers, in New-England, for the Worshipping of God, Whereof

22 have been Banished upon pain of Death.

03 have been Martyred.

03 have had their Right Ears cut.

01 hath been burned in the Hand with the letter H.

31 persons have received 650 stripes.

01 was beat while his Body was like a jelly.

Several were beat with Pitched Ropes.

Five Appeals made to England were denied by the Rulers of Boston.

One thousand forty four pounds of goods hath been taken from them (being poor men) for meeting together in the fear of the Lord, and for keeping the Commands of Christ.

One now lyeth in Iron-fetters, condemned to dye.[36]

The second major way Quaker suffering became "officially" expressed within their tradition was the "Meeting for Sufferings." In 1756 Philadelphia Friends established a Meeting for Sufferings patterned after the London model.[37] This meeting was meant to serve as a body of Friends organized to look after Quaker interests and needs between yearly meetings. In this case the Meeting for Sufferings was specifically established to care for Quakers who met with extreme hardship, even murder, on the American frontier. Eventually the Meeting for Sufferings expanded its domain by responding to sufferings not limited to Quakers, such as the sufferings endured by slaves. Trueblood writes that "just as, in the early days, there were "Sufferings" because of imprisonment, now there were other sufferings. The interest in those who suffered was by no means limited to Quakers and soon included the suffering slaves. All of the interests of Quakers at home and abroad were finally involved."[38]

Within the American Protestant experience the Quaker tradition is a premier example of dangerous memory—a dangerous and subversive tradition which embodies the remembrance of suffering and freedom. There is, however, another tradition within American Protestanism which, with the possible exception of the Native American Indian, is the epitome of the experience of suffering and the search for freedom on American soil. This tradition is the experience of the black American churches.

The Black Protestant Experience

Within American Protestantism the black experience stands alone in its capacity to evoke dangerous memory. Unlike the vast majority of immigrants whose vision of freedom saw America as a promised land and a "new" Eden, blacks were introduced to America in bondage—unwillingly uprooted, systematically enslaved, and brutally deprived of their African cultural and religious heritage. Martin Marty puts it well when he says, "As slaves, they became commodities without rights, unable to develop memories in continuity with their religious past."[39] Marty goes on to state that "the Protestant empire was built at the expense of black inhabitants. They were either overlooked, intentionally neglected, enslaved, expatriated, or exterminated."[40] Yet black Americans have become a significant and unique religious body within American Protestantism, and evangelical Christianity has played a leading role in black life, keeping alive their memory of suffering and their search for freedom.

At first white colonialists were reluctant to evangelize black slaves. Some did not believe that blacks were included in God's redemptive design and others were fearful that Christianity would instill thoughts of freedom and equality in black minds and hearts, but others, according to Ahlstrom, "found it easier to justify enslavement of heathen than of fellow children of God."[41] Not until the Great Awakening between 1790 and 1815 did Baptists and Methodists mount a serious effort to evangelize black slaves. These efforts were moderately successful and in 1790 the Methodist church claimed nearly 12,000 black members.

More important, however, was the emergence of two independent black churches resulting from two secessions in Philadelphia and New York. Under the leadership of Richard Allen, the first black to be ordained a Methodist deacon, the African Methodist Episcopal Church was formed in Philadelphia in 1816 after years of black-white friction. In a similar situation in New York the AME Zion Church was founded in 1821. By the turn of the century both black national churches combined claimed three quarters of a million members.

There is little doubt that evangelical Christianity has played a central role in the black American experience. According to Ahlstrom, after emancipation "the church was by far the most important black institution after the family."[42] Even before emancipation there is good reason to believe that Christianity functioned very powerfully in providing a sense of community and identity for black slaves. Marty writes that in 1847 a number of whites in Charleston, South Carolina, expressed great fear "that religious instruction would give blacks 'plentitude of freedom of thought, word, and action in the church' so that they would establish organized community."[43] There is also good evidence to suggest that Christianity was a significant factor in the slave revolts led by Gabriel Prosser (1880), Denmark Vesey (1822), and Nat Turner (1831).

Prior to emancipation, black Christianity was a powerful and sustaining "invisible" institution where reading the Bible and the experience of bondage intersected, providing black slaves with a medium for expressing their suppressed yearning for freedom. "Spirituals," a hallmark of black Christianity, were songs of intense faith, hope, and freedom often expressing the toil and bondage of the black experience. Ahlstrom writes that "revivalistic Protestant Christianity became the chief means by which the African slave—bereft of his native culture, language, and religion—defined and explained his personal and social existence in America."[44]

After emancipation the black churches quickly became the primary means whereby a structured social existence emerged for Southern blacks. Alhstrom claims that "the little churches of the rural South were a psychological and social necessity—the more so because they institutionalized the only area in which a fair measure of Negro freedom remained."[45] The black churches were havens in a hostile world and, most importantly, they provided a means for preserving a sense of identity and racial solidarity. Remembering his own upbringing in rural Arkansas during the 1940s and 1950s, James Cone writes,

In the context of Macedonia African Methodist Episcopal Church, resistance to white injustice was joined with faith in

God's righteousness. . . .Religion was . . . the source of identity and survival, on the one hand, and the source of empowerment in the struggle for freedom on the other. . . . God was the reality to which the people turned for identity and worth because the existing social, political, and economic structures said that they were nobody.[46]

Within the Protestant experience black Christianity continues as a living memorial and a dangerous memory that our social transformation is far from complete. In our own midst, the black experience is a constant reminder of God's "preferential option" as the One who hears the cries of the oppressed and delivers them out of the hands of Egypt.

Abolitionism and Social Gospel

The American Protestant story also contains a strong and vibrant tradition of freedom—a potentially "subversive" memory of emancipatory interests and causes. This Protestant search for freedom is best exemplified in the abolitionist movement and the Social Gospel.

The Quakers were at the forefront of antislavery sentiment in America, and they were indeed the early forerunners of the abolitionist movement. One of the earliest and best-known antislavery Quakers was John Woolman, a New Jersey tailor born in 1720. Early on in his life Wollman became convinced that slavery was morally wrong. These sentiments coalesced in a small book published in 1754 entitled *Some Considerations on the Keeping of Negroes*. In this and other writings, such as *Journal*, Woolman articulated the inseparable link between Christianity and the necessity of freedom for all. He saw slavery as a grievous sin which must be opposed and was particularly haunted by the great human suffering caused by the slave trade. Trueblood writes that Woolman, in his *Journal*, "mentioned the bloodshed in America, the 'lives destroyed through insupportable Stench and other hardships in crossing the Sea' and that through 'extreme oppression Many Slaves are brought to an untimely end.' What saddened him . . . was the fact that all of this suffering was produced for the sake of financial gain."[47] Well over a hundred years before the Civil War Woolman saw the system of slavery "as a dark gloominess hanging over the Land" and predicted that "sin of such depth . . . would bring sorrow and pain, even to subsequent gererations."[48]

Second only to the Quakers in the abolitionist movement were the Methodists. Influenced by William Lloyd Garrison and John Wesley's own *Thoughts Upon Slavery,* Methodist abolitionism combined evangelical revivals with antislavery sentiment to produce an abolitionist crusade. Methodist abolitionism emerged first in New England under the leadership of La Roy Sunderland, the Methodist minister at Andover, Massachusettes, followed shortly by George Storrs and the colorful radical Orange Scott, both of whom were Methodist ministers. Under their fiery and vigorous leadership numerous antislavery societies were formed and they even won the New England and New Hampshire Methodist Conferences over to the abolitionist cause. Though often accused of "insurrectionary" practices, Methodist abolitionists were undaunted in their call for immediate and complete emancipation of black slaves. Speaking of Orange Scott, Donald Mathews writes,

> As a seasoned revivalist, Scott had a vision if not a plan—a vision of the immediate emancipation of the slaves, the immediate provision for their education, the immediate passage of laws to guarantee them civil and legal rights so that "at the earliest possible period, consistent with the best good of the slaves, they should be FULLY EMANCIPATED."[49]

There is no doubt that the Methodist abolitionists "disturbed" the peace of the Methodist Episcopal Church. Indeed, according to Mathews, the church was "shaken" as "its genteel and Southern accommodations with conscience were under embarrassing and persistent attack. Abolitionists offered a radical alternative to all compromise between conscience and sin by insisting that Negroes had a right to their own persons and destinies."[50]

According to Ahlstrom abolitionism was the "decisive prelude" to the Social Gospel in that "both were characterized by a readiness to harness the churches and a tendency to subordinate every other interest of the church to the one great national policy question of the day."[51] Under such diverse influences as the Puritan conviction that remaking society was the church's concern; the liberal theology of Albrecht Ritschl and certain "homegrown" American radicals like Henry George (*Poverty and Progress,* 1879), the American Protestant tradition gave birth to the Social Gospel in the late nineteenth and early-twentieth centuries. Martin Marty claims that the Social Gospel was the "first movement which demonstrated that Protestant thought was coming to terms with the way power was organized in urban America."[52] Under the intellectual guidance of such men as Washington Gladden, Josiah Strong, and Walter Rauschenbusch, the Social Gospel promoted a scathing critique of capitalism as incompatible with Christianity. Gladden's message was simple. He called upon the churches to concern themselves with social injustice by working, through example and advocacy, for the transformation of American economic life bringing it "under the laws of God's kingdom."[53] Following Gladden's lead, Rauschenbusch, also convinced of the centrality of God's kingdom, declared capitalism a social sin. He accused capitalism of destroying the "organismic character" of Christian society because it "tempts, defeats, drains, and degrades, and leaves men stunted, cowed, and shamed in their manhood."[54] For Rauschenbusch capitalism produced "a mammonistic organization with which Christianity can never be content" and a spirit "antagonistic to the spirit of Christianity."[55]

The aim of this brief sketch of the Catholic and Protestant story in the U.S. is to underscore the claim that there exists embedded in our journey a tradition of suffering and action for social justice. Using the language of Johann Metz, one could name this a "dangerous" or "subversive" tradition. The task of Christian religious education is to reclaim this tradition, calling it to mind as the remembrance of suffering and freedom for the purpose of sponsoring contemporary Christians to action for social transformation. However, a "dangerous tradition" alone is insufficient. Dangerous memory must also be rooted in the biblical and theological tradition.

Dangerous Memory: Biblical-Theological Foundations

The basis for understanding dangerous memory biblically and theologically is the Exodus, Israel's emancipation and redemption "out of the land of Egypt." The Exodus-event was the foundational experience in the life and memory of the Israelite community. The Exodus-event provided the historical ground for the Israelite community's experience of emancipation-redemption through the salvific activity of Yahweh who is revealed as a God of justice and righteousness with a special "predisposition" toward the poor and oppressed. This core experience is underscored in Israel's ancient confession of faith preserved for us by the Deuteronomist: "We cried to the Lord the God of our fathers, and the Lord heard our voice and saw our affliction, our toil, and our oppression; and he brought us out of Egypt with a mighty hand and an outstretched arm with great terror, with signs and wonders" (Dt. 26: 5-9).

For the people of Israel the memory of Exodus as the remembrance of slavery and redemption became embedded in cult and code. Cultically the Exodus became memorialized in the celebration of Passover, the primary ritual celebration of Israel's redemption.[56] In Exodus 13:3 we read: "Moses said to the people, 'Remember this day on which you came out of the Land of Egypt, out of the state of slavery, how the Lord freed you by the strength of his hand, no unleaven bread shall be eaten.' " The writer here, most likely the Deuteronomist, is concerned that the Exodus tradition be passed on to later generations and that, in the celebration of Passover, the Exodus from Egypt will be actualized and experienced. Preserved here is the notion that Israel's remembrance includes both the memory of suffering and freedom.

The remembrance of the Exodus is also embedded in Israel's Covenant Code. We have evidence of this in Exodus 22:21-27. In verse 21 the phrase "for you were strangers in the land of Egypt" is a reminding formula, the purpose of which is to provide the motivation for obeying the admonition. The language is adopted from Israel's cultic confession and implies that Israel's oppression in Egypt and emancipation serves as the theological foundation for Israel's social responsibility to the poor and oppressed.

Israel's remembrance, however, receives most attention in the Book of Deuteronomy where we can explicitly speak of a "theology of remembrance." The Deuteronomist's special concern is to keep the memory of the Exodus alive within the

Israelite community. For example, many of the reminding formulas found in the Book of Exodus are believed to be Deuteronomic expansions.

The Deuteronomist utilizes the notion of remembrance in several ways.[57] First, memory is historical and is used to provide the link between the *present* generation and the redemptive events of the *past*. Second, the remembrance of Israel'a emancipation from slavery provides the basis for observing the commandments.[58] In this case remembrance not only provokes action but one acts in order to evoke historical memory. Third, memory also functions to actualize the past in the present. In this case when Israel celebrates Passover in order to remember its suffering and freedom, Israel is participating again in Exodus.

Remembrance is also incorporated in the New Testament experience. A primary example would be the admonition of Jesus to "do this in remembrance of me." Here remembrance functions within the context of Eucharist and is reinterpreted by the early Christian community to refer to the "passover" of Jesus' death and resurrection. Again the notion of remembrance is imbued with the memory of suffering and freedom. In this case, however, remembrance is historical and eschatological in anticipation of the fulfillment of the future promise of God's reign.

Building upon this biblical tradition and drawing upon insights from the Frankfurt School of critical theory, Johann Metz has attempted to utilize memory and narrative as practical categories for theological reflection. In *Faith in History and Society*, memory and narrative are developed as essential components of a practical fundamental theology. Metz understands memory in two ways. First, memory is a basic category of practical critical reason, and, second, memory is primarily the remembrance of suffering and freedom. Narrative is inextricably linked to memory because the articulation of the memory of suffering and freedom is always practical. That is, the articulation of the memory takes the form of dangerous and liberating stories.[59] Memory is "dangerous" for Metz because of its capacity to subvert existing ideologies and unjust social structures and because it contains the possibility for promoting an emancipatory praxis for freedom and justice.[60]

Theologically Metz sees memory and narrative as practical categories of salvation. Specifically, and within the Christian context, memory is a definite salvific memory referring to the "dangerous memory of the freedom of Jesus Christ." The dangerous memory of Jesus Christ focuses on the centrality of Jesus' life, death, and resurrection for Christian faith. For Metz the memory of freedom in Jesus is rooted in Jesus' own life and vision: Jesus' proclamation of the Kingdom, Jesus' solidarity with victims, Jesus' suffering and death, and Jesus' liberation from death through the resurrection. In this theological context, the church, as the sacrament of Jesus Christ, becomes the public expression of the dangerous memory of Jesus. As the public witness to the memory of Jesus, the church must constantly remind the world of God's freedom eschatologically won in the death and resurrection of Jesus. In doing so, Metz claims that the church has the responsibility of "making present" our collective historical memory of suffering and freedom. Here, in the "making present," the theological and pedagogical tasks merge and becomes the special concern of Christian religious education.

Dangerous Memory: Educational Foundations

I am not aware of any warrants in educational writings of the past or present for discussing "dangerous memory" within the educational enterprise. However, education always attends to the "remembrance of things past" especially in relation to curriculum theory and development. Curriculum theory is always concerned with making present the inherited disciplines and knowledge of the *past*.

In his effort to remake curricular language, Dwayne Huebner identifies several aspects of human temporality aimed at promoting greater intentionality in our educational praxis.[61] One of these aspects is memory and tradition. Memories and traditions refer to what John Dewey called the "funded capital of civilization," understood by Huebner as the "collective wealth" of a people. Education is the process whereby the memories and traditions of the past are maintained and protected against loss and forgetting. Huebner claims, "Without education traditions and memories would be forgotten, hope would be ignored and futures would remain unclaimed."[62] The task of the educator is to "care for the past, conserve it so it will not be forgotten or lost for use or reference."[63]

Memories and traditions alone however, are incomplete. The past is always acted upon in some fashion; it never stands in a vacuum or comes to us untampered or "neutral." This consideration leads to Huebner's second aspect of human temporality: the activity of interpretation or hermeneutics. For Huebner, hermeneutical activity provides the link between past, present, and future and between the self and others. Hermeneutical activity is also, at the same time, a political activity because it deals with the crucial question of what past, what collective memories and traditions will be made present and for what purpose.

Past memories and traditions, along with hermeneutical activity of the present, always occur within Heubner's third aspect of human temporality: community or society. For Huebner, community is a "caring collectivity in which individuals share memories and intentions."[64] Without education, collective memories are forgotten and the community can no longer maintain itself, resulting in disintegration, nonidentity, and the foreclosure of its historical future.

Huebner's search for a new curricular language provides a basis for discussing memory and remembrance as a constitutive dimension of the pedagogical process. While he does not use the language of dangerous memory, Huebner does recognize the hermeneutical and political nature of curricular theory and practice. Dangerous memory brings an intentionally critical and possibly emancipatory capacity to the process of remembering within education.

A basis also exists for discussing dangerous memory within the field of Christian religious education. Thomas Groome's approach of "shared Christian praxis" provides some insights on how memory can function within this context.[65] Groome's approach attempts to address and incorporate the importance of memory as a category of critical reason. Within his pedagogical framework memory occurs within the second and third movement.

A major component of the second movement is the activity

of critical reflection. Building on the work of Freire and Habermas, Groome proposes three purposes of critical reflection,
one of which is to critically remember the past in the present.
In Groome's perspective the interests, the ideologies, and the
assumptions of present action can be critiqued only when the
personal and social genesis of present action is brought to
consciousness.[66] This requires the use of memory. Analytical
memory invites people to unmask the genesis of their person-
al/social reality and to uncover the controlling interests and
ideologies that constitute their present situation. Memory here
is used to reappropriate the past, both one's own and society's,
that has been forgotten or submerged. The danger of a forgotten past is that it maintains the unconscious power to shape
our present and future. The use of critical memory in remembrance holds the potential for freeing us from a controlling past
by bringing to consciousness the social genesis of our present
action. Within Groome's second movement memory functions
on a psycho-social level.

Memory is also utilized in the third movement during which
the Christian Story and Vision is made accessible to the participants. Here the Story/Vision is called to memory and reclaimed
as constitutive for knowing God and experiencing salvation.
Groome writes that "remembering and representing the Story is
an essential part of the Jewish and Christian process of knowing
God" and that "we experience salvation for our time by remembering and reencountering the Story of God's saving
deeds."[67] In this capacity memory is primarily historical because the Story is rooted in historical events. Moreover, the use
of memory in the third movement reveals memory's political
and hermeneutical dimension. In the process of remembering
the Story the question arises as to what *version* will be made
present. The decision to make one version present and not
another is a political decision, and at this point the political
nature of curriculum and the function of memory emerges. The
remembrance of things past in curriculum and Storytelling also
reveals the hermeneutical side of memory. In remembering the
version of the Story the interpretive process is already at work
guided by the overall interest and goal of the pedagogical process. In the next section I will return to Groome's "shared

praxis" approach as a possible framework for understanding dangerous memory as a pedagogical strategy within a U.S. Catholic-Protestant context.

Dangerous Memory in a U.S. Context: Toward a Strategy

The purpose of the preceding sections was to lay a foundation for understanding dangerous memory, both theologically and educationally (within the U.S. Catholic-Protestant experience). The task of this concluding section is to define dangerous memory within a U.S. context and to suggest a strategy for its use as a pedagogical principle for educating for justice and social transformation.

My understanding of dangerous memory embodies several facets of meaning. First, dangerous memory embodies the remembrance of suffering and injustice. Here dangerous memory refers to the history of suffering and/or the traditions of suffering and injustice embedded in a people's collective story. Second, dangerous memory embodies the remembrance of those stories, symbols, and personal-collective voices which stood to alleviate suffering and injustice in the name of compassion and human freedom. In this capacity dangerous memory is also the memory of freedom.[68] While dangerous memory is oriented toward the past, the memory of freedom contains a forward-looking dimension because the memory of freedom recalls the voices of freedom who might inspire and become for us models around which our future action might take shape. Third, dangerous memory has a narrative structure meaning and is therefore communicated in a practical manner, that is, by way of stories. Johann Metz writes, "It [dangerous memory] takes place in dangerous stories in which the interest in freedom is introduced, identified, and presented in narrative form."[69]

There are several reasons for the appropriate utilization of dangerous memory in a U.S. setting. First, in the Catholic context, Andrew Greeley's research indicates that while the Catholic community is predominantly middle-class, it is not far removed from the immigrant past. In 1974, 60 percent of U.S. Catholics were third or fourth generation while the remaining 40 percent were first or second generation.[70] In other words, for most Catholics, personally and collectively, the formative process of the immigrant experience is not that historically distant from consciousness. This creates the possibility that dangerous memory can be revived and utilized to bridge the span of time between contemporary U.S. Catholics and their not too distant relatives of the past.

A second reason for the possible efficaciousness of dangerous memory lies in Marcus Hansen's "principle of third generation interest."[71] That is, what the son or daughter of the immigrant wishes to forget, the grandson wishes to remember. The third generation reveals an openness and a willingness to remember the past for the sake of a "remembered heritage." While Herberg claims that this remembrance usually takes shape in reidentification with one's religious tradition, to pedagogically utilize this "third generation interest" by promoting the "dangerous" elements embedded in the U.S. Catholic story might be possible.

Third, dangerous memory is appropriate within a U.S. Catholic and Protestant context because embedded in our story is a dangerous tradition of suffering and freedom. Dangerous memory encompasses three aspects of this tradition within the U.S. First, dangerous memory refers to the disturbing socio-economic conditions of the "Old World" and the experience of displacement that brought many immigrants to these shores. In this case dangerous memory contains the "exodus story" of Catholic and Protestant immigrants. Second, dangerous memory refers to the actual experience of injustice in the U.S.: the struggle, hardship, poverty, exploitation, marginalization, and bondage that many Christians encountered. Third, dangerous memory refers to the church's response to injustice: the search for freedom and social justice. In this context dangerous memory is understood as the church's historical praxis for freedom and justice; dangerous memory embodies a tradition of U.S. Catholic and Protestant voices, activists, and movements that supported and worked for social transformation.[72]

As a pedagogical principle for religious education for social justice, dangerous memory refers to the intentional process of remembering the past traditions of suffering and the attempts to alleviate those sufferings for the expressed purpose of provoking a present praxis for freedom in the hope of the future kingdom of shalom. In other words, within the context of educating for justice and social transformation, dangerous memory attends to the past as the remembrance of suffering and freedom, to the present as a praxis for freedom in the memory of suffering, and to the future in the memory of suffering as a vision of God's kingdom of peace and justice.

In this pedagogical capacity, the principle of dangerous memory functions on three levels: theological, socio-historical, and personal-psychological. At the theological level is what Metz calls the "dangerous memory of the Freedom of Jesus Christ." This dangerous memory embodies the dangerous and subversive content of the Jesus tradition especially focused on Jesus' suffering, death, and resurrection. This dangerous memory also includes those theological-biblical traditions that possess potential critical and liberating characteristics such as the Exodus tradition, the prophetic tradition, the meaning and use of parable and kingdom in the proclamation of Jesus, and the Catholic human rights tradition. Also included here would be political theology, especially those attempts by various theologians to develop an indigenous political theology for North America, what Coleman calls an "American Strategic Theology."

As a socio-historical concept, dangerous memory means that contemporary Catholics and Protestants stand within that collective tradition of suffering, freedom, and commitment to social transformation. The pedagogical process would actively promote the remembrance of the "dangerous" contents of the Catholic-Protestant story in the U.S.

Finally, as a personal-psychological concept, dangerous memory means that the self-formative process, containing the tradition of suffering and freedom, can be critically remembered and personally appropriated. The dangerous memory is dangerous in that it holds the potential power of converting us to the necessity of justice and social responsibility in our time. In other words, if the past story of the U.S. Catholic and Protestant community is critically remembered and imagined, the story can become dangerous because it can unlock the possibility for new and creative action for justice. My claim is that the church's past story in the U.S. holds the potential for becoming a subversive tradition and a dangerous memory today.

Groome's approach of shared praxis offers a helpful paradigm for envisioning the possibilities for dangerous memory as
a pedagogical principle for social justice education. Within
Groome's framework the strategic principle of dangerous memory can specifically occur in the second and third movements.
A major component of the second movement is the activity of
critical reflection. Memory is utilized here to reappropriate
one's formative past which has been forgotten or submerged.
One's formative past becomes dangerous when it radically in-
trudes and calls into question our complacent and comfortable
present. Therefore, within the second movement, dangerous
memory occurs in the context of critical reflection and is experienced in its personal psycho-social dimension. Within a pedagogy for justice, dangerous memory would invite, not only
reflection upon the genesis of one's present action as articulated by Groome, but also the remembrance of personal and
social suffering. To do this the educator would have to provide
focusing questions or activities to help the participants uncover
personal, collective, or generational memories of suffering and
freedom and/or experiences or interests in forgetting suffering.
A helpful activity might be to encourage "research" into one's
family heritage to uncover family "memories" of poverty, slavery, immigration, or social activism for freedom. Particularly
insightful could be the "oral history" of grandparents or great
grandparents. The specific purpose would be to assist the contemporary student to make connections through remembering
their own personal and familial traditions of suffering and freedom.

Another second movement activity could be a personal time-
line, often done in artistic fashion, whereby the student traces
or highlights what he/she considers experiences of suffering,
injustice, or freedom. The educator could then be asked (if
allowed) probing questions to promote critical reflection on the
social, political, and economic context of the student's personal
history. The overall aim would be to evoke "dangerous remembering" by encouraging participants to come to a critical awareness of the social conditioning, interests, and assumptions that
are embedded in their present action or inaction for justice. As
in the other movements of shared praxis the responses should

be shared in dialogue. In this movement personal "storytelling" is often a disclosure experience and requires reverent listening.

Dangerous memory can also occur within the context of Groome's third movement, which is the opportunity for the participants to encounter the church's Story and Vision. First of all, dangerous memory determines what version of the Story and Vision is to be made accessible and how this accessibility is to be achieved. As a pedagogical principle for justice education dangerous memory requires that the critical and subversive features of our Story be made accessible for remembrance. In this setting the Story is constituted by the remembrance of suffering and freedom. The Vision, on the other hand, becomes the future in the memory of suffering or an anticipatory memory of the kingdom as a future for "the suffering, the hopeless, the oppressed, the injured, and the useless of this earth."[73]

I see three components of dangerous memory operative in the third movement given the context of justice education in a Catholic-Protestant setting. The first component is theological. That is, the third movement should make present the church's biblical-theological Story and Vision of justice. This component would include biblical and theological perspectives on the meaning and centrality of justice, including the Catholic human rights tradition and Protestant social ethics as well as the various theologies of liberation. This component could be made accessible in any number of ways including lecture, guest speakers or resource people, Bible readings such as Exodus 3:1-15 or Luke 4:16-24, and readings in social ethics and/or liberation theology.[74]

The second component is essentially socio-historical and would involve the retelling of the U.S. Catholic-Protestant story of suffering, injustice, and freedom. Besides the memory of suffering, that the church's search for freedom and justice be retold in the hope of providing role models and paradigms for social transformation and action for justice is important. Any old and original writings from those who suffered and searched for justice in our past would be most helpful in making this component of the third movement present. Other readings could include John Woolman's *Journal,* Wesley's *Thoughts Upon Slavery,* the Social Creed of the Methodist Churches, or the Bishop's Program of 1919. Jay Dolan's *Immigrant Church* or even the movie, "On the Waterfront," could be used in a Catholic setting to recall the experience of immigrant struggle and suffering. Certainly Harriet Beecher Stowe's great novel, *Uncle Tom's Cabin,* would be most appropriate reading.

The third component of this movement should be actual "field experience." That is, participants should have the opportunity to experience first-hand situations of suffering and injustice and what is currently being done to alleviate them. This is a constitutive component of the Story of suffering and injustice as that Story presently takes shape in our midst. The pedagogical value of field experience, what I would call "an experience of contrast," is that field experience holds the potential of challenging one's stereotypes, interests, and assumptions about those who are suffering socio-economic injustice by removing suffering and injustice from the abstract-impersonal level to the level of personal experience. In doing so, field experience has the possibility of promoting critical reflection on, and critical awareness of, suffering and injustice and positive political action for social transformation. That the educator be prepared to offer concrete and realizable opportunities for participants to invest positive energy is imperative. Many church conferences, dioceses, and church-affiliated social agencies have volunteer or internship programs which would be ideal as an experience of contrast.[75] The value of field experience should not be underestimated since oftentimes "classroom" experience alone does not promote the kind of critical reflection and action (praxis) necessary to promote social transformation.

My hope is that this brief reflection underscores the creative possibilities that dangerous memory might hold as a strategic principle for educating for justice and social responsibility. As Christian religious educators continue to search for new and better ways to educate their people for social and political responsibility in public life, dangerous memory is offered here as one response to this continuing task and challenge. I encourage and welcome those who see some merit in dangerous memory to reflect upon dangerous memory in light of their own denominational and religious context for the common goal we share is a just and peaceful future that is more consistent with the vision of God's kingdom of shalom.

Notes

1. *Justice in the World,* National Conference of Catholic Bishops (Washington, D.C.: U.S.C.C. Publications Office, 1972), p. 34.

2. I realize that the use of "middle class" is problematic given the fact that as a social class designation its meaning in a U.S. context is still much debated among sociologists. I am using it to refer to people with whom we work who are economically secure and do not suffer any economic deprivation.

3. I am using "dangerous memory" as used and defined by Johann Baptist Metz, *Faith in History and Society* (New York: Seabury, 1980), pp. 109-110, 195-196.

4. Edward Duff, "The Church and American Public Life," in *Contemporary Catholicism in the United States,* ed. Philip Gleason (Notre Dame, Ind.: University of Notre Dame Press, 1969), p. 98.

5. These ethnic-immigrants arrived with little or nothing in the way of economically usable resources. Consequently Philip Gleason correctly asserts that "from the onset of mass immigration before the Civil War until the middle of the present century, Catholics were predominantly a low-status, working-class population." Philip Gleason, "The Crisis of Americanization," in *Contemporary Catholicism in the United States,* p. 9.

6. David O'Brien, *The Renewal of American Catholicism* (New York: Oxford University Press, 1972), pp. 208-209.

7. Americanization refers to the process of assimilation or cultural integration in the American context.

8. O'Brien, *The Renewal of American Catholicism,* p. 61.

9. Joseph Fichter, "The Americanization of Catholicism," in *Roman Catholicism and the American Way of Life,* ed. Thomas McAvoy (Notre Dame, Ind.: University of Notre Dame Press, 1960), pp. 124-125.

10. John L. Thomas, "The American Catholic Family," in *Contemporary Catholicism in the United States,* p. 220.

11. There are three significant reasons for the rapid Catholic success in the U.S. First, Catholics took advantage of educational opportunities, especially Catholic education. Second, Catholics benefited from passage of New Deal legislation, particularly the GI Bill of Rights. Finally, Catholics benefited, in large numbers, from the labor movement and the church's support of organized labor.

12. Andrew Greeley, *The American Catholic, A Social Portrait* (New York: Basic Books, 1977), p. 46.

13. Ibid.

14. Ibid., p. 47.

15. Will Herberg, *Protestant, Catholic, Jew* (New York: Doubleday, 1960), p. 158.

16. Ibid., p. 75.

17. Ibid., p. 180.

18. The issue of a middle-class religious ideology is an important

one if Christian religious educators are interested in promoting social responsibility and action for justice. For an insightful reflection on middle-class ideology see Gregory Baum, "Middle Class Religion in America," *Concilium, Christianity and the Bourgeoisie,* ed. J. B. Metz (New York: Seabury, 1979).

19. Social amnesia means the loss of socio-historical memory. My analysis of Catholic assimilation suggests social amnesia is a constitutive component of that process because assimilation involved both generational distance from the original immigrant-ghetto experience and upward-class mobility.

20. John Coleman, *An American Strategic Theology* (New York: Paulist, 1982), p. 159.

21. Coleman, for one, levels the blame at Catholic educational institutions. In similar fashion David O'Brien offers his own indictment against American Catholic education. See O'Brien, *The Renewal of American Catholicism,* p. 224.

22. The reader should keep in mind that I am using U.S. Catholicism as a "case study" because it is the context with which I am most familiar and comfortable. I do believe, however, that dangerous memory has applications to other ethnic and religious traditions. After all, none of us can claim to be "natives" to these shores except the Native American Indian. The quest for freedom and justice and the experience of suffering is deeply embedded in our common yet diverse traditions.

23. Herberg, *Protestant, Catholic, Jew,* p. 136.

24. Oscar Handlin has identified four major causes for this cataclysmic upheaval. See Oscar Handlin, *Boston's Immigrants* (Cambridge, Mass.: Harvard University Press, 1959), pp. 26ff.

25. Perhaps there is no better or more extreme example of these oppressive conditions than the Irish experience. As a somewhat dispassionate observer of the Irish situation, Handlin writes, "Westward from Ireland went four and a half million. On that crowded island a remorselessly rising population, avaricious absentee landlords, English policy that discouraged the growth of industry early stimulated emigration." See Oscar Handlin, *The Uprooted* (Boston: Little, Brown, 1952), p. 35.

26. Saul Alinsky, "The Urban Immigrant," in *Roman Catholicism and the American Way of Life,* p. 143.

27. See Jay P. Dolan, *The Immigrant Church* (Baltimore: Johns Hopkins University Press, 1975) and Handlin, *Boston's Immigrants.*

28. Dolan, *The Immigrant Church,* p. 33.

29. Foy's paper was a fine attempt to critically analyze the socioeconomic situation and propose some progressive solutions. Foy maintained that the capitalist program of industrial centralization was perpetuated not by nature but by civil law. He believed that governmental support insured the success of the capitalist endeavor at the

expense of the toiling masses. See Aaron I. Abell, *American Catholic Thought on Social Questions* (New York: Bobbs-Merrill, 1968), pp. 193-194.

30. Mary Harris Jones is truly one of the most colorful and controversial figures on American Catholic history. Unfortunately given her sex, age, and church-status, little has been written about her in "official" histories of U.S. Catholicism. However, in my opinion she stands along with Dorothy Day as one of several heroines in the U.S. Catholic church's "subversive tradition" for social justice. For further reading on Mary Harris Jones I recommend her biography by Dale Fetherling, *Mother Jones, the Miner's Angel* (Carbondale, Ill.: Southern Illinois University Press, 1974).

31. Neil Betten, *Catholic Activism and the Industrial Worker* (Gainsville: University Presses of Florida, 1976), p. x.

32. I am using the language "usable past" as Letty Russell uses it. See Letty M. Russell, *Human Liberation in a Feminist Perspective—A Theology* (Philadelphia: Westminster, 1974), p. 72ff. I also regret that this section does not contain an account of the feminist struggle within American Protestantism. It stands as an important and timely example of a tradition of suffering and freedom. Women such as Antoinette Brown, Phoebe Palmer, Catherine Mumford Booth, and Elizabeth Cady Stanton deserve more than a footnote. Unfortunately time and space prevent me from doing more. My apologies.

33. Ibid. p. 81.

34. D. Elton Trueblood, *The People Called Quakers* (Richmond, Ind.: Friends United Press, 1976), p. 2.

35. Ibid., p. 4.

36. Hugh Barbour and Arthur Roberts, *Early Quaker Writings* (Grand Rapids, Mich.: Eerdmans, 1973), p. 137.

37. Trueblood, *The People Called Quakers,* p. 150.

38. Ibid., p. 151.

39. Martin E. Marty, *Protestantism in the United States* (New York: Scribner, 1986), p. 31.

40. Ibid., p. 30.

41. Sydney E. Ahlstrom, *A Religious History of the American People* (New Haven: Yale University Press, 1973), p. 699.

42. Ibid., p. 710.

43. Marty, *Protestantism in the United States,* p. 35.

44. Ahlstrom, *A Religious History of the American People,* p. 704.

45. Ibid., p. 709.

46. James H. Cone, *My Soul Looks Back* (Maryknoll, N. Y.: Orbis, 1986), pp. 22-23.

47. Trueblood, *The People Called Quakers,* p. 158.

48. Ibid., pp. 157, 161.

49. Donald G. Mathews, *Slavery and Methodism* (Princeton, N. J.: Princeton University Press, 1965), p. 124.

50. Ibid., p. 146.
51. Ahlstrom, *A Religious History of the American People*, p. 787.
52. Marty, *Protestantism in the United States*, p. 203.
53. Alhstrom, *A Religious History of the American People*, p. 795.
54. Marty, *Protestantism in the United States*, p. 204.
55. Ibid., pp. 204-205.
56. See Exodus 12:1-13:16.
57. See Brevard Childs, *Memory and Tradition in Israel*, Studies in Biblical Theology, No. 37, 1962.
58. Ibid., p. 53.
59. Metz, *Faith in History and Society*, p. 110.
60. Ibid., pp. 109-110.
61. See Dwayne Huebner, "Toward a Remaking of Curricular Language," *Heightened Consciousness, Cultural Revolution and Curriculum Theory*, ed. William Pinar (Berkeley: McCutchan Publishing, 1974).
62. Ibid., p. 41.
63. Ibid.
64. Ibid., p. 37.
65. In his approach of shared Christian praxis Groome proposes five movements. They are 1.) naming present action, 2.) the participants' stories and visions, 3.) the church's story and vision, 4.) dialectical hermeneutic between the story and participants' stories and 5.) dialectical hermeneutic between the Vision and participants' visions. For a complete discussion of these five movements including concrete examples of each see Thomas H. Groome, *Christian Religious Education* (New York: Harper & Row, 1980), pp. 207-232.
66. Ibid., p. 186.
67. Ibid., p. 192.
68. Johann Metz states that "in its practical intention, the memory of freedom is primarily a memoria passionis, a memory of suffering." See Metz, *Faith in History and Society*, p. 195.
69. Ibid., p. 196.
70. Greeley, *The American Catholic*, p. 38.
71. Marcus L. Hansen, *The Problem of the Third Generation Immigrant* (Rock Island, Ill.: Augustana Historical Society Publication, 1938), p. 7ff.
72. Dangerous memory can never refer exclusively to the sufferings of a particular group such as ethnic-immigrant Catholics. Because of its "privileged status" the U.S. Catholic community must attend to the past and present sufferings of others nationally and internationally. In other words, there are present demands of dangerous memory which require us to remember the suffering and injustice in our midst.
73. Metz, *Faith in History and Society*, p. 117.
74. Readings in the theologies of liberation which represent the black, feminist, and Hispanic perspectives are: James H. Cone, *My*

Soul Looks Back (Maryknoll, N. Y.: Orbis, 1986); Virgilio Elizondo, *Galilean Journey* (Maryknoll, N. Y.: Orbis, 1983), and Russell, *Human Liberation in a Feminist Perspective.*

75. An example of what I am suggesting here is the Urban Plunge program at the University of Portland. It is an intense weekend experience for college undergraduates whereby they live and work in the inner city with those who are ministering to the urban poor and homeless. For more detailed information about this exciting and challenging program contact the Office of Volunteer Service at the University of Portland in Portland, Oregon.

REFERENCES

There are many resources in social education that will enable further explanation of the relationship between religious faith and social justice. Most religious groups and judicatories maintain resource centers of such material. The following resources are suggestive of the possibilities.

I. A Social Theory of Religious Education

Bibliography

Bernstein, Richard J. *Praxis and Action.* Philadelphia: University of Pennsylvania Press, 1971.

Karier, Clarence J. *The Individual, Society, and Education.* 2nd ed. Urbana: University of Illinois Press (second edition), 1967. A history of American education which focuses on the issues of the social functions of education.

Groome, Thomas H. *Christian Religious Education.* San Francisco: Harper & Row, 1980.

Resources

Elliott, Charles. *Comfortable Compassion? Poverty, Power and the Church.* New York: Paulist Press, 1987. This book guides readers into these issues by examining the reasons for the failure of so much church and secular development work.

Galdamez, Pablo. *Faith of a People: The Life of a Basic Christian Community in El Salvador, 1970-1980.* Maryknoll: Orbis Books, 1986. Pablo Galdamez, a Catholic priest, describes the growth and ex-

234

periences of one community of poor Christians. His story recounts community's commitment to create a new reality for both the church and society in a country torn by inequalities and repression. *Hammering Swords into Ploughshares: Essays in Honor of Archbishop Mpilo Desmond Tutu.* Ed. Buti Tlhagale and Itumeleng Mosala. Grand Rapids, Mich.: Eerdmans, 1987.

The Journey: From Faith to Action in Brazil. Elkhart, Ind.: Church World Service, 1984.

II. THE CHANGING FAMILY

BIBLIOGRAPHY

Berger, Brigitte, and Peter L. Berger. *The War Over the Family: Capturing the Middle Ground.* Garden City, N. Y.: Anchor Press/Doubleday, 1983.

Gittens, Diana. *The Family in Question: Changing Households and Familiar Ideologies.* Atlantic Highlands, N. J.: Humanities Press International, Inc., 1986.

Hauerwas, Stanley. *A Community of Character: Toward a Constructive Christian Social Ethic.* Notre Dame: University of Notre Dame Press, 1981.

Todd, Emmanuel. *The Explanation of Ideology: Family Structures and Social Systems.* Trans. David Garrioch. Oxford, England: Basil Blackwell, Ltd., 1985.

Yorburg, Betty. *Families and Societies: Survival or Extinction?* New York: Columbia University Press, 1983.

RESOURCES

For students interested in a guide to the religious education of children, a useful small book is John Westerhoff, *Bringing up Children in the Christian Faith.* Minneapolis: Winston Press, 1980.

Lois Seifert. *Our Family Night In: Workbook of Family Covenant Living.* Nashville: The Upper Room, 1981. This is an example of the kind of intergenerational curricular resources available that can be used effectively for special educational events with families.

James McGinnis. *Educating for Peace and Justice.* St. Louis: Institute for Peace and Justice, 1985. The Institute has a series of study guides for family groupings on Peace and Justice issues. For information, write 4144 Lindell Boulevard, #400, St. Louis 63108.

There are few resources available to guide congregations in the creation of family networks. The small group is emphasized in John and Adrienne Carr, *The Pilgrimmate Project: Renewing Our Sense of God's Presence and Purpose.* Nashville: Discipleship Resources, 1987. It, however, can be used to establish networks among adults that can later be easily expanded to include their children.

A selection of contemporary films on video could be utilized to examine the issues of family living today. Among these are *Breakfast Club*, *Sixteen Candles*, *Kramer vs. Kramer*, and *Mr. Mom*. More classical films to consider are *The Grapes of Wrath*, *The Red Balloon*, *Small Change*, and *The Graduate*.

III. WOMEN AND MEN IN THE SOCIAL ORDER: CHALLENGE TO RELIGIOUS EDUCATION

BIBLIOGRAPHY

Allison, Caroline. *It's Like Holding the Keys to Your Own Jail: Women of Namibia*. Geneva: World Council of Churches, 1986.
Fiorenza, Elisabeth Schüssler. *Bread Not Stone: The Challenge of Feminist Biblical Interpretation*. Boston: Beacon Press, 1984.
Moltmann-Wendel, Elisabeth. *The Women Around Jesus*. New York: Crossroad Publishing Co., 1982.
Morton, Nelle. *The Journey is Home*. Boston: Beacon Press, 1985.
Ruether, Rosemary Radford. *New Woman New Earth: Sexist Ideologies and Human Liberation*. New York: Seabury Press, 1975.
Russell, Letty M. *The Future of Partnership*. Philadelphia: Westminster Press, 1979.

RESOURCES

"Killing Us Softly." Film addressing sexism in advertising. Available from Cambridge Documentary Films, Inc., Box 385, Cambridge, Mass. 02139.
Bausch, Michael G. and Ruth C. Duck, eds. *Everflowing Streams: Songs for Worship*. New York: Pilgrim Press, 1981. Contains 83 hymns and songs in inclusive language; companion to *Bread for the Journey*.
Duck, Ruth C., ed. *Bread for the Journey: Resources for Worship*. New York: Pilgrim Press, 1981. Offers liturgical resources for Christian sacraments, rites, and seasons of church year.
Neufer Emswiler, Sharon and Tom, eds. *Sisters and Brothers Sing*. Normal, Ill.: Illinois State University, Wesley Foundation, 1977. Offers 33 contemporary and traditional songs in inclusive language. A supplement is also available: *Put on Your Party Clothes*.
Neufer Emswiler, Sharon and Tom. *Women and Worship: A Guide to Non-Sexist Hymns, Prayers and Liturgies*. San Francisco: Harper & Row, 1984.
United Church of Canada. *The Words We Sing: An Inclusive Language Guide to 'The Hymn Book'*. Toronto: CANEC, United Church of Canada. The booklet offers guides for inclusive language, some revised hymns, and a workshop model.
The Inclusive-Language Lectionary Committee, National Council of

Churches of Christ in the United States. *Inclusive-Language Lectionary: Readings for Year A*. Philadelphia: Westminster Press, 1986. See also: *Inclusive-Language Lectionary: Readings for Year B* (1987) and *Inclusive-Language Lectionary: Readings for Year C* (1985).

IV. A HUMAN WORLD ORDER

BIBLIOGRAPHY

Arias, Esther and Mortimer. *The Cry of My People: Out of Captivity in Latin America*. New York: Friendship Press, 1980.

The Challenge of Peace: God's Promise and Our Response. A Pastoral Letter on War and Peace. National Conference of Catholic Bishops. Washington, D.C.: U.S. Catholic Conference, 1983.

Evans, Alice Frazer, Robert A. Evans and William Bean Kennedy. *Pedagogies for The Non-Poor*. Maryknoll, N.Y.: Orbis Books, 1987.

Nelson, Jack A. *Hunger For Justice: The Politics of Food and Faith*. Maryknoll, N.Y.: Orbis Books, 1980.

Johnson, David M., ed. *Justice and Peace Education*. Maryknoll, N.Y.: Orbis Books, 1986.

RESOURCES

Alternatives. P.O. Box 429, Ellenwood, Georgia 30049. Resources to encourage responsible celebrations and conscientious ways of living; bookstore; quarterly newsletter.

"Education Newsletter." Office of Education, World Council of Churches, 150 rte de Ferney, 1211 Geneva 20, Switzerland. Variety of articles and resource listing on education and social issues.

"Gods of Metal." Film which analyzes the arms race from a Christian perspective, showing the economic and social effects on people in the U.S. and the Third World. Nominated for an Academy Award. Publisher: Maryknoll. Source: Ecu-Film, 810 12th Avenue, South, Nashville, TN 37203.

Global Education Associates. 552 Park Avenue, East Orange, N.J. 07017. Publications, educational programs, newsletter, consulting, speakers, media, and research projects committed to creating a more just, peaceful, and human world order.

"How Do We Live In A Hungry World." Film which focuses on people from different parts of the country with different backgrounds whose concerns about shortages and inequitable distribution of resources in the world have prompted them to alter their lifestyle in response to the problem. Source: Ecu-Film (see above).

Institute for Peace and Justice. 4144 Lindell Boulevard, St. Louis, Mo. 63108. Resources, educational programs, curriculum for building shalom.

Plowshares Institute. Simsbury, Conn.

V. POLITICS AND THE RELIGIOUS CONSCIOUSNESS

BIBLIOGRAPHY

Diggins, John P. *The Lost Soul of American Politics: Virtue, Self-Interest, and the Foundations of Liberalism.* Lake Station, Ind.: Basic Books, 1984.

McBrien, Richard P. *Ceasar's Coin: Religion and Politics in America.* New York: Macmillan, 1987.

McIntyre, C.T., ed. *Herbert Butterfield's Writings in Christianity and History.* New York: Oxford University Press, 1979.

Segre, Dan Vittorio. *Memoirs of a Fortunate Jew: An Italian Story.* Adler and Adler, 1986.

Thompson, Kenneth, ed. *Herbert Butterfield: The Ethics of History and Politics.* Lanham, Maryland: University Press of America, 1980.

Tracy, David. *The Analogical Imagination.* New York: Crossroad, 1981.

RESOURCES

Literature is a source to deal with the ambiguity of values and the nature of the political consciousness.

Bloom, Harold, ed. *Flannery O'Connor.* Edgemont, Pa.: Chelsea House, 1986.

Melville, Herman. *Billy Budd, Sailor and Other Stories.* New York: Penguin, 1986.

Updike, John. *Roger's Version.* New York: Knopf, 1986.

Films that might be utilized in either the classroom or in individual viewing and analysis are:

Billy Budd—A rendering of Herman Melville's story of the "pure" Billy, who nevertheless "must hang" because he has violated the law. An examination of ambiguity as one man struggles to choose between two moralities.

Citizen Kane—Power and politics for the sake of power. This is a classic in American cinema.

McCabe and Mrs. Miller—Robert Altman's examination of life in a frontier community blends religion and community organization in a provocative manner.

Power—A film with Richard Gere which talks with wisdom about modern politics and how media shapes our decisions.

VI. TRANSFORMATION AT WORK

BIBLIOGRAPHY

Gillett, Richard. *The Human Enterprise.* Kansas City, Mo.: Leaven Press, 1985.

Kanter, Rosabeth Moss. *Men and Women of the Corporation.* New York: Basic Books, 1977.

Raines, John and Donna Day-Lower. *Modern Work and Human Meaning.* Philadelphia: Westminster Press, 1986.

Richardson, Elliott. *Work in America: Report of a Special Task Force to the Secretary of Health, Education and Welfare.* Cambridge, Mass.: MIT Press, 1978.

Stackhouse, Max L. *Public Theology and Political Economy: Christian Stewardship in Modern Society.* Grand Rapids, Mich.: Eerdmans, 1987.

RESOURCES

OIKOS Project on Work, Family and Faith, Candler School of Theology, Emory University, Atlanta, Ga. 30322. Research and adult education.

Search for Justice (Oblate Media Images). Available from Paulist Press. Five videotapes exploring issues raised by the U.S. Catholic Bishops' Pastoral Letter on Catholic Social Teaching and the U.S. Economy.

Trinity Center for Ethics and Corporate Policy, 74 Trinity Place, New York, N.Y. 10006-2088. Resources and programs for approaching issues in managerial ethics.

VII. THE ECOLOGY OF HUMAN EXISTENCE: LIVING WITHIN THE NATURAL ORDER

BIBLIOGRAPHY

Brown, Lester, ed. *State of the World.* 1984 through 1988. Worldwatch Ins. New York: Norton.

Cobb, John and Charles Birch. *The Liberation of Life.* Oxford, England: Oxford University Press, 1983.

Freudenberger, C. Dean and Paul Minus. *Christian Responsibility in a Hungry World,* Nashville, Abingdon Press, 1974.

Moltmann, Jürgen. *God in Creation: A New Theology of Creation and the Spirit of God.* San Francisco: Harper & Row, 1985.

World Council of Churches. *Anticipation: The Future of Man and Society in a World of Science-Based Technology.* Geneva: WCC, 1970-1983.

RESOURCES

A World Hungry. A Filmstrip by The Franciscans Communication Center, Los Angeles, 1975.

World Council of Churches. *One World.* No. 125, Geneva, May, 1987.

VIII. Dangerous Memories:
Toward a Pedagogy of Social Transformation

Bibliography

Cone, James H. *My Soul Looks Back*. Maryknoll, N.Y.: Orbis Books, 1986.

Dolan, Jay P. *The Immigrant Church*. Baltimore: Johns Hopkins University Press, 1975.

Marty, Martin E. *Protestanism in the United States*. New York: Scribner Book Company, 1986.

Metz, Johann B. *Faith in History and Society*. New York: Seabury Press, 1980.

Pinar, William, ed. *Heightened Consciousness, Cultural Revolution, and Curriculum Theory* Berkeley: McCutcheon Publishing, 1974.

Resources

Bread for the World, 802 Rhode Island Avenue, NE, Washington, D.C. 20018. Bread for the World defines itself as a "Christian citizen's movement" whose members seek government policies that address the basic causes of hunger. As an ecumenical Christian political lobby, BFW is one concrete example in which Christians can be encouraged to invest their energy in working for social transformation. BFW also has an intern program and a covenant church program. More information can be secured from BFW at the above address.

Dickens, Charles. *A Christmas Carol*. Dir. Clive Donner. CBS Television. New York, N.Y., December 17, 1984. *A Christmas Carol* by Charles Dickens could be used as a Christmas time or Advent resource in a parish or school social justice program. The 1984 CBS television movie starring George C. Scott is an excellent video remake of Dickens' classic tale. It is a good portrayal of the power of remembrance and imagination (the ghosts of Christmas past, present, and future) to promote conversion to a life of compassion for the poor. It is also a good historical "period piece" for discussion the poverty and suffering caused by early industrial capitalism in mid-nineteenth century England.

On the Waterfront. Dir. Elia Kazan. Columbia Pictures. 1954. In a Catholic context *On the Waterfront* is an excellent movie-resource since its historical setting is Catholic ethnic-immigrant participation in the corrupt longshoremen unions of the Lower East-Side in New York City where the Jesuits had a labor school during the 1930s and 1940s. The film could be used as part of a "third movement" presentation on the church's Past Story of searching for freedom and justice.

About the Authors

Allen J. Moore is Professor of Religion and Personality and Education, as well as Dean, at the School of Theology at Claremont, Claremont, California. A selected list of his writings includes *The Young Adult Generation*, "The Family Relations of Older Persons" in *Ministry With the Aging*, and "Liberation and the Future of Christian Education" in *Contemporary Approaches to Christian Education.*

Charles R. Foster is Professor of Christian Education at the Candler School of Theology, Emory University. Graduate School. His writings include *Teaching in the Community of Faith, The Church in the Education of the Public*, and *The Ministry of the Volunteer Teacher.* A continuing research interest reflected in this chapter has to do with the history of family.

Mary Elizabeth Moore is Professor of Christian Education and Theology at the School of Theology at Claremont, Claremont, California. She teaches courses in educational ministry, feminist theology, psychology of religion, and spirituality. Her publications include *Education for Continuity and Change: A Traditioning Model for Christian Religious Education* and *Called to Serve: The United Methodist Diaconate*, along with essays published in collections.

Gerald F. Mische is president and co-founder of Global Education Associates, a network of associates in over sixty countries. After working in a community development leadership project in Central America, Gerald co-founded and was first director of the Association for International Development—a nonprofit organization that trained and placed people in socio-economic self-help programs in twenty-two countries in Africa, Asia, and Latin America. He is the co-author of the book, *Toward a Human World Order*.

James M. Wall is editor of Christian Century, a weekly magazine of news and opinion. Prior to assuming that position in 1972, Wall was editor of the *Christian Advocate*, a publication of the United Methodist Church. An ordained clergyman in that denomination, Wall has authored a book on film, and is the editor of four other books on film. He also writes on public affairs and religion. He has been active in politics, serving as state chairman of President Jimmy Carter's Illinois campaign in 1976.

William Johnson Everett is Director of Advanced Studies and Associate Professor of Ecclesiology at the Candler School of Theology, Emory University. He is co-director of the OIKOS Project on Work, Family and Faith. He is the author of *Blessed Be the Bond: Christian Perspectives on Marriage and Family*, and *God's Federal Republic* as well as numerous articles in the field of religion and society.

C. Dean Freudenberger has been a student of international agriculture development and Christian social ethics for the past thirty years. He received his formal training in agronomy at the California State Polytechnic University at San Luis Obispo, followed by work in ethics at the Boston University School of Theology. After eleven years of agricultural missionary service in Zaire he returned to Boston University to complete his Ph.D. He teaches in international development studies, ecumenics, and rural ministry at the School of Theology Claremont, California. Among his writings is *Food for Tommorow?*

Russell A. Butkus is Assistant Professor of Theology and Education and Director of the Program in Religious Education at the University of Portland, Portland, Oregon. He has contributed numerous articles and essays to learned journals and collections, including *Ecucation for Peace and Justice*.

Index of Names

Index of Subjects